# Clojure Data Analysis Cookbook
## Second Edition

Dive into data analysis with Clojure through over 100 practical recipes for every stage of the analysis and collection process

**Eric Rochester**

[PACKT] open source*
PUBLISHING   community experience distilled

BIRMINGHAM - MUMBAI

# Clojure Data Analysis Cookbook
## Second Edition

First published: March 2013

Second edition: January 2015

Production reference: 1220115

Published by Packt Publishing Ltd.
Livery Place
35 Livery Street
Birmingham B3 2PB, UK.

ISBN 978-1-78439-029-7

www.packtpub.com

# Credits

**Author**
Eric Rochester

**Reviewers**
Vitomir Kovanovic

Muktabh Mayank Srivastava

Federico Tomassetti

**Commissioning Editor**
Ashwin Nair

**Acquisition Editor**
Sam Wood

**Content Development Editor**
Parita Khedekar

**Technical Editor**
Ryan Kochery

**Copy Editors**
Dipti Kapadia

Puja Lalwani

Vikrant Phadke

**Project Coordinator**
Neha Thakur

**Proofreaders**
Ameesha Green

Joel T. Johnson

Samantha Lyon

**Indexer**
Priya Sane

**Graphics**
Sheetal Aute

Disha Haria

**Production Coordinator**
Nitesh Thakur

**Cover Work**
Nitesh Thakur

# About the Author

**Eric Rochester** enjoys reading, writing, and spending time with his wife and kids. When he's not doing these things, he programs in a variety of languages and platforms, including websites and systems in Python, and libraries for linguistics and statistics in C#. Currently, he is exploring functional programming languages, including Clojure and Haskell. He works at Scholars' Lab in the library at the University of Virginia, helping humanities professors and graduate students realize their digitally informed research agendas. He is also the author of *Mastering Clojure Data Analysis, Packt Publishing*.

I'd like to thank everyone. My technical reviewers proved invaluable. Also, thank you to the editorial staff at Packt Publishing. This book is much stronger because of all of their feedback, and any remaining deficiencies are mine alone.

A special thanks to Jackie, Melina, and Micah. They've been patient and supportive while I worked on this project. It is, in every way, for them.

# About the Reviewers

**Vitomir Kovanovic** is a PhD student at the School of Informatics, University of Edinburgh, Edinburgh, UK. He received an MSc degree in computer science and software engineering in 2011, and BSc in information systems and business administration in 2009 from the University of Belgrade, Serbia. His research interests include learning analytics, educational data mining, and online education. He is a member of the Society for Learning Analytics Research and a member of program committees of several conferences and journals in technology-enhanced learning. In his PhD research, he focuses on the use of trace data for understanding the effects of technology use on the quality of the social learning process and learning outcomes. For more information, visit `http://vitomir.kovanovic.info/`

**Muktabh Mayank Srivastava** is a data scientist and the cofounder of ParallelDots.com. Previously, he helped in solving many complex data analysis and machine learning problems for clients from different domains such as healthcare, retail, procurement, automation, Bitcoin, social recommendation engines, geolocation fact-finding, customer profiling, and so on.

His new venture is ParallelDots. It is a tool that allows any content archive to be presented in a story using advanced techniques of NLP and machine learning. For publishers and bloggers, it automatically creates a timeline of any event using their archive and presents it in an interactive, intuitive, and easy-to-navigate interface on their webpage. You can find him on LinkedIn at `http://in.linkedin.com/in/muktabh/` and on Twitter at `@muktabh` / `@ParallelDots`.

**Federico Tomassetti** has been programming since he was a child and has a PhD in software engineering. He works as a consultant on model-driven development and domain-specific languages, writes technical articles, teaches programming, and works as a full-stack software engineer.

He has experience working in Italy, Germany, and Ireland, and he is currently working at Groupon International.

You can read about his projects on `http://federico-tomassetti.it/` or `https://github.com/ftomassetti/`.

# www.PacktPub.com

## Support files, eBooks, discount offers, and more

For support files and downloads related to your book, please visit www.PacktPub.com.

Did you know that Packt offers eBook versions of every book published, with PDF and ePub files available? You can upgrade to the eBook version at www.PacktPub.com and as a print book customer, you are entitled to a discount on the eBook copy. Get in touch with us at service@packtpub.com for more details.

At www.PacktPub.com, you can also read a collection of free technical articles, sign up for a range of free newsletters and receive exclusive discounts and offers on Packt books and eBooks.

https://www2.packtpub.com/books/subscription/packtlib

Do you need instant solutions to your IT questions? PacktLib is Packt's online digital book library. Here, you can search, access, and read Packt's entire library of books.

## Why subscribe?

- ▶ Fully searchable across every book published by Packt
- ▶ Copy and paste, print, and bookmark content
- ▶ On demand and accessible via a web browser

## Free access for Packt account holders

If you have an account with Packt at www.PacktPub.com, you can use this to access PacktLib today and view 9 entirely free books. Simply use your login credentials for immediate access.

# Table of Contents

# Preface

Welcome to the second edition of *Clojure Data Analysis Cookbook*! It seems that books become obsolete almost as quickly as software does, so here we have the opportunity to keep things up-to-date and useful.

Moreover, the state of the art of data analysis is also still evolving and changing. The techniques and technologies are being refined and improved. Hopefully, this book will capture some of that. I've also added a new chapter on how to work with unstructured textual data.

In spite of these changes, some things have stayed the same. Clojure has further proven itself to be an excellent environment to work with data. As a member of the lisp family of languages, it inherits a flexibility and power that is hard to match. The concurrency and parallelization features have further proven themselves as great tools for developing software and analyzing data.

Clojure's usefulness for data analysis is further improved by a number of strong libraries. Incanter provides a practical environment to work with data and perform statistical analysis. Cascalog is an easy-to-use wrapper over Hadoop and Cascading. Finally, when you're ready to publish your results, ClojureScript, an implementation of Clojure that generates JavaScript, can help you to visualize your data in an effective and persuasive way.

Moreover, Clojure runs on the Java Virtual Machine (JVM), so any libraries written for Java are available too. This gives Clojure an incredible amount of breadth and power.

I hope that this book will give you the tools and techniques you need to get answers from your data.

# What this book covers

*Chapter 1, Importing Data for Analysis*, covers how to read data from a variety of sources, including CSV files, web pages, and linked semantic web data.

*Chapter 2, Cleaning and Validating Data*, presents strategies and implementations to normalize dates, fix spelling, and work with large datasets. Getting data into a useable shape is an important, but often overlooked, stage of data analysis.

*Chapter 3, Managing Complexity with Concurrent Programming*, covers Clojure's concurrency features and how you can use them to simplify your programs.

*Chapter 4, Improving Performance with Parallel Programming*, covers how to use Clojure's parallel processing capabilities to speed up the processing of data.

*Chapter 5, Distributed Data Processing with Cascalog*, covers how to use Cascalog as a wrapper over Hadoop and the Cascading library to process large amounts of data distributed over multiple computers.

*Chapter 6, Working with Incanter Datasets*, covers the basics of working with Incanter datasets. Datasets are the core data structures used by Incanter, and understanding them is necessary in order to use Incanter effectively.

*Chapter 7, Statistical Data Analysis with Incanter*, covers a variety of statistical processes and tests used in data analysis. Some of these are quite simple, such as generating summary statistics. Others are more complex, such as performing linear regressions and auditing data with Benford's Law.

*Chapter 8, Working with Mathematica and R*, talks about how to set up Clojure in order to talk to Mathematica or R. These are powerful data analysis systems, and we might want to use them sometimes. This chapter will show you how to get these systems to work together, as well as some tasks that you can perform once they are communicating.

*Chapter 9, Clustering, Classifying, and Working with Weka*, covers more advanced machine learning techniques. In this chapter, we'll primarily use the Weka machine learning library. Some recipes will discuss how to use it and the data structures its built on, while other recipes will demonstrate machine learning algorithms.

*Chapter 10, Working with Unstructured and Textual Data*, looks at tools and techniques used to extract information from the reams of unstructured, textual data.

*Chapter 11, Graphing in Incanter*, shows you how to generate graphs and other visualizations in Incanter. These can be important for exploring and learning about your data and also for publishing and presenting your results.

*Chapter 12, Creating Charts for the Web*, shows you how to set up a simple web application in order to present findings from data analysis. It will include a number of recipes that leverage the powerful D3 visualization library.

# What you need for this book

One piece of software required for this book is the Java Development Kit (JDK), which you can obtain from `http://www.oracle.com/technetwork/java/javase/downloads/index.html`. JDK is necessary to run and develop on the Java platform.

The other major piece of software that you'll need is Leiningen 2, which you can download and install from `http://leiningen.org/`. Leiningen 2 is a tool used to manage Clojure projects and their dependencies. It has become the de facto standard project tool in the Clojure community.

Throughout this book, we'll use a number of other Clojure and Java libraries, including Clojure itself. Leiningen will take care of downloading these for us as we need them.

You'll also need a text editor or Integrated Development Environment (IDE). If you already have a text editor of your choice, you can probably use it. See `http://clojure.org/getting_started` for tips and plugins for using your particular favorite environment. If you don't have a preference, I'd suggest that you take a look at using Eclipse with Counterclockwise. There are instructions to this set up at `https://code.google.com/p/counterclockwise/`.

That is all that's required. However, at various places throughout the book, some recipes will access other software. The recipes in *Chapter 8, Working with Mathematica and R*, that are related to Mathematica will require Mathematica, obviously, and those that are related to R will require that. However, these programs won't be used in the rest of the book, and whether you're interested in those recipes might depend on whether you already have this software.

# Who this book is for

This book is for programmers or data scientists who are familiar with Clojure and want to use it in their data analysis processes. This isn't a tutorial on Clojure—there are already a number of excellent introductory books out there—so you'll need to be familiar with the language, but you don't need to be an expert.

Likewise, you don't have to be an expert on data analysis, although you should probably be familiar with its tasks, processes, and techniques. While you might be able to glean enough from these recipes to get started with, for it to be truly effective, you'll want to get a more thorough introduction to this field.

# Conventions

In this book, you will find a number of styles of text that distinguish between different kinds of information. Here are some examples of these styles, and an explanation of their meaning.

Code words in text, database table names, folder names, filenames, file extensions, pathnames, dummy URLs, user input, and Twitter handles are shown as follows: "Now, there will be a new subdirectory named `getting-data`.

A block of code is set as follows:

```
(defproject getting-data "0.1.0-SNAPSHOT"
  :description "FIXME: write description"
  :url "http://example.com/FIXME"
  :license {:name "Eclipse Public License"
            :url "http://www.eclipse.org/legal/epl-v10.html"}
  :dependencies [[org.clojure/clojure "1.6.0"]])
```

When we wish to draw your attention to a particular part of a code block, the relevant lines or items are set in bold:

```
(defn watch-debugging
  [input-file]
  (let [reader (agent
                  (seque
                    (mapcat
                      lazy-read-csv
                      input-files)))
        caster (agent nil)
        sink (agent [])
        counter (ref 0)
        done (ref false)]
    (add-watch caster :counter
               (partial watch-caster counter))
    (add-watch caster :debug debug-watch)
    (send reader read-row caster sink done)
    (wait-for-it 250 done)
    {:results @sink
     :count-watcher @counter}))
```

Any command-line input or output is written as follows:

```
$ lein new getting-data
Generating a project called getting-data based on the default template.
To see other templates (app, lein plugin, etc), try lein help new.
```

**New terms** and **important words** are shown in bold. Words that you see on the screen, in menus or dialog boxes for example, appear in the text like this: "Take a look at the Hadoop website for the **Getting Started** documentation of your version. Get a single node setup working".

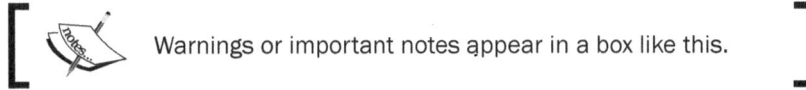

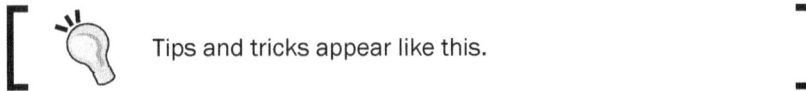

> Warnings or important notes appear in a box like this.

> Tips and tricks appear like this.

# Reader feedback

Feedback from our readers is always welcome. Let us know what you think about this book—what you liked or may have disliked. Reader feedback is important for us to develop titles that you really get the most out of.

To send us general feedback, simply send an e-mail to feedback@packtpub.com, and mention the book title via the subject of your message.

If there is a topic that you have expertise in and you are interested in either writing or contributing to a book, see our author guide on www.packtpub.com/authors.

# Customer support

Now that you are the proud owner of a Packt book, we have a number of things to help you to get the most from your purchase.

## Downloading the example code

You can download the example code files for all Packt books you have purchased from your account at http://www.packtpub.com. If you purchased this book elsewhere, you can visit http://www.packtpub.com/support and register to have the files e-mailed directly to you.

## Downloading the color images of this book

We also provide you a PDF file that has color images of the screenshots/diagrams used in this book. The color images will help you better understand the changes in the output. You can download this file from: `https://www.packtpub.com/sites/default/files/downloads/B03480_coloredimages.pdf`.

## Errata

Although we have taken every care to ensure the accuracy of our content, mistakes do happen. If you find a mistake in one of our books—maybe a mistake in the text or the code—we would be grateful if you could report this to us. By doing so, you can save other readers from frustration and help us improve subsequent versions of this book. If you find any errata, please report them by visiting `http://www.packtpub.com/submit-errata`, selecting your book, clicking on the **Errata Submission Form** link, and entering the details of your errata. Once your errata are verified, your submission will be accepted and the errata will be uploaded to our website or added to any list of existing errata under the Errata section of that title.

To view the previously submitted errata, go to `https://www.packtpub.com/books/content/support` and enter the name of the book in the search field. The required information will appear under the **Errata** section.

## Piracy

Piracy of copyright material on the Internet is an ongoing problem across all media. At Packt, we take the protection of our copyright and licenses very seriously. If you come across any illegal copies of our works, in any form, on the Internet, please provide us with the location address or website name immediately so that we can pursue a remedy.

Please contact us at `copyright@packtpub.com` with a link to the suspected pirated material.

We appreciate your help in protecting our authors, and our ability to bring you valuable content.

## Questions

You can contact us at `questions@packtpub.com` if you are having a problem with any aspect of the book, and we will do our best to address it.

# 1
# Importing Data for Analysis

In this chapter, we will cover the following recipes:

- ▶ Creating a new project
- ▶ Reading CSV data into Incanter datasets
- ▶ Reading JSON data into Incanter datasets
- ▶ Reading data from Excel with Incanter
- ▶ Reading data from JDBC databases
- ▶ Reading XML data into Incanter datasets
- ▶ Scraping data from tables in web pages
- ▶ Scraping textual data from web pages
- ▶ Reading RDF data
- ▶ Querying RDF data with SPARQL
- ▶ Aggregating data from different formats

## Introduction

There's not much data analysis that can be done without data, so the first step in any project is to evaluate the data we have and the data that we need. Once we have some idea of what we'll need, we have to figure out how to get it.

Many of the recipes in this chapter and in this book use **Incanter** (http://incanter.org/) to import the data and target Incanter datasets. Incanter is a library that is used for statistical analysis and graphics in Clojure (similar to R) an open source language for statistical computing (http://www.r-project.org/). Incanter might not be suitable for every task (for example, we'll use the **Weka library** for machine learning later) but it is still an important part of our toolkit for doing data analysis in Clojure. This chapter has a collection of recipes that can be used to gather data and make it accessible to Clojure.

For the very first recipe, we'll take a look at how to start a new project. We'll start with very simple formats such as **comma-separated values** (**CSV**) and move into reading data from relational databases using JDBC. We'll examine more complicated data sources, such as web scraping and linked data (RDF).

# Creating a new project

Over the course of this book, we're going to use a number of third-party libraries and external dependencies. We will need a tool to download them and track them. We also need a tool to set up the environment and start a **REPL** (**read-eval-print-loop** or interactive interpreter) that can access our code or to execute our program. REPLs allow you to program interactively. It's a great environment for exploratory programming, irrespective of whether that means exploring library APIs or exploring data.

We'll use Leiningen for this (http://leiningen.org/). This has become a standard package automation and management system.

## Getting ready

Visit the Leiningen site and download the `lein` script. This will download the Leiningen JAR file when it's needed. The instructions are clear, and it's a simple process.

## How to do it...

To generate a new project, use the `lein new` command, passing the name of the project to it:

```
$ lein new getting-data
Generating a project called getting-data based on the default template.
To see other templates (app, lein plugin, etc), try lein help new.
```

There will be a new subdirectory named `getting-data`. It will contain files with stubs for the `getting-data.core` namespace and for tests.

## How it works...

The new project directory also contains a file named `project.clj`. This file contains metadata about the project, such as its name, version, license, and more. It also contains a list of the dependencies that our code will use, as shown in the following snippet. The specifications that this file uses allow it to search Maven repositories and directories of Clojure libraries (Clojars, `https://clojars.org/`) in order to download the project's dependencies. Thus, it integrates well with Java's own packaging system as developed with Maven (`http://maven.apache.org/`).

```
(defproject getting-data "0.1.0-SNAPSHOT"
  :description "FIXME: write description"
  :url "http://example.com/FIXME"
  :license {:name "Eclipse Public License"
            :url "http://www.eclipse.org/legal/epl-v10.html"}
  :dependencies [[org.clojure/clojure "1.6.0"]])
```

In the *Getting ready* section of each recipe, we'll see the libraries that we need to list in the `:dependencies` section of this file. Then, when you run any `lein` command, it will download the dependencies first.

# Reading CSV data into Incanter datasets

One of the simplest data formats is comma-separated values (CSV), and you'll find that it's everywhere. Excel reads and writes CSV directly, as do most databases. Also, because it's really just plain text, it's easy to generate CSV files or to access them from any programming language.

## Getting ready

First, let's make sure that we have the correct libraries loaded. Here's how the project Leiningen (`https://github.com/technomancy/leiningen`) `project.clj` file should look (although you might be able to use more up-to-date versions of the dependencies):

```
(defproject getting-data "0.1.0-SNAPSHOT"
  :dependencies [[org.clojure/clojure "1.6.0"]
                 [incanter "1.5.5"]])
```

Also, in your REPL or your file, include these lines:

```
(use 'incanter.core
     'incanter.io)
```

Finally, downloaded a list of rest area locations from POI Factory at `http://www.poi-factory.com/node/6643`. The data is in a file named `data/RestAreasCombined(Ver.BN).csv`. The version designation might be different though, as the file is updated. You'll also need to register on the site in order to download the data. The file contains this data, which is the location and description of the rest stops along the highway:

```
-67.834062,46.141129,"REST AREA-FOLLOW SIGNS SB I-95 MM305","RR, PT,
Pets, HF"
-67.845906,46.138084,"REST AREA-FOLLOW SIGNS NB I-95 MM305","RR, PT,
Pets, HF"
-68.498471,45.659781,"TURNOUT NB I-95 MM249","Scenic Vista-NO
FACILITIES"
-68.534061,45.598464,"REST AREA SB I-95 MM240","RR, PT, Pets, HF"
```

In the project directory, we have to create a subdirectory named `data` and place the file in this subdirectory.

I also created a copy of this file with a row listing the names of the columns and named it `RestAreasCombined(Ver.BN)-headers.csv`.

## How to do it...

1. Now, use the `incanter.io/read-dataset` function in your REPL:

```
user=> (read-dataset "data/RestAreasCombined(Ver.BJ).csv")
```

```
|      :col0 |     :col1 |                              :col2
|                    :col3 |
|------------+-----------+-------------------------------------------+-
--------------------------|
| -67.834062 | 46.141129 | REST AREA-FOLLOW SIGNS SB I-95 MM305 |
RR, PT, Pets, HF |
| -67.845906 | 46.138084 | REST AREA-FOLLOW SIGNS NB I-95 MM305 |
RR, PT, Pets, HF |
| -68.498471 | 45.659781 |             TURNOUT NB I-95 MM249 |
Scenic Vista-NO FACILITIES |
| -68.534061 | 45.598464 |             REST AREA SB I-95 MM240 |
RR, PT, Pets, HF |
| -68.539034 | 45.594001 |             REST AREA NB I-95 MM240 |
RR, PT, Pets, HF |
    ...
```

2. If we have a header row in the CSV file, then we include `:header true` in the call to `read-dataset`:

```
user=> (read-dataset "data/RestAreasCombined(Ver.BJ)-headers.csv"
:header true)
```

```
| :longitude | :latitude |                                            :name
|                         :codes |
|-----------+-----------+-------------------------------------+-
--------------------------|
| -67.834062 | 46.141129 | REST AREA-FOLLOW SIGNS SB I-95 MM305 |
RR, PT, Pets, HF |
| -67.845906 | 46.138084 | REST AREA-FOLLOW SIGNS NB I-95 MM305 |
RR, PT, Pets, HF |
| -68.498471 | 45.659781 |                 TURNOUT NB I-95 MM249 |
Scenic Vista-NO FACILITIES |
| -68.534061 | 45.598464 |                 REST AREA SB I-95 MM240 |
RR, PT, Pets, HF |
| -68.539034 | 45.594001 |                 REST AREA NB I-95 MM240 |
RR, PT, Pets, HF |
...
```

## How it works...

Together, Clojure and Incanter make a lot of common tasks easy, which is shown in the *How to do it* section of this recipe.

We've taken some external data, in this case from a CSV file, and loaded it into an Incanter dataset. In Incanter, a dataset is a table, similar to a sheet in a spreadsheet or a database table. Each column has one field of data, and each row has an observation of data. Some columns will contain string data (all of the columns in this example did), some will contain dates, and some will contain numeric data. Incanter tries to automatically detect when a column contains numeric data and coverts it to a Java `int` or `double`. Incanter takes away a lot of the effort involved with importing data.

## There's more...

For more information about Incanter datasets, see *Chapter 6, Working with Incanter Datasets*.

# Reading JSON data into Incanter datasets

Another data format that's becoming increasingly popular is **JavaScript Object Notation**
(**JSON**, http://json.org/). Like CSV, this is a plain text format, so it's easy for programs to
work with. It provides more information about the data than CSV does, but at the cost of being
more verbose. It also allows the data to be structured in more complicated ways, such as
hierarchies or sequences of hierarchies.

Because JSON is a much richer data model than CSV, we might need to transform the
data. In that case, we can just pull out the information we're interested in and flatten the
nested maps before we pass it to Incanter. In this recipe, however, we'll just work with fairly
simple data structures.

## Getting ready

First, here are the contents of the Leiningen `project.clj` file:

```
(defproject getting-data "0.1.0-SNAPSHOT"
  :dependencies [[org.clojure/clojure "1.6.0"]
                 [incanter "1.5.5"]
                 [org.clojure/data.json "0.2.5"]])
```

Use these libraries in your REPL or program (inside an `ns` form):

```
(require '[incanter.core :as i]
         '[clojure.data.json :as json]
         '[clojure.java.io :as io])
(import '[java.io EOFException])
```

Moreover, you need some data. For this, I have a file named `delicious-rss-214k.json`
and placed it in the folder named data. It contains a number of top-level JSON objects.
For example, the first one starts like this:

```
{
    "guidislink": false,
    "link": "http://designreviver.com/tips/a-collection-of-wordpress-
tutorials-tips-and-themes/",
    "title_detail": {
        "base": "http://feeds.delicious.com/v2/rss/
recent?min=1&count=100",
        "value": "A Collection of Wordpress Tutorials, Tips and Themes
| Design Reviver",
        "language": null,
        "type": "text/plain"
    },
    "author": "mccarrd4",
    ...
```

You can download this data file from Infochimps at `http://www.ericrochester.com/clj-data-analysis/data/delicious-rss-214k.json.xz`. You'll need to decompress it into the data directory.

## How to do it...

Once everything's in place, we'll need a couple of functions to make it easier to handle the multiple JSON objects at the top level of the file:

1.  We'll need a function that attempts to call a function on an instance of `java.io.Reader` and returns `nil` if there's an `EOFException`, in case there's a problem reading the file:

```
(defn test-eof [reader f]
  (try
    (f reader)
    (catch EOFException e
      nil)))
```

2.  Now, we'll build on this to repeatedly parse a JSON document from an instance of `java.io.Reader`. We do this by repeatedly calling `test-eof` until eof or until it returns `nil`, accumulating the returned values as we go:

```
(defn read-all-json [reader]
  (loop [accum []]
    (if-let [record (test-eof reader json/read)]
      (recur (conj accum record))
      accum)))
```

3.  Finally, we'll perform the previously mentioned two steps to read the data from the file:

```
(def d (i/to-dataset
         (with-open
           [r (io/reader
                "data/delicious-rss-214k.json")]
           (read-all-json r))))
```

This binds d to a new dataset that contains the information read in from the JSON documents.

## How it works...

Similar to all **Lisp's** (**List Processing**), Clojure is usually read from the inside out and from right to left. Let's break it down. `clojure.java.io/reader` opens the file for reading. `read-all-json` parses all of the JSON documents in the file into a sequence. In this case, it returns a vector of the maps. `incanter.core/to-dataset` takes a sequence of maps and returns an Incanter dataset. This dataset will use the keys in the maps as column names, and it will convert the data values into a matrix. Actually, `to-dataset` can accept many different data structures. Try `doc to-dataset` in the REPL (`doc` shows the documentation string attached to the function), or see the Incanter documentation at `http://data-sorcery.org/contents/` for more information.

# Reading data from Excel with Incanter

We've seen how Incanter makes a lot of common data-processing tasks very simple, and reading an Excel spreadsheet is another example of this.

## Getting ready

First, make sure that your Leiningen `project.clj` file contains the right dependencies:

```
(defproject getting-data "0.1.0-SNAPSHOT"
  :dependencies [[org.clojure/clojure "1.6.0"]
                 [incanter "1.5.5"]]])
```

Also, make sure that you've loaded those packages into the REPL or script:

```
(use 'incanter.core
     'incanter.excel)
```

Find the Excel spreadsheet you want to work on. The file name of my spreadsheet is `data/small-sample-header.xls`, as shown in the following screenshot. You can download this from `http://www.ericrochester.com/clj-data-analysis/data/small-sample-header.xls`.

## How to do it...

Now, all you need to do is call `incanter.excel/read-xls`:

```
user=> (read-xls "data/small-sample-header.xls")
```

```
| given-name | surname |  relation |
|------------+---------+-----------|
|      Gomez |  Addams |    father |
|   Morticia |  Addams |    mother |
|   Pugsley  |  Addams |   brother |
```

## How it works...

This can read standard Excel files (.xls) and the XML-based file format introduced in Excel 2003 (.xlsx).

# Reading data from JDBC databases

Reading data from a relational database is only slightly more complicated than reading from Excel, and much of the extra complication involves connecting to the database.

Fortunately, there's a Clojure-contributed package that sits on top of **JDBC** (the **Java database connector** API, `http://www.oracle.com/technetwork/java/javase/jdbc/index.html`) and makes working with databases much easier. In this example, we'll load a table from an SQLite database (`http://www.sqlite.org/`), which stores the database in a single file.

## Getting ready

First, list the dependencies in your Leiningen `project.clj` file. We will also need to include the database driver library. For this example, it is `org.xerial/sqlite-jdbc`:

```
(defproject getting-data "0.1.0-SNAPSHOT"
  :dependencies [[org.clojure/clojure "1.6.0"]
                 [incanter "1.5.5"]
                 [org.clojure/java.jdbc "0.3.3"]
                 [org.xerial/sqlite-jdbc "3.7.15-M1"]])
```

Then, load the modules into your REPL or script file:

```
(require '[incanter.core :as i]
         '[clojure.java.jdbc :as j])
```

Finally, get the database connection information. I have my data in an SQLite database file named `data/small-sample.sqlite`, as shown in the following screenshot. You can download this from `http://www.ericrochester.com/clj-data-analysis/data/small-sample.sqlite`.

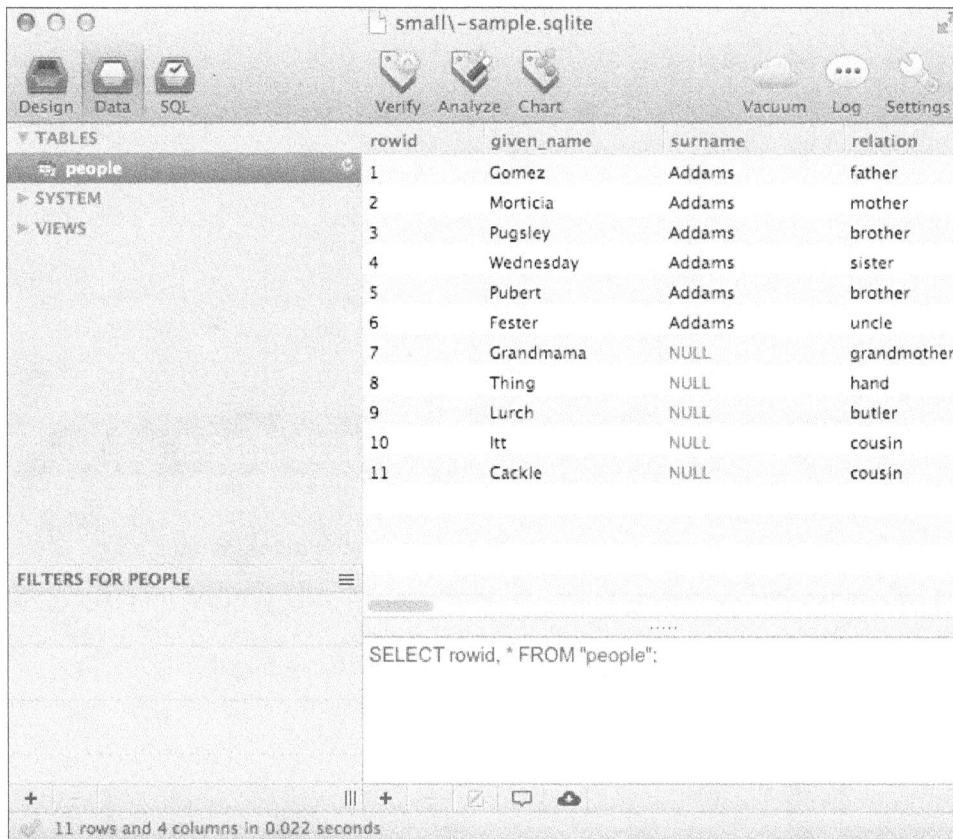

## How to do it...

Loading the data is not complicated, but we'll make it easier with a wrapper function:

1. We'll create a function that takes a database connection map and a table name and returns a dataset created from this table:

```
(defn load-table-data
  "This loads the data from a database table."
  [db table-name]
  (i/to-dataset
    (j/query db (str "SELECT * FROM " table-name ";"))))
```

2. Next, we define a database map with the connection parameters suitable for our database:

```
(defdb {:subprotocol "sqlite"
        :subname "data/small-sample.sqlite"
        :classname "org.sqlite.JDBC"})
```

3. Finally, call `load-table-data` with `db` and a table name as a symbol or string:

```
user=> (load-table-data db 'people)

|   :relation |  :surname | :given_name |
|-------------+-----------+-------------|
|      father |    Addams |       Gomez |
|      mother |    Addams |     Morticia |
|      brother |   Addams |     Pugsley |||
...
```

## How it works...

The `load-table-data` function passes the database connection information directly through to `clojure.java.jdbc/query.query`. It creates an SQL query that returns all of the fields in the table that is passed in. Each row of the result is a sequence of hashes mapping column names to data values. This sequence is wrapped in a dataset by `incanter.core/to-dataset`.

## See also

Connecting to different database systems using JDBC isn't necessarily a difficult task, but it's dependent on which database you wish to connect to. Oracle has a tutorial for how to work with JDBC at `http://docs.oracle.com/javase/tutorial/jdbc/basics`, and the documentation for the `clojure.java.jdbc` library has some good information too (`http://clojure.github.com/java.jdbc/`). If you're trying to find out what the connection string looks like for a database system, there are lists available online. The list at `http://www.java2s.com/Tutorial/Java/0340__Database/AListofJDBCDriversconnectionstringdrivername.htm` includes the major drivers.

# Reading XML data into Incanter datasets

One of the most popular formats for data is XML. Some people love it, while some hate it. However, almost everyone has to deal with it at some point. While Clojure can use Java's XML libraries, it also has its own package which provides a more natural way to work with XML in Clojure.

## Getting ready

First, include these dependencies in your Leiningen `project.clj` file:

```
(defproject getting-data "0.1.0-SNAPSHOT"
  :dependencies [[org.clojure/clojure "1.6.0"]
                 [incanter "1.5.5"]]])
```

Use these libraries in your REPL or program:

```
(require '[incanter.core :as i]
         '[clojure.xml :as xml]
         '[clojure.zip :as zip])
```

Then, find a data file. I visited the website for the Open Data Catalog for Washington, D.C. (http://data.octo.dc.gov/), and downloaded the data for the 2013 crime incidents. I moved this file to data/crime_incidents_2013_plain.xml. This is how the contents of the file look:

```
<?xml version="1.0" encoding="iso-8859-1"?>
<dcst:ReportedCrimes
    xmlns:dcst="http://dc.gov/dcstat/types/1.0/">
  <dcst:ReportedCrime
    xmlns:dcst="http://dc.gov/dcstat/types/1.0/">
      <dcst:ccn><![CDATA[04104147]]></dcst:ccn>
      <dcst:reportdatetime>
        2013-04-16T00:00:00-04:00
      </dcst:reportdatetime>
  ...
```

## How to do it...

Now, let's see how to load this file into an Incanter dataset:

1. The solution for this recipe is a little more complicated, so we'll wrap it into a function:

```
(defn load-xml-data [xml-file first-data next-data]
  (let [data-map (fn [node]
                   [(:tag node) (first (:content node))])]
    (->>
      (xml/parse xml-file)
      zip/xml-zip
      first-data
      (iterate next-data)
      (take-while #(not (nil? %)))
      (map zip/children)
      (map #(mapcat data-map %))
      (map #(apply array-map %))
         i/to-dataset)))
```

2. We can call the function like this. Because there are so many columns, we'll just verify the data that is loaded by looking at the column names and the row count:

```
user=> (def d
         (load-xml-data "data/crime_incidents_2013_plain.xml"
                        zip/down zip/right))
user=> (i/col-names d)
[:dcst:ccn :dcst:reportdatetime :dcst:shift :dcst:offense
:dcst:method :dcst:lastmodifieddate :dcst:blocksiteaddress
:dcst:blockxcoord :dcst:blockycoord :dcst:ward :dcst:anc
:dcst:district :dcst:psa :dcst:neighborhoodcluster :dcst:busi
nessimprovementdistrict :dcst:block_group :dcst:census_tract
:dcst:voting_precinct :dcst:start_date :dcst:end_date]
user=> (i/nrow d)
35826
```

This looks good. This gives you the number of crimes reported in the dataset.

## How it works...

This recipe follows a typical pipeline for working with XML:

1. Parsing an XML data file
2. Extracting the data nodes
3. Converting the data nodes into a sequence of maps representing the data
4. Converting the data into an Incanter dataset

`load-xml-data` implements this process. This takes three parameters:

▶ The input filename

▶ A function that takes the root node of the parsed XML and returns the first data node

▶ A function that takes a data node and returns the next data node or nil, if there are no more nodes

First, the function parses the XML file and wraps it in a **zipper** (we'll talk more about zippers in the next section). Then, it uses the two functions that are passed in to extract all of the data nodes as a sequence. For each data node, the function retrieves that node's child nodes and converts them into a series of tag name / content pairs. The pairs for each data node are converted into a map, and the sequence of maps is converted into an Incanter dataset.

## There's more...

We used a couple of interesting data structures or constructs in this recipe. Both are common in functional programming or Lisp, but neither have made their way into more mainstream programming. We should spend a minute with them.

### Navigating structures with zippers

The first thing that happens to the parsed XML is that it gets passed to `clojure.zip/xml-zip`. Zippers are standard data structures that encapsulate the data at a position in a tree structure, as well as the information necessary to navigate back out. This takes Clojure's native XML data structure and turns it into something that can be navigated quickly using commands such as `clojure.zip/down` and `clojure.zip/right`. Being a functional programming language, Clojure encourages you to use immutable data structures, and zippers provide an efficient, natural way to navigate and modify a tree-like structure, such as an XML document.

Zippers are very useful and interesting, and understanding them can help you understand and work better with immutable data structures. For more information on zippers, the Clojure-doc page is helpful (`http://clojure-doc.org/articles/tutorials/parsing_xml_with_zippers.html`). However, if you would rather dive into the deep end, see Gerard Huet's paper, *The Zipper* (`http://www.st.cs.uni-saarland.de/edu/seminare/2005/advanced-fp/docs/huet-zipper.pdf`).

### Processing in a pipeline

We used the `->>` macro to express our process as a pipeline. For deeply nested function calls, this macro lets you read it from the left-hand side to the right-hand side, and this makes the process's data flow and series of transformations much more clear.

We can do this in Clojure because of its macro system. `->>` simply rewrites the calls into Clojure's native, nested format as the form is read. The first parameter of the macro is inserted into the next expression as the last parameter. This structure is inserted into the third expression as the last parameter, and so on, until the end of the form. Let's trace this through a few steps. Say, we start off with the expression `(->> x first (map length) (apply +))`. As Clojure builds the final expression, here's each intermediate step (the elements to be combined are highlighted at each stage):

1. `(->> x first (map length) (apply +))`
2. `(->>(first x) (map length) (apply +))`
3. `(->>(map length (first x)) (apply +))`
4. `(apply + (map length (first x)))`

## Comparing XML and JSON

XML and JSON (from the *Reading JSON data into Incanter datasets* recipe) are very similar. Arguably, much of the popularity of JSON is driven by disillusionment with XML's verboseness.

When we're dealing with these formats in Clojure, the biggest difference is that JSON is converted directly to native Clojure data structures that mirror the data, such as maps and vectors Meanwhile, XML is read into record types that reflect the structure of XML, not the structure of the data.

In other words, the keys of the maps for JSON will come from the domains, `first_name` or `age`, for instance. However, the keys of the maps for XML will come from the data format, such as **tag**, **attribute**, or **children**, and the tag and attribute names will come from the domain. This extra level of abstraction makes XML more unwieldy.

# Scraping data from tables in web pages

There's data everywhere on the Internet. Unfortunately, a lot of it is difficult to reach. It's buried in tables, articles, or deeply nested `div` tags. Web scraping (writing a program that walks over a web page and extracts data from it) is brittle and laborious, but it's often the only way to free this data so it can be used in our analyses. This recipe describes how to load a web page and dig down into its contents so that you can pull the data out.

To do this, we're going to use the Enlive (`https://github.com/cgrand/enlive/wiki`) library. This uses a **domain specific language** (**DSL**, a set of commands that make a small set of tasks very easy and natural) based on CSS selectors to locate elements within a web page. This library can also be used for templating. In this case, we'll just use it to get data back out of a web page.

## Getting ready

First, you have to add Enlive to the dependencies in the `project.clj` file:

```
(defproject getting-data "0.1.0-SNAPSHOT"
  :dependencies [[org.clojure/clojure "1.6.0"]
                 [incanter "1.5.5"]
                 [enlive "1.1.5"]]])
```

Next, use these packages in your REPL or script:

```
(require '[clojure.string :as string]
         '[net.cgrand.enlive-html :as html]
         '[incanter.core :as i])
(import [java.net URL])
```

Finally, identify the file to scrape the data from. I've put up a file at `http://www.ericrochester.com/clj-data-analysis/data/small-sample-table.html`, which looks like this:

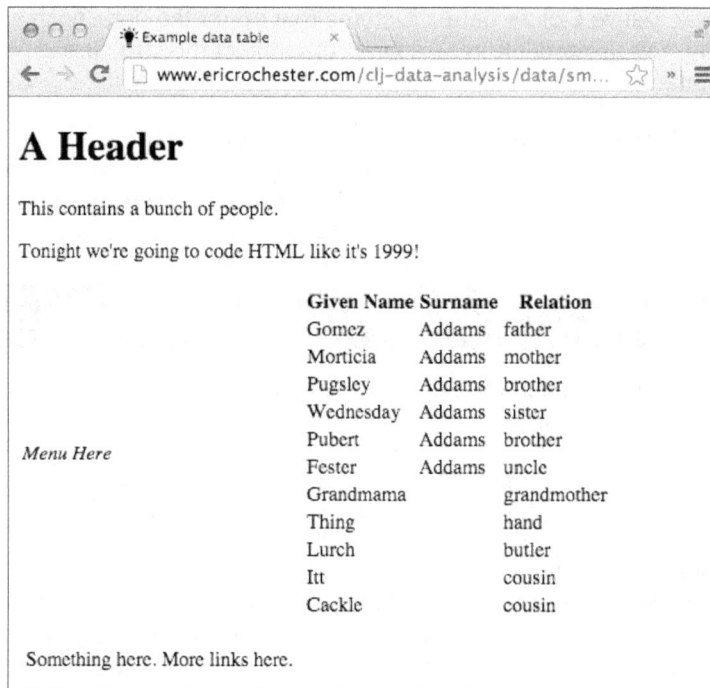

It's intentionally stripped down, and it makes use of tables for layout (hence the comment about 1999).

## How to do it...

1. Since this task is a little complicated, let's pull out the steps into several functions:

```
(defn to-keyword
  "This takes a string and returns a normalized keyword."
  [input]
  (->input
    string/lower-case
    (string/replace \space \-)
    keyword))


(defn load-data
  "This loads the data from a table at a URL."
  [url]
  (let [page (html/html-resource (URL. url))
        table (html/select page [:table#data])
        headers (->>
                    (html/select table [:tr :th])
                    (map html/text)
                    (map to-keyword)
                    vec)
        rows (->> (html/select table [:tr])
               (map #(html/select % [:td]))
               (map #(map html/text %))
               (filterseq))]
    (i/dataset headers rows))))))
```

2. Now, call `load-data` with the URL you want to load data from:

```
user=> (load-data (str "http://www.ericrochester.com/"
        "clj-data-analysis/data/small-sample-table.html"))
| :given-name | :surname | :relation |
|-------------+----------+-----------|
|       Gomez |   Addams |    father |
|    Morticia |   Addams |    mother |
|     Pugsley |   Addams |   brother |
|   Wednesday |   Addams |    sister |
  ...
```

## How it works...

The `let` bindings in `load-data` tell the story here. Let's talk about them one by one.

The first binding has Enlive download the resource and parse it into Enlive's internal representation:

```
(let [page (html/html-resource (URL. url))
```

The next binding selects the table with the `data` ID:

```
table (html/select page [:table#data])
```

Now, select of all the header cells from the table, extract the text from them, convert each to a keyword, and then convert the entire sequence into a vector. This gives headers for the dataset:

```
headers (->>
          (html/select table [:tr :th])
          (map html/text)
          (map to-keyword)
          vec)
```

First, select each row individually. The next two steps are wrapped in `map` so that the cells in each row stay grouped together. In these steps, select the data cells in each row and extract the text from each. Last, use `filterseq`, which removes any rows with no data, such as the header row:

```
rows (->> (html/select table [:tr])
          (map #(html/select % [:td]))
          (map #(map html/text %))
          (filterseq))]
```

Here's another view of this data. In this image, you can see some of the code from this web page. The variable names and select expressions are placed beside the HTML structures that they match. Hopefully, this makes it more clear how the select expressions correspond to the HTML elements:

Finally, convert everything to a dataset. `incanter.core/dataset` is a lower level constructor than `incanter.core/to-dataset`. It requires you to pass in the column names and data matrix as separate sequences:

```
(i/dataset headers rows)))
```

It's important to realize that the code, as presented here, is the result of a lot of trial and error. Screen scraping usually is. Generally, I download the page and save it, so I don't have to keep requesting it from the web server. Next, I start the REPL and parse the web page there. Then, I can take a look at the web page and HTML with the browser's view source function, and I can examine the data from the web page interactively in the REPL. While working, I copy and paste the code back and forth between the REPL and my text editor, as it's convenient. This workflow and environment (sometimes called REPL-driven-development) makes screen scraping (a fiddly, difficult task at the best of times) almost enjoyable.

## See also

- ▸ The next recipe, *Scraping textual data from web pages*, has a more involved example of data scraping on an HTML page
- ▸ The *Aggregating data from different formats* recipe has a practical, real-life example of data scraping in a table

# Scraping textual data from web pages

Not all of the data on the Web is in tables, as in our last recipe. In general, the process to access this nontabular data might be more complicated, depending on how the page is structured.

## Getting ready

First, we'll use the same dependencies and the `require` statements as we did in the last recipe, *Scraping data from tables in web pages*.

Next, we'll identify the file to scrape the data from. I've put up a file at `http://www.ericrochester.com/clj-data-analysis/data/small-sample-list.html`.

This is a much more modern example of a web page. Instead of using tables, it marks up the text with the `section` and `article` tags and other features from HTML5, which help convey what the text means, not just how it should look.

As the screenshot shows, this page contains a list of sections, and each section contains a list of characters:

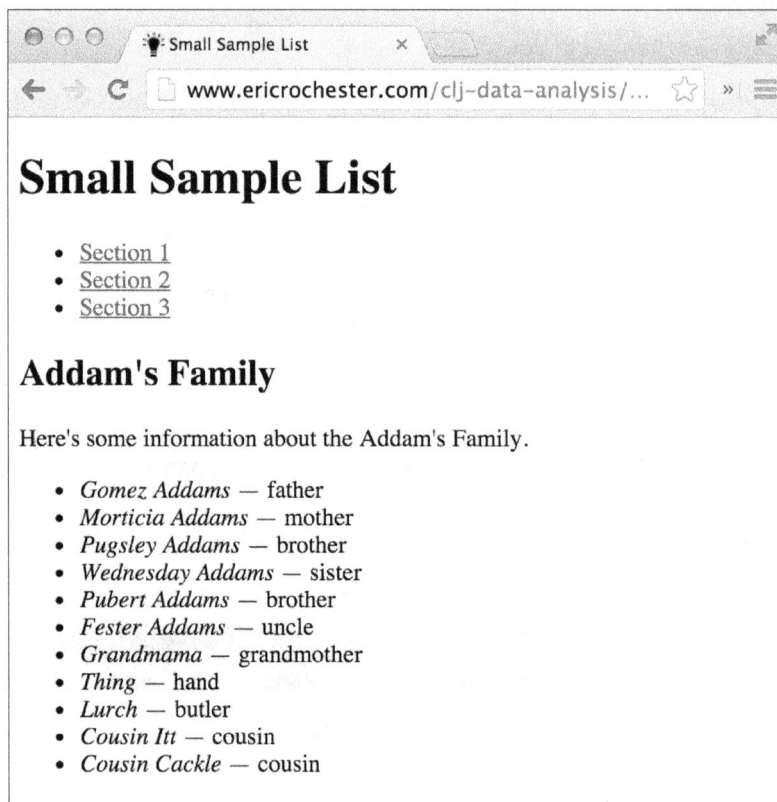

## How to do it...

1. Since this is more complicated, we'll break the task down into a set of smaller functions:

```
(defn get-family
  "This takes an article element and returns the family
  name."
  [article]
  (string/join
    (map html/text (html/select article [:header :h2]))))
```

```
(defn get-person
  "This takes a list item and returns a map of the person's
  name and relationship."
  [li]
  (let [[{pnames :content} rel] (:content li)]
    {:name (apply str pnames)
     :relationship (string/trim rel)}))

(defn get-rows
  "This takes an article and returns the person mappings,
  with the family name added."
  [article]
  (let [family (get-family article)]
    (map #(assoc % :family family)
         (map get-person
              (html/select article [:ul :li])))))

(defn load-data
  "This downloads the HTML page and pulls the data out of
  it."
  [html-url]
  (let [html (html/html-resource (URL. html-url))
        articles (html/select html [:article])]
    (i/to-dataset (mapcat get-rows articles))))
```

2. Now that these functions are defined, we just call `load-data` with the URL that we want to scrape:

```
user=> (load-data (str "http://www.ericrochester.com/"
                       "clj-data-analysis/data/"
                       "small-sample-list.html"))
|         :family |           :name | :relationship |
|-----------------+-----------------+---------------|
| Addam's Family |    Gomez Addams |      — father |
| Addam's Family | Morticia Addams |      — mother |
| Addam's Family |  Pugsley Addams |     — brother |
...
```

## How it works...

After examining the web page, each family is wrapped in an `article` tag that contains a header with an `h2` tag. `get-family` pulls that tag out and returns its text.

`get-person` processes each person. The people in each family are in an unordered list (`ul`), and each person is in an `li` tag. The person's name itself is in an `em` tag. `let` gets the contents of the `li` tag and decomposes it in order to pull out the name and relationship strings. `get-person` puts both pieces of information into a map and returns it.

`get-rows` processes each `article` tag. It calls `get-family` to get that information from the header, gets the list item for each person, calls `get-person` on the list item, and adds the family to each person's mapping.

Here's how the HTML structures correspond to the functions that process them. Each function name is mentioned beside the elements it parses:

```
<article>
  <header>
    <h2 id='addams'>Addam's Family</h2>   get-family
  </header>
  <p>Here's some information about the Addam's Family.</p>
  <ul>
    <li><em>Gomez Addams</em> &mdash; father</li>
    <li><em>Morticia Addams</em> &mdash; mother</li>   get-rows
    <li><em>Pugsley Addams</em> &mdash; brother</li>
    <li><em>Wednesday Addams</em> &mdash; sister</li>
    <li><em>Pubert Addams</em> &mdash; brother</li>
    <li><em>Fester Addams</em> &mdash; uncle</li>
    <li><em>Grandmama</em> &mdash; grandmother</li>
    <li><em>Thing</em> &mdash; hand</li>
    <li><em>Lurch</em> &mdash; butler</li>
    <li><em>Cousin Itt</em> &mdash; cousin</li>
    <li><em>Cousin Cackle</em> &mdash; cousin</li>
  </ul>                       get-person
</article>
```

Finally, `load-data` ties the process together by downloading and parsing the HTML file and pulling the `article` tags from it. It then calls `get-rows` to create the data mappings and converts the output to a dataset.

# Reading RDF data

More and more data is going up on the Internet using linked data in a variety of formats such as microformats, RDFa, and RDF/XML.

Linked data represents entities as consistent URLs and includes links to other databases of the linked data. In a sense, it's the computer equivalent of human-readable web pages. Often, these formats are used for open data, such as the data published by some governments, like in the UK and elsewhere.

Linked data adds a lot of flexibility and power, but it also introduces more complexity. Often, to work effectively with linked data, we need to start a triple store of some kind. In this recipe and the next three, we'll use Sesame (`http://rdf4j.org/`) and the `kr` Clojure library (`https://github.com/drlivingston/kr`).

## Getting ready

First, we need to make sure that the dependencies are listed in our Leiningen `project.clj` file:

```
(defproject getting-data "0.1.0-SNAPSHOT"
  :dependencies [[org.clojure/clojure "1.6.0"]
                 [incanter "1.5.5"]
                 [edu.ucdenver.ccp/kr-sesame-core "1.4.17"]
                 [org.clojure/tools.logging "0.3.0"]
                 [org.slf4j/slf4j-simple "1.7.7"]])
```

We'll execute these packages to have these loaded into our script or REPL:

```
(use 'incanter.core
     'edu.ucdenver.ccp.kr.kb
     'edu.ucdenver.ccp.kr.rdf
     'edu.ucdenver.ccp.kr.sparql
     'edu.ucdenver.ccp.kr.sesame.kb
     'clojure.set)
(import [java.io File])
```

For this example, we'll get data from the Telegraphis Linked Data assets. We'll pull down the database of currencies at `http://telegraphis.net/data/currencies/currencies.ttl`. Just to be safe, I've downloaded that file and saved it as `data/currencies.ttl`, and we'll access it from there.

We'll store the data, at least temporarily, in a Sesame data store (`http://notes.3kbo.com/sesame`) that allows us to easily store and query linked data.

## How to do it...

The longest part of this process will be to define the data. The libraries we're using do all of the heavy lifting, as shown in the steps given below:

1.  First, we will create the triple store and register the namespaces that the data uses. We'll bind this triple store to the name `tstore`:

```
(defn kb-memstore
  "This creates a Sesame triple store in memory."
  []
  (kb :sesame-mem))
(defn init-kb [kb-store]
  (register-namespaces
    kb-store
    '(("geographis"
        "http://telegraphis.net/ontology/geography/geography#")
      ("code"
        "http://telegraphis.net/ontology/measurement/code#")
      ("money"
        "http://telegraphis.net/ontology/money/money#")
      ("owl"
        "http://www.w3.org/2002/07/owl#")
      ("rdf"
        "http://www.w3.org/1999/02/22-rdf-syntax-ns#")
      ("xsd"
        "http://www.w3.org/2001/XMLSchema#")
      ("currency"
        "http://telegraphis.net/data/currencies/")
      ("dbpedia" "http://dbpedia.org/resource/")
      ("dbpedia-ont" "http://dbpedia.org/ontology/")
      ("dbpedia-prop" "http://dbpedia.org/property/")
      ("err" "http://ericrochester.com/"))))

(def t-store (init-kb (kb-memstore)))
```

2. After taking a look at the data some more, we can identify what data we want to pull out and start to formulate a query. We'll use the kr library's (`https://github.com/drlivingston/kr`) query DSL and bind it to the name q:

```
(def q '((?/c rdf/type money/Currency)
         (?/c money/name ?/full_name)
         (?/c money/shortName ?/name)
         (?/c money/symbol ?/symbol)
         (?/c money/minorName ?/minor_name)
         (?/c money/minorExponent ?/minor_exp)
         (?/c money/isoAlpha ?/iso)
         (?/c money/currencyOf ?/country)))
```

3. Now, we need a function that takes a result map and converts the variable names in the query into column names in the output dataset. The `header-keyword` and `fix-headers` functions will do this:

```
(defn header-keyword
  "This converts a query symbol to a keyword."
  [header-symbol]
  (keyword (.replace (name header-symbol) \_ \-)))
(defn fix-headers
  "This changes all of the keys in the map to make them
  valid header keywords."
  [coll]
  (into {}
        (map (fn [[k v]] [(header-keyword k) v])
             coll)))
```

4. As usual, once all of the pieces are in place, the function that ties everything together is short:

```
(defn load-data
  [krdf-file q]
  (load-rdf-file k rdf-file)
  (to-dataset (map fix-headers (query k q))))
```

5. Also, using this function is just as simple:

```
user=> (sel d :rows (range 3)
           :cols [:full-name :name :iso :symbol])
```

|                          | :full-name |   :name |  :iso | :symbol |
| ------------------------ | ---------- | ------- | ----- | ------- |
| United Arab Emirates dirham |         |  dirham |   AED |      ｄ |
|          Afghan afghani  |            | afghani |   AFN |      ｊ |
|            Albanian lek  |            |     lek |   ALL |       L |

## How it works...

First, here's some background information. **Resource Description Format** (**RDF**) isn't an XML format, although it's often written using XML. (There are other formats as well, such as N3 and Turtle.) RDF sees the world as a set of statements. Each statement has at least three parts (a triple): a subject, predicate, and object. The subject and predicate must be URIs. (URIs are like URLs, only more general. For example, `uri:7890` is a valid URI.) Objects can be a literal or a URI. The URIs form a graph. They are linked to each other and make statements about each other. This is where the *linked* in *linked data* comes from.

If you want more information about linked data, `http://linkeddata.org/guides-and-tutorials` has some good recommendations.

Now, about our recipe. From a high level, the process we used here is pretty simple, given as follows:

1. Create a triple store (`kb-memstore` and `init-kb`)
2. Load the data (`load-data`)
3. Query the data to pull out only what you want (`q` and `load-data`)
4. Transform it into a format that Incanter can ingest easily (`rekey` and `col-map`)
5. Finally, create the Incanter dataset (`load-data`)

The newest thing here is the query format. `kb` uses a nice SPARQL-like DSL to express the queries. In fact, it's so easy to use that we'll deal with it instead of working with raw RDF. The items starting with `?/` are variables which will be used as keys for the result maps. The other items look like `rdf-namespace/value`. The namespace is taken from the registered namespaces defined in `init-kb`. These are different from Clojure's namespaces, although they serve a similar function for your data: to partition and provide context.

## See also

The next few recipes, *Querying RDF data with SPARQL* and *Aggregating data from different formats*, build on this recipe and will use much of the same set up and techniques.

# Querying RDF data with SPARQL

For the last recipe, *Reading RDF data*, the **embedded domain-specific language** (**EDSL**) used for the query gets converted to SPARQL, which is the query language for many linked data systems. If you squint just right at the query, it looks kind of like a SPARQL WHERE clause. For example, you can query DBPedia to get information about a city, such as its population, location, and other data. It's a simple query, but a query nevertheless.

This worked great when we had access to the raw data in our own triple store. However, if we need to access a remote SPARQL endpoint directly, it's more complicated.

For this recipe, we'll query DBPedia (http://dbpedia.org) for information on the United Arab Emirates currency, which is the Dirham. DBPedia extracts structured information from Wikipedia (the summary boxes) and republishes it as RDF. Just as Wikipedia is a useful first-stop for humans to get information about something, DBPedia is a good starting point for computer programs that want to gather data about a domain.

## Getting ready

First, we need to make sure that the dependencies are listed in our Leiningen project.clj file:

```
(defproject getting-data "0.1.0-SNAPSHOT"
  :dependencies [[org.clojure/clojure "1.6.0"]
                 [incanter "1.5.5"]
                 [edu.ucdenver.ccp/kr-sesame-core "1.4.17"]
                 [org.clojure/tools.logging "0.3.0"]
                 [org.slf4j/slf4j-simple "1.7.7"]])
```

Then, load the Clojure and Java libraries we'll use:

```
(require '[clojure.java.io :as io]
         '[clojure.xml :as xml]
         '[clojure.pprint :as pp]
         '[clojure.zip :as zip])
(use 'incanter.core
     'edu.ucdenver.ccp.kr.kb
     'edu.ucdenver.ccp.kr.rdf
     'edu.ucdenver.ccp.kr.sparql
     'edu.ucdenver.ccp.kr.sesame.kb
     'clojure.set)
(import [java.io File]
        [java.net URL URLEncoder])
```

## How to do it...

As we work through this, we'll define a series of functions. Finally, we'll create one function, `load-data`, to orchestrate everything, and we'll finish by doing the following:

1.  We have to create a Sesame triple store and initialize it with the namespaces we'll use. For both of these, we'll use the `kb-memstore` and `init-kb` functions from *Reading RDF data*. We define a function that takes a URI for a subject in the triple store and constructs a SPARQL query that returns at most 200 statements about this subject. The function then filters out any statements with non-English strings for objects, but it allows everything else:

```
(defn make-query
  "This creates a query that returns all of the
  triples related to asubject URI. It
  filters out non-English strings."
  ([subject kb]
   (binding [*kb* kb
             *select-limit* 200]
     (sparql-select-query
       (list '(~subject ?/p ?/o)
             '(:or (:not (:isLiteral ?/o))
                   (!= (:datatype ?/o) rdf/langString)
                   (= (:lang ?/o) ["en"])))))))
```

2.  Now that we have the query, we'll need to encode it into a URL in order to retrieve the results:

```
(defn make-query-uri
  "This constructs a URI for the query."
  ([base-uri query]
   (URL. (str base-uri
              "?format="
              (URLEncoder/encode "text/xml")
              "&query=" (URLEncoder/encode query)))))
```

3.  Once we get a result, we'll parse the XML file, wrap it in a zipper, and navigate to the first result. All of this will be in a function that we'll write in a minute. Right now, the next function will take this first result node and return a list of all the results:

```
(defn result-seq
  "This takes the first result and returns a sequence
  of this node, plus all of the nodes to the right of
  it."
  ([first-result]
   (cons (zip/node first-result)
         (zip/rights first-result))))
```

4. The following set of functions takes each result node and returns a key-value pair (`result-to-kv`). It uses `binding-str` to pull the results out of the XML. Then, `accum-hash` pushes the key-value pairs into a map. Keys that occur more than once have their values accumulated in a vector:

```
(defn binding-str
  "This takes a binding, pulls out the first tag's
  content, and concatenates it into a string."
  ([b]
    (apply str (:content (first (:content b))))))

(defn result-to-kv
  "This takes a result node and creates a key-value
  vector pair from it."
  ([r]
    (let [[p o] (:content r)]
      [(binding-str p) (binding-str o)])))

(defn accum-hash
  ([m [k v]]
    (if-let [current (m k)]
      (assoc m k (str current \space v))
      (assoc m k v))))
```

5. For the last utility function, we'll define `rekey`. This will convert the keys of a map based on another map:

```
(defn rekey
  "This just flips the arguments for
  clojure.set/rename-keys to make it more
  convenient."
  ([k-map map]
    (rename-keys
      (select-keys map (keys k-map)) k-map)))
```

6. Let's now add a function that takes a SPARQL endpoint and subject and returns a sequence of result nodes. This will use several of the functions we've just defined:

```
(defn query-sparql-results
  "This queries a SPARQL endpoint and returns a
  sequence of result nodes."
  ([sparql-uri subject kb]
    (->> kb
      ;; Build the URI query string.
      (make-query subject)
      (make-query-uri sparql-uri)
```

```
;; Get the results, parse the XML,
;; and return the zipper.
io/input-stream
xml/parse
zip/xml-zip
;; Find the first child.
zip/down
zip/right
zip/down
;; Convert all children into a sequence.
result-seq)))
```

7. Finally, we can pull everything together. Here's `load-data`:

```
(defn load-data
  "This loads the data about a currency for the
  given URI."
  [sparql-uri subject col-map]
  (->>
    ;; Initialize the triple store.
    (kb-memstore)
    init-kb
    ;; Get the results.
    (query-sparql-results sparql-uri subject)
    ;; Generate a mapping.
    (map result-to-kv)
    (reduce accum-hash {})
    ;; Translate the keys in the map.
    (rekey col-map)
    ;; And create a dataset.
    to-dataset))
```

8. Now, let's use this data. We can define a set of variables to make it easier to reference the namespaces we'll use. We'll use these to create the mapping to column names:

```
(def rdfs "http://www.w3.org/2000/01/rdf-schema#")
(def dbpedia "http:///dbpedia.org/resource/")
(def dbpedia-ont "http://dbpedia.org/ontology/")
(def dbpedia-prop "http://dbpedia.org/property/")

(def col-map {(str rdfs 'label) :name,
  (str dbpedia-prop 'usingCountries) :country
  (str dbpedia-prop 'peggedWith) :pegged-with
  (str dbpedia-prop 'symbol) :symbol
  (str dbpedia-prop 'usedBanknotes) :used-banknotes
  (str dbpedia-prop 'usedCoins) :used-coins
  (str dbpedia-prop 'inflationRate) :inflation})
```

9. We call `load-data` with the DBPedia SPARQL endpoint, the resource we want information about (as a symbol), and the column map:

```
user=> (def d (load-data "http://dbpedia.org/sparql"
                  (symbol (str dbpedia dbpedia "United_Arab_
Emirates_dirham"))
                  col-map))
user=> (sel d :cols [:country :name :symbol])
```

| :country | :name | :symbol |
|----------------------|-----------------------------|---------|
| United Arab Emirates | United Arab Emirates dirham | ﺩ |

## How it works...

The only part of this recipe that has to do with SPARQL, really, is the `make-query` function. It uses the `sparql-select-query` function to generate a SPARQL query string from the query pattern. This pattern has to be interpreted in the context of the triple store that has the namespaces defined. This context is set using the `binding` command. We can see how this function works by calling it from the REPL by itself:

```
user=> (println
         (make-query
           (symbol (str dbpedia "/United_Arab_Emirates_dirham"))
           (init-kb (kb-memstore))))
PREFIX rdf: <http://www.w3.org/1999/02/22-rdf-syntax-ns#>
SELECT ?p ?o
WHERE {  <http://dbpedia.org/resource/United_Arab_Emirates_dirham> ?p
?o .
 FILTER (  ( ! isLiteral(?o)
 || ( datatype(?o)  !=<http://www.w3.org/1999/02/22-rdf-syntax-
ns#langString> )
 || ( lang(?o)  = "en" )  )
 )
} LIMIT 200
```

The rest of the recipe is concerned with parsing the XML format of the results, and in many ways, it's similar to the last recipe.

## There's more...

For more information on RDF and linked data, see the previous recipe, *Reading RDF data*.

# Aggregating data from different formats

Being able to aggregate data from many linked data sources is good, but most data isn't already formatted for the semantic Web. Fortunately, linked data's flexible and dynamic data model facilitates the integration of data from multiple sources.

For this recipe, we'll combine several previous recipes. We'll load currency data from RDF, as we did in the *Reading RDF data* recipe. We'll also scrape the exchange rate data from X-Rates (http://www.x-rates.com) to get information out of a table, just as we did in the *Scraping data from tables in web pages* recipe. Finally, we'll dump everything into a triple store and pull it back out, as we did in the last recipe.

## Getting ready

First, make sure your Leiningen `project.clj` file has the right dependencies:

```
(defproject getting-data "0.1.0-SNAPSHOT"
  :dependencies [[org.clojure/clojure "1.6.0"]
                 [incanter "1.5.5"]
                 [enlive "1.1.5"]
                 [edu.ucdenver.ccp/kr-sesame-core "1.4.17"]
                 [org.clojure/tools.logging "0.3.0"]
                 [org.slf4j/slf4j-simple "1.7.7"]
                 [clj-time "0.7.0"]])
```

We need to declare that we'll use these libraries in our script or REPL:

```
(require '(clojure.java [io :as io]))
(require '(clojure [xml :as xml]
                   [string :as string]
                   [zip :as zip]))
(require '(net.cgrand [enlive-html :as html]))
(use 'incanter.core
     'clj-time.coerce
     '[clj-time.format :only (formatter formatters parse unparse)]
     'edu.ucdenver.ccp.kr.kb
     'edu.ucdenver.ccp.kr.rdf
     'edu.ucdenver.ccp.kr.sparql
     'edu.ucdenver.ccp.kr.sesame.kb)

(import [java.io File]
        [java.net URL URLEncoder])
```

Finally, make sure that you have the file, `data/currencies.ttl`, which we've been using since *Reading RDF data*.

## How to do it...

Since this is a longer recipe, we'll build it up in segments. At the end, we'll tie everything together.

### Creating the triple store

To begin with, we'll create the triple store. This has become pretty standard. In fact, we'll use the same version of `kb-memstore` and `init-kb` that we've been using from the *Reading RDF data* recipe.

### Scraping exchange rates

The first data that we'll pull into the triple store is the current exchange rates:

1.  This is where things get interesting. We'll pull out the timestamp. The first function finds it, and the second function normalizes it into a standard format:

```
(defn find-time-stamp
  ([module-content]
   (second
     (map html/text
          (html/select module-content
                       [:span.ratesTimestamp]))))))

(def time-stamp-format
     (formatter "MMM dd, yyyy HH:mm 'UTC'"))

(defn normalize-date
  ([date-time]
   (unparse (formatters :date-time)
            (parse time-stamp-format date-time))))
```

2.  We'll drill down to get the countries and their exchange rates:

```
(defn find-data
  ([module-content]
   (html/select module-content
                [:table.tablesorter.ratesTable
                 :tbody :tr])))

(defn td->code
  ([td]
   (let [code (-> td
```

```
                    (html/select [:a])
                    first
                    :attrs
                    :href
                    (string/split #"=")
                    last)]
          (symbol "currency" (str code "#" code)))))))

(defn get-td-a
  ([td]
   (->> td
     :content
     (mapcat :content)
     string/join
     read-string)))

(defn get-data
  ([row]
   (let [[td-header td-to td-from]
         (filter map? (:content row))]
     {:currency (td->code td-to)
      :exchange-to (get-td-a td-to)
      :exchange-from (get-td-a td-from)})))
```

3. This function takes the data extracted from the HTML page and generates a list of RDF triples:

```
(defn data->statements
  ([time-stamp data]
   (let [{:keys [currency exchange-to]} data]
     (list [currency 'err/exchangeRate exchange-to]
           [currency 'err/exchangeWith
            'currency/USD#USD]
           [currency 'err/exchangeRateDate
            [time-stamp 'xsd/dateTime]])))))
```

4. This function ties all of the processes that we just defined together by pulling the data out of the web page, converting it to triples, and adding them to the database:

```
(defn load-exchange-data
  "This downloads the HTML page and pulls the data out
  of it."
  [kb html-url]
```

```
(let [html (html/html-resource html-url)
      div (html/select html [:div.moduleContent])
      time-stamp (normalize-date
                   (find-time-stamp div))]
  (add-statements
    kb
    (mapcat (partial data->statements time-stamp)
            (map get-data (find-data div)))))))
```

That's a mouthful, but now that we can get all of the data into a triple store, we just need to pull everything back out and into Incanter.

## Loading currency data and tying it all together

Bringing the two data sources together and exporting it to Incanter is fairly easy at this point:

```
(defn aggregate-data
  "This controls the process and returns the aggregated data."
  [kb data-file data-url q col-map]
  (load-rdf-file kb (File. data-file))
  (load-exchange-data kb (URL. data-url))
  (to-dataset (map (partial rekey col-map) (query kb q))))
```

We'll need to do a lot of the set up we've done before. Here, we'll bind the triple store, the query, and the column map to names so that we can refer to them easily:

```
(def t-store (init-kb (kb-memstore)))

(def q
  '((?/c rdf/type money/Currency)
    (?/c money/name ?/name)
    (?/c money/shortName ?/shortName)
    (?/c money/isoAlpha ?/iso)
    (?/c money/minorName ?/minorName)
    (?/c money/minorExponent ?/minorExponent)
    (:optional
      ((?/c err/exchangeRate ?/exchangeRate)
       (?/c err/exchangeWith ?/exchangeWith)
       (?/c err/exchangeRateDate ?/exchangeRateDate)))))

(def col-map {'?/name :fullname
              '?/iso :iso
              '?/shortName :name
              '?/minorName :minor-name
```

```
                '?/minorExponent :minor-exp
                '?/exchangeRate :exchange-rate
                '?/exchangeWith :exchange-with
                '?/exchangeRateDate :exchange-date})
```

The specific URL that we're going to scrape is `http://www.x-rates.com/table/?from=USD&amount=1.00`. Let's go ahead and put everything together:

```
user=> (def d
         (aggregate-data t-store "data/currencies.ttl"
            "http://www.x-rates.com/table/?from=USD&amount=1.00"
            q col-map))
user=> (sel d :rows (range 3)
         :cols [:fullname :name :exchange-rate])

|                            :fullname | :name  | :exchange-rate |
|--------------------------------------+--------+----------------|
| United Arab Emirates dirham | dirham |       3.672845 |
| United Arab Emirates dirham | dirham |       3.672845 |
| United Arab Emirates dirham | dirham |       3.672849 |
...
```

As you will see, some of the data from `currencies.ttl` doesn't have exchange data (the ones that start with `nil`). We can look in other sources for that, or decide that some of those currencies don't matter for our project.

## How it works...

A lot of this is just a slightly more complicated version of what we've seen before, pulled together into one recipe. The complicated part is scraping the web page, which is driven by the structure of the page itself.

After taking a look at the source for the page and playing with it on the REPL, the page's structure was clear. First, we needed to pull the timestamp off the top of the table that lists the exchange rates. Then, we walked over the table and pulled the data from each row. Both the data tables (the short and long ones) are in a `div` element with a `moduleContent` class, so everything begins there.

Next, we drilled down from the module's content into the rows of the `rates` table. Inside each row, we pulled out the currency code and returned it as a symbol in the currency namespace. We also drilled down to the exchange rates and returned them as floats. Then, we put everything into a map and converted it to triple vectors, which we added to the triple store.

## See also

▶ For more information on how we pulled in the main currency data and worked with the triple store, see the *Reading RDF data* recipe.

▶ For more information on how we scraped the data from the web page, see *Scraping data from tables in web pages*.

▶ For more information on the SPARQL query, see *Reading RDF data with SPARQL*.

# 2
# Cleaning and Validating Data

In this chapter, we will cover the following recipes:

- ▶ Cleaning data with regular expressions
- ▶ Maintaining consistency with synonym maps
- ▶ Identifying and removing duplicate data
- ▶ Regularizing numbers
- ▶ Calculating relative values
- ▶ Parsing dates and times
- ▶ Lazily processing very large data sets
- ▶ Sampling from very large data sets
- ▶ Fixing spelling errors
- ▶ Parsing custom data formats
- ▶ Validating data with Valip

## Introduction

You probably won't spend as much time to get the data as you will in trying to get it into shape. Raw data is often inconsistent, duplicated, or full of holes. Addresses might be missing, years and dates might be formatted in a thousand different ways, or names might be entered into the wrong fields. You'll have to fix these issues before the data is usable.

This is often an iterative, interactive process. If it's a very large dataset, I might create a sample to work with at this stage. Generally, I start by examining the data files. Once I find a problem, I try to code a solution, which I run on the dataset. After each change, I archive the data, either using a ZIP file or, if the data files are small enough, a version control system. Using a version control system is a good option because I can track the code to transform the data along with the data itself and I can also include comments about what I'm doing. Then, I take a look at the data again, and the entire process starts again. Once I've moved on to analyze the entire collection of data, I might find more issues or I might need to change the data somehow in order to make it easier to analyze, and I'm back in the data cleansing loop once more.

Clojure is an excellent tool for this kind of work, because a REPL is a great environment to explore data and fix it interactively. Also, because many of its sequence functions are lazy by default, Clojure makes it easy to work with a lot of data.

This chapter will highlight a few of the many features that Clojure has to clean data. Initially, we'll take a look at regular expressions and some other basic tools. Then, we'll move on to how we can normalize specific kinds of values. The next few recipes will turn our attention to the process of how to handle very large data sets. Finally, we'll take a look at some more sophisticated ways to fix data where we will write a simple spell checker and a custom parser. Finally, the last recipe will introduce you to a Clojure library that has a good DSL to write tests in order to validate your data.

# Cleaning data with regular expressions

Often, cleaning data involves text transformations. Some, such as adding or removing a set and static strings, are pretty simple. Others, such as parsing a complex data format such as JSON or XML, requires a complete parser. However, many fall within a middle range of complexity. These need more processing power than simple string manipulation, but full-fledged parsing is too much. For these tasks, regular expressions are often useful.

Probably, the most basic and pervasive tool to clean data of any kind is a regular expression. Although they're overused sometimes, regular expressions truly are the best tool for the job many times. Moreover, Clojure has a built-in syntax for compiled regular expressions, so they are convenient too.

In this example, we'll write a function that normalizes U.S. phone numbers.

## Getting ready

For this recipe, we will only require a very basic `project.clj` file. It should have these lines:

```
(defproject cleaning-data "0.1.0-SNAPSHOT"
  :dependencies [[org.clojure/clojure "1.6.0"]])
```

We also only need to have the `clojure.string` library available for our script or REPL. We will get this by using:

```
(require '[clojure.string :as string])
```

## How to do it...

1. First, let's define a regular expression:

```
(def phone-regex
  #"(?x)
  (\d{3})        # Area code.
  \D{0,2}        # Separator. Probably one of \(, \), \-, \space.
  (\d{3})        # Prefix.
  \D?            # Separator.
  (\d{4})
  ")
```

2. Now, we'll define a function that uses this regular expression to pull apart a string that contains a phone number and put it back together in the form of *(999)555-1212*. If the string doesn't appear to be a phone number, it returns `nil`:

```
(defn clean-us-phone [phone]
  (when-let [[_ area-code prefix post]
             (re-find phone-regex phone)]
    (str \( area-code \) prefix \- post)))
```

3. The function works the way we expected:

```
user=> (clean-us-phone "123-456-7890")
"(123)456-7890"
user=> (clean-us-phone "1 2 3 a b c 0 9 8 7")
nil
```

## How it works...

The most complicated part of this process is the regular expression. Let's break it down:

- ▶ `(?x)`: This is a flag that doesn't match anything by itself. Instead, it allows you to spread out the regular expression. The flag will ignore whitespaces and comments. Writing regular expressions in this way makes them considerably easier to read and work with, especially when you are trying to remember what it does after six months.

- ▶ `(\d{3})`: This matches three digits.

- ▶ `\D{0,2}`: This matches zero to two non-numeric characters. This is to allow optional separators between the area code and the prefix.

- `(\d{3})`: This matches another three digits.
- `\D?`: This is an optional non-numeric character. This allows a dash or something similar.
- `(\d{4})`: This matches the final four digits of the phone number.

The items in parentheses are captured by the regular expression. If there are no groups within the parentheses in the regular expression, `re-find` just returns a matching string. If there are groups, it returns a vector. The entire matching string is the first element, and the groups follow in the order in which they appear in the regular expression. In this recipe, we use the groups that are returned to build the output.

## There's more...

Regular expressions are complex, and heavy books have been written about them. Here are some more resources:

- The JavaDocs for the Pattern class (`http://docs.oracle.com/javase/6/docs/api/java/util/regex/Pattern.html`). This summarizes the syntax of Java's style of regular expressions.
- Oracle's Java tutorial on regular expressions (`http://docs.oracle.com/javase/tutorial/essential/regex/`).
- RegexPlant's online tester (`http://www.regexplanet.com/advanced/java/index.html`). However, the REPL is usually what I use to build and test regular expressions.

## See also

Jamie Zawinski is credited with this saying:

> *Some people, when confronted with a problem, think, "I know, I'll use regular expressions." Now they have two problems.*

Regular expressions are a complex, dense, and often fiddly tool. Sometimes, they are the right tool, but sometimes they are not. We'll see a more powerful, and often better, solution in the *Parsing custom data formats* recipe.

# Maintaining consistency with synonym maps

One common problem with data is inconsistency. Sometimes, a value is capitalized, while sometimes it is not. Sometimes it is abbreviated, and sometimes it is full. At times, there is a misspelling.

When it's an open domain, such as words in a free-text field, the problem can be quite difficult. However, when the data represents a limited vocabulary (such as US state names, for our example here) there's a simple trick that can help. While it's common to use full state names, standard postal codes are also often used. A mapping from common forms or mistakes to a normalized form is an easy way to fix variants in a field.

## Getting ready

For the `project.clj` file, we'll use a very simple configuration:

```
(defproject cleaning-data "0.1.0-SNAPSHOT"
  :dependencies [[org.clojure/clojure "1.6.0"]])
```

We just need to make sure that the `clojure.string/upper-case` function is available to us:

```
(use '[clojure.string :only (upper-case)])
```

## How to do it...

1. For this recipe, we'll define the synonym map and a function to use it. Then, we'll see it in action. We'll define the mapping to a normalized form. I will not list all of the states here, but you should get the idea:

```
(def state-synonyms
  {"ALABAMA" "AL",
   "ALASKA" "AK",
   "ARIZONA" "AZ",
   ...
   "WISCONSIN" "WI",
   "WYOMING" "WY"})
```

2. We'll wrap it in a function that makes the input uppercased before querying the mapping, as shown here:

```
(defn normalize-state [state]
  (let [uc-state (upper-case state)]
    (state-synonyms uc-state uc-state)))
```

3. Then, we just call `normalize-state` with the strings we want to fix:

```
user=> (map normalize-state
         ["Alabama" "OR" "Va" "Fla"])
("AL" "OR" "VA" "FL")
```

## How it works...

The only wrinkle here is that we have to normalize the input a little by making sure that it's uppercased before we can apply the mapping of synonyms to it. Otherwise, we'd also need to have an entry for any possible way in which the input can be capitalized.

## See also

  ▶  The *Fixing spelling errors* recipe later in this chapter

# Identifying and removing duplicate data

One problem when cleaning up data is dealing with duplicates. How do we find them? What do we do with them once we have them? While a part of this process can be automated, often merging duplicated data is a manual task, because a person has to look at potential matches and determine whether they are duplicates or not and determining what needs to be done with the overlapping data. We can code heuristics, of course, but at some point, a person needs to make the final call.

The first question that needs to be answered is what constitutes identity for the data. If you have two items of data, which fields do you have to look at in order to determine whether they are duplicates? Then, you must determine how close they need to be.

For this recipe, we'll examine some data and decide on duplicates by doing a fuzzy comparison of the name fields. We'll simply return all of the pairs that appear to be duplicates.

## Getting ready

First, we need to add the library to do the fuzzy string matching to our Leiningen `project.clj` file:

```
(defproject cleaning-data "0.1.0-SNAPSHOT"
  :dependencies [[org.clojure/clojure "1.6.0"]
                 [clj-diff "1.0.0-SNAPSHOT"]])
```

And to make sure that's available to our script or REPL:

```
(use 'clj-diff.core)
```

## How to do it...

We'll first define a function to test for fuzzy equality. Then, we'll write another function that uses fuzzy equality to test whether two records match.

1. Here are the main parameters for fuzzy string matching. We'll see how to use these later in the recipe:

```
(def fuzzy-max-diff 2)
(def fuzzy-percent-diff 0.1)
(def fuzzy-dist edit-distance)
```

2. Now, we can define a function that uses these parameters to determine whether two strings are equal to each other:

```
(defn fuzzy= [a b]
  (let [dist (fuzzy-dist a b)]
    (or (<= dist fuzzy-max-diff)
        (<= (/ dist (min (count a) (count b)))
            fuzzy-percent-diff))))
```

3. Building on this, we can write a function that determines whether two records are the same. It also takes one or more key functions, which returns the values that the items should be compared on:

```
(defn records-match
  [key-fn a b]
  (let [kfns (if (sequential? key-fn) key-fn [key-fn])
        rfn (fn [prev next-fn]
              (and prev (fuzzy= (next-fn a)
                                (next-fn b))))]
    (reduce rfn true kfns)))
```

4. These should allow you to test whether two records are approximately equal. Let's create some data to test this out:

```
(def data
  {:mulder {:given-name "Fox" :surname "Mulder"}
   :molder {:given-name "Fox" :surname "Molder"}
   :mulder2 {:given-name "fox" :surname "mulder"}
   :scully {:given-name "Dana" :surname "Scully"}
   :scully2 {:given-name "Dan" :surname "Scully"}})
```

5. Now, we can test some of these for *equality*:

```
user=> (records-match [:given-name :surname]
                      (data :mulder) (data :molder))
true
user=> (records-match [:given-name :surname]
                      (data :mulder) (data :mulder2))
true
user=> (records-match [:given-name :surname]
                      (data :scully) (data :scully2))
true
user=> (records-match [:given-name :surname]
                      (data :mulder) (data :scully))
false
```

## How it works...

The fuzzy string matching function uses several parameters. Let's take a look at each individually:

```
(def fuzzy-dist edit-distance)
```

`fuzzy-dist` is a function that returns a similarity metric for the two strings. Lower numbers indicate that the two strings are more similar. In this case, we're using `clj-diff.core/edit-distance`. The `edit-distance` parameter is the number of editing operations (usually inserting and deleting a single character, with a change being a combination of these) required to transform one string into another. For example, here are the edit distances of a few simple strings:

```
user=> (edit-distance "abc" "bc")
1
user=> (edit-distance "abc" "abcd")
1
user=> (edit-distance "abc" "bac")
2
user=> (edit-distance "abc" "bbc")
2
```

Based off of these values, the maximum allowable distance is determined by the following two parameters:

```
(def fuzzy-max-diff 2)
```

First, for equality, the distance has to be at most `fuzzy-max-diff`. Setting it to 2 allows replacements, which are generally two changes (delete and insert):

```
(def fuzzy-percent-diff 0.1)
```

The maximum distance can also be a percentage of the length of the shortest input string. In this case, we're using 10 percent as the maximum difference value that 2 can be.

If either of these two conditions is met, the strings are determined to be the same. This leads to two scenarios. No matter the length of the string, if only two characters change, it's the same. This is problematic for very short strings.

On the other hand, a hard maximum distance doesn't work for very long strings either. If, say for example, the value is 200 characters or more, you'll want to allow more absolute characters of difference than you would for a string of 20 characters. `fuzzy-percent-diff` provides this flexibility.

## There's more...

As I mentioned, this will not handle short strings very well. For example, it will judge *ace* and *are* to be the same. We can make the logic more complicated by adding a clause that says only to use `fuzzy-max-diff` if the length of the string is greater than some value.

In this recipe, we used `clj-diff.core/edit-distance`. This measures the number of changes that need to be made in order to transform one string into the other with the single-character operations `insert` and `delete`. Another option is to use `clj-diff.core/levenshtein-distance`, which also uses a single-character `replace` operation.

# Regularizing numbers

If we need to read in numbers as strings, we have to worry about how they're formatted. However, we'll probably want the computer to deal with them as *numbers*, not as strings, and this can't happen if the string contains a comma or period to separate the thousands place. This allows the numbers to be sorted and to be available for mathematical functions.

In this recipe, we'll write a short function that takes a number string and returns the number. The function will strip out all of the extra punctuation inside the number and only leave the last separator. Hopefully, this will be the one that marks the decimal place.

Of course, the version of this function, which we'll see here, only works in locales that use commas to separate thousands and periods to separate decimals. However, it would be relatively easy to write versions that will work in any particular locale.

## Getting ready

For this recipe, we're back to the most simple `project.clj` files:

```
(defproject cleaning-data "0.1.0-SNAPSHOT"
  :dependencies [[org.clojure/clojure "1.6.0"]])
```

To write this function, we just need to have access to the `clojure.string` library:

```
(require '[clojure.string :as string])
```

## How to do it...

1. The function itself is pretty short, shown as follows:

```
(defn normalize-number [n]
    (let [v (string/split n #"[,.]")
          [pre post] (split-at (dec (count v)) v)]
      (Double/parseDouble (apply str (concat pre [\.] post)))))
```

2. Also, using the function is straightforward:

```
user=> (normalize-number "1,000.00")
1000.0
user=> (normalize-number "1.000,00")
1000.0
user=> (normalize-number "3.1415")
3.1415
```

## How it works...

This function is fairly simple. So, let's take it apart, step by step:

1. We take the input and use a regular expression to split it on every comma and period. This handles both the thousands separators and decimals for most locales, expressions that use comma for thousands and periods for decimals, and vice versa:

```
(string/split n #"[,.]")
```

2. We take the split input and partition it into the integer part (everything up to the last element) and the fractional part (the last element):

```
(split-at (dec (count v)) v)
```

3. We join them back together as a new string, using a period for the decimal and leaving out any thousands separators:

```
(apply str (concat pre [\.] post))
```

4. We use the standard Java Double class to parse this into a `double`:

```
(Double/parseDouble …)
```

This version of the function assumes that the numbers are represented with a decimal component. If that's not the case, there will be problems:

```
user=> (normalize-number "1,000")
1.0
```

How will you go about fixing this? It might be easier to have separate versions of this function for integers and floats. In the end, you need to know your data in order to decide how to best handle it.

# Calculating relative values

One way to normalize values is to scale frequencies by the sizes of their groups. For example, say the word *truth* appears three times in a document. This means one thing if the document has thirty words. It means something else if the document has 300 or 3,000 words. Moreover, if the dataset has documents of all these lengths, how do you compare the frequencies for words across documents?

One way to do this is to rescale the frequency counts. In some cases, we can just scale the terms by the length of the documents. Or, if we want better results, we might use something more complicated such as **term frequency-inverse document frequency (TF-IDF)**.

For this recipe, we'll rescale some term frequencies by the total word count for their document.

## Getting ready

We don't need much for this recipe. We'll use the minimal `project.clj` file, which is listed here:

```
(defproject cleaning-data "0.1.0-SNAPSHOT"
  :dependencies [[org.clojure/clojure "1.6.0"]])
```

However, it will be easier if we have a 'pretty-printer' available in the REPL:

```
(require '[clojure.pprint :as pp])
```

## How to do it...

Actually, let's frame this problem in a more abstract manner. If each datum is a map, we can rescale one key (`:frequency`) by the total of this key's values in the group defined by another key (`:document`). This is a more general approach and should be useful in more situations.

1.  Let's define a function that rescales by a key's total in a collection. It assigns the scaled value to a new key (`dest`):

    ```
    (defn rescale-by-total [src dest coll]
      (let [total (reduce + (map src coll))
            update #(assoc % dest (/ (% src) total))]
        (map update coll)))
    ```

2.  Now, let's use this function in order to define a function to rescale by a group:

```
(defn rescale-by-group [src group dest coll]
  (->> coll
       (sort-by group)
       (group-by group)
       vals
       (mapcat #(rescale-by-total src dest %))))
```

3.  We can easily make up some data to test this:

```
(def word-counts
  [{:word 'the, :freq 92, :doc 'a}
   {:word 'a, :freq 76,:doc 'a}
   {:word 'jack, :freq 4,:doc 'a}
   {:word 'the, :freq 3,:doc 'b}
   {:word 'a, :freq 2,:doc 'b}
   {:word 'mary, :freq 1,:doc 'b}])
```

Now, we can see how it works:

```
user=> (pp/pprint (rescale-by-group :freq :doc :scaled
                                    word-counts))
({:freq 92, :word the, :scaled 23/43, :doc a}
 {:freq 76, :word a, :scaled 19/43, :doc a}
 {:freq 4, :word jack, :scaled 1/43, :doc a}
 {:freq 3, :word the, :scaled 1/2, :doc b}
 {:freq 2, :word a, :scaled 1/3, :doc b}
 {:freq 1, :word mary, :scaled 1/6, :doc b})
```

We can immediately see that the scaled values are more easily comparable. The scaled frequencies for *the*, for example, are approximately in line with each other in the way that the raw frequencies just aren't (0.53 and 0.5 versus 92 and 3). Of course, since this isn't a real dataset, the frequencies are meaningless, but this still illustrates the method and how it improves the dataset.

## How it works...

For each function, we pass in a couple of keys: a source key and a destination key. The first function, `rescale-by-total`, totals the values for the source key, and then sets the destination key to the ratio of the source key for that item and the total for the source key in all of the items in the collection.

The second function, `rescale-by-group`, uses another key: the group key. It sorts and groups the items by group key and then passes each group to `rescale-by-total`.

# Parsing dates and times

One difficult issue when normalizing and cleaning up data is how to deal with time. People enter dates and times in a bewildering variety of formats; some of them are ambiguous, and some of them are vague. However, we have to do our best to interpret them and normalize them into a standard format.

In this recipe, we'll define a function that attempts to parse a date into a standard string format. We'll use the `clj-time` Clojure library, which is a wrapper around the Joda Java library (`http://joda-time.sourceforge.net/`).

## Getting ready

First, we need to declare our dependencies in the Leiningen `project.clj` file:

```
(defproject cleaning-data "0.1.0-SNAPSHOT"
  :dependencies [[org.clojure/clojure "1.6.0"]
                 [clj-time "0.9.0-beta1"]])
```

Then, we need to load these dependencies into our script or REPL. We'll exclude `second` from `clj-time` to keep it from clashing with `clojure.core/second`:

```
(use '[clj-time.core :exclude (extend second)]
     '[clj-time.format])
```

## How to do it...

In order to solve this problem, we'll specify a sequence of date/time formats and walk through them. The first that doesn't throw an exception will be the one that we'll use.

1. Here's a list of formats that you can try:

```
(def ^:dynamic *default-formats*
  [:date
   :date-hour-minute
   :date-hour-minute-second
   :date-hour-minute-second-ms
   :date-time
   :date-time-no-ms
   :rfc822
   "YYYY-MM-dd HH:mm"
   "YYYY-MM-dd HH:mm:ss"
   "dd/MM/YYYY"
   "YYYY/MM/dd"
   "d MMM YYYY"])
```

2. Notice that some of these are keywords and some are strings. Each needs to be handled differently. We'll define a protocol with the method ->formatter, which attempts to convert each type to a date formatter, and the protocol for both the types to be represented in the format list:

```
(defprotocol ToFormatter
  (->formatter [fmt]))

(extend-protocol ToFormatter
  java.lang.String
  (->formatter [fmt]
 (formatter fmt))
  clojure.lang.Keyword
  (->formatter [fmt] (formatters fmt)))
```

3. Next, parse-or-nil will take a format and a date string, attempt to parse the date string, and return nil if there are any errors:

```
(defn parse-or-nil [fmt date-str]
  (try
    (parse (->formatter fmt) date-str)
    (catch Exception ex
      nil)))
```

4. With these in place, here is normalize-datetime. We just attempt to parse a date string with all of the formats, filter out any nil values, and return the first non-nil. Because Clojure's lists are lazy, this will stop processing as soon as one format succeeds:

```
(defn normalize-datetime [date-str]
  (first
    (remove nil?
            (map #(parse-or-nil % date-str)
                 *default-formats*))))
```

Now we can try this out:

```
user=> (normalize-datetime "2012-09-12")
#<DateTime 2012-09-12T00:00:00.000Z>
user=> (normalize-datetime "2012/09/12")
#<DateTime 2012-09-12T00:00:00.000Z>
user=> (normalize-datetime "28 Sep 2012")
#<DateTime 2012-09-28T00:00:00.000Z>
user=> (normalize-datetime "2012-09-28 13:45")
#<DateTime 2012-09-28T13:45:00.000Z>
```

## There's more...

This approach to parse dates has a number of problems. For example, because some date formats are ambiguous, the first match might not be the correct one.

However, trying out a list of formats is probably about the best we can do. Knowing something about our data allows us to prioritize the list appropriately, and we can augment it with ad hoc formats as we run across new data. We might also need to normalize data from different sources (for instance, U.S. date formats versus the rest of the world) before we merge the data together.

# Lazily processing very large data sets

One of the good features of Clojure is that most of its sequence-processing functions are lazy. This allows us to handle very large datasets with very little effort. However, when combined with readings from files and other I/O, there are several things that you need to watch out for.

In this recipe, we'll take a look at several ways to safely and lazily read a CSV file. By default, the `clojure.data.csv/read-csv` is lazy, so how do you maintain this feature while closing the file at the right time?

## Getting ready

We'll use a `project.clj` file that includes a dependency on the Clojure CSV library:

```
(defproject cleaning-data "0.1.0-SNAPSHOT"
  :dependencies [[org.clojure/clojure "1.6.0"]
                 [org.clojure/data.csv "0.1.2"]])
```

We need to load the libraries that we're going to use into the REPL:

```
(require '[clojure.data.csv :as csv]
         '[clojure.java.io :as io])
```

## How to do it...

We'll try several solutions and consider their strengths and weaknesses:

1.  Let's start with the most straightforward way:
    ```
    (defn lazy-read-bad-1 [csv-file]
      (with-open [in-file (io/reader csv-file)]
        (csv/read-csv in-file)))
    user=> (lazy-read-bad-1 "data/small-sample.csv")
    IOException Stream closed  java.io.BufferedReader.ensureOpen
    (BufferedReader.java:97)
    ```

Oops! At the point where the function returns the lazy sequence, it hasn't read any data yet. However, when exiting the `with-open` form, the file is automatically closed. What happened?

First, the file is opened and passed to `read-csv`, which returns a lazy sequence. The lazy sequence is returned from `with-open`, which closes the file. Finally, the REPL tries to print out this lazy sequence. Now, `read-csv` tries to pull data from the file. However, at this point the file is closed, so the `IOException` is raised.

This is a pretty common problem for the first draft of a function. It especially seems to bite me whenever I'm doing database reads, for some reason.

2. So, in order to fix this, we'll just force all of the lines to be read:

```
(defn lazy-read-bad-2 [csv-file]
  (with-open [in-file (io/reader csv-file)]
    (doall
      (csv/read-csv in-file))))
```

This will return data, but everything gets loaded into the memory. Now, we have safety but no laziness.

3. Here's how we can get both:

```
(defn lazy-read-ok [csv-file]
  (with-open [in-file (io/reader csv-file)]
    (frequencies
      (map #(nth % 2) (csv/read-csv in-file)))))
```

This is one way to do it. Now, we've moved what we're going to do to the data into the function that reads it. This works, but it has a poor separation of concerns. It is both reading and processing the data, and we really should break these into two functions.

4. Let's try it one more time:

```
(defn lazy-read-csv [csv-file]
  (let [in-file (io/reader csv-file)
        csv-seq (csv/read-csv in-file)
        lazy (fn lazy [wrapped]
               (lazy-seq
                 (if-let [s (seq wrapped)]
                   (cons (first s) (lazy (rest s)))
                   (.close in-file))))]
    (lazy csv-seq)))
```

This works! Let's talk about why.

## How it works...

The last version of the function, `lazy-read-csv`, works because it takes the lazy sequence that `csv/read-csv` produces and wraps it in another sequence that closes the input file when there is no more data coming out of the CSV file. This is complicated because we're working with two levels of input: reading from the file and reading CSV. When the higher-level task (reading CSV) is completed, it triggers an operation on the lower level (reading the file). This allows you to read files that don't fit into the memory and process their data on the fly.

However, with this function, we again have a nice, simple interface that we can present to callers while keeping the complexity hidden.

Unfortunately, this still has one glaring problem: if we're not going to read the entire file (say we're only interested in the first 100 lines or something) the file handle won't get closed. For the use cases in which only a part of the file will be read, `lazy-read-ok` is probably the best option.

# Sampling from very large data sets

One way to deal with very large data sets is to sample. This can be especially useful when we're getting started and want to explore a dataset. A good sample can tell us what's in the full dataset and what we'll need to do in order to clean and process it. Samples are used in any kind of survey or election exit polling.

In this recipe, we'll see a couple of ways of creating samples.

## Getting ready

We'll use a basic `project.clj` file:

```
(defproject cleaning-data "0.1.0-SNAPSHOT"
  :dependencies [[org.clojure/clojure "1.6.0"]])
```

## How to do it...

There are two ways to sample from a stream of values. If you want 10 percent of the larger population, you can just take every tenth item. If you want 1,000 out of who knows how many items, the process is a little more complicated.

## Sampling by percentage

1. Performing a rough sampling by percentage is pretty simple:

```
(defn sample-percent
  [k coll]  (filter (fn [_] (<= (rand) k)) coll))
```

2. Using it is also simple:

```
user=> (sample-percent 0.01 (range 1000))
(141 146 155 292 598 624 629 640 759 815 852 889)
user=> (count *1)
12
```

## Sampling exactly

Sampling for an exact count is a little more complicated. We'll use Donald Knuth's algorithm from *The Art of Computer Programming, Volume 2*. This takes the sample off the front of the input sequence, and then from this point, each new item from the input has a chance of *sample-size / size-of-collection-so-far* randomly replacing one existing item in the sample. To implement this, we'll need one helper function which takes a map and a new key-value pair. It removes a random key from the map and inserts the new pair:

```
(defn rand-replace
  [m k v]  (assoc (dissoc m (rand-nth (keys m))) k v))
```

We'll also need another small utility to create an infinite range that begins at a given place:

```
(defn range-from [x] (map (partial + x) (range)))
```

Now, we use this to create the function that does the sampling:

```
(defn sample-amount [k coll]
  (->> coll
    (drop k)
    (map vector (range-from (inc k)))
    (filter #(<= (rand) (/ k (first %))))
    (reduce rand-replace
            (into {} (map vector (range k) (take k coll))))
    (sort-by first)
    (map second)))
```

Using this is as simple as using the first function though:

```
user=> (sample-amount 10 (range 1000))
(70 246 309 430 460 464 471 547 955 976)
user=> (count *1)
10
```

## How it works...

Sampling by percentage just compares the percentage against a random value for each item in the collection. If the random number is less than the value, it saves the item. Notice though, that since it's random, the exact number that it pulls out doesn't necessarily match the parameter exactly. In this case, 1 percent.

Sampling by a set amount is more complicated. We keep a map of the sample, keyed by each item's position in the original sequence. Originally, we populate this map with the first items off the sequence. Afterwards, we walk through the rest of the collection. For each item, we randomly decide whether to keep it or not. If we do keep it, we randomly swap it with one item that is currently in the sample.

Let's see what this looks like in the code:

1.  Initially, we want to take the sample off the front of the collection. The processing pipeline in `sample-amount` will work over the rest of the collection, so we'll begin by dropping the initial sample off the front:

```
(defn sample-amount [k coll]
  (->> coll
       (drop k)
```

2.  In order to figure out each subsequent item's probability of being chosen for the sample, we need to have its position in the collection. We can get this by associating each item with its position in a vector pair:

```
       (map vector (range-from (inc k)))
```

3.  Now, filter out all of the items whose position number, divided by the sample size, is less than a random number. This randomly replaces each item based on its position, as outlined in the algorithm:

```
       (filter #(<= (rand) (/ k (first %))))
```

4.  At this point, we start building the final sample as a hash map that maps each item's position in the original collection with the item itself. We use `rand-replace` to swap out an item from the sample `Hashmap` for each item that passed the random filter in Step 3:

```
       (reduce rand-replace
               (into {}
                     (map vector (range k) (take k coll))))
```

5.  Once the reduce call is made, we can sort the hash-map by position:

```
       (sort-by first)
```

6. Finally, we throw away the positions and return a sequence of a sample of the items from the original collection:

```
(map second)))
```

# Fixing spelling errors

One of the issues that we'll need to deal with at some point is spelling errors. Especially when you're trying to work with raw text, spelling errors can throw a wrench in the works.

At one time, spell checkers were major pieces of software with lots of optimizations to run in the constrained environments that were once everyday desktops. Now, that's not the case. Peter Norvig has published a piece on the Internet titled *How to Write a Spelling Corrector* (`http://norvig.com/spell-correct.html`). This shows how to take some text that is assumed to be spelled correctly and generate a spell checker built on it. He included a 21-line implementation in Python.

For this recipe, we'll convert the Python code to Clojure. Our version will be longer, but less dense. We can certainly implement it more concisely than we will do it, but it will be helpful for our explanation to break it out more.

## Getting ready

We'll use the minimal `project.clj` file that we've seen in several recipes already in this chapter:

```
(defproject cleaning-data "0.1.0-SNAPSHOT"
  :dependencies [[org.clojure/clojure "1.6.0"]])
```

We require `clojure.string` and one function from `clojure.set`:

```
(require '[clojure.string :as string])
(use '[clojure.set :only (union)])
```

## How to do it...

This algorithm works by comparing a set of permutations of a word against a map of correctly spelled words and their frequencies. The spelling that occurs most frequently wins:

1. We need a function to tokenize a string into words. We'll use a regular expression for this:

```
(defn words
```

```
[text]
 (re-seq #"[a-z]+" (string/lower-case text)))
```

2. The training data structure is just a map of words and their frequencies:

```
(defn train
 [feats] (frequencies feats))
```

3. Now, we can train our spell checker. We'll use the dataset that Norvig has linked to in his article (http://norvig.com/big.txt), which I've downloaded locally:

```
(def n-words
    (train (words (slurp "data/big.txt"))))
(def alphabet
   "abcdefghijklmnopqrstuvwxyz")
```

4. We need to define some operations on the words in our training corpus:

```
(defn split-word [word i]
  [(.substring word 0 i) (.substring word i)])
(defn delete-char [[w1 w2]]
  (str w1 (.substring w2 1)))
(defn transpose-split [[w1 w2]]
  (str w1 (second w2) (first w2) (.substring w2 2)))
(defn replace-split [[w1 w2]]
  (let [w2-0 (.substring w2 1)]
    (map #(str w1 % w2-0) alphabet)))
(defn insert-split [[w1 w2]]
  (map #(str w1 % w2) alphabet))
```

5. We're now ready to define the two functions that are the heart of the algorithm. The first function calculates all of the possible edits that can be made to a word, based on the operators we just defined:

```
(defn edits-1 [word]
  (let [splits (map (partial split-word word)
                    (range (inc (count word))))
        long-splits (filter #(> (count (second %)) 1)
                            splits)
        deletes (map delete-char long-splits)
        transposes (map transpose-split long-splits)
        replaces (mapcat replace-split long-splits)
        inserts (remove nil?
                        (mapcat insert-split splits))]
    (set (concat deletes transposes
                 replaces inserts)))))
```

6. The second primary function gets the edits of the edits of a word, but only if they're known in the training set:

```
(defn known-edits-2 [word]
  (set (filter (partial contains? n-words)
               (apply union
                      (map #(edits-1 %)
                           (edits-1 word))))))
```

7. Now, we need another utility function that takes a sequence of words and returns the set of those seen in the training corpus:

```
(defn known [words]
  (set (filter (partial contains? n-words) words)))
```

8. Finally, we can put it all together to create the `correct` function:

```
(defn correct [word]
  (let [candidate-thunks [#(known (list word))
                          #(known (edits-1 word))
                          #(known-edits-2 word)
                          #(list word)]]
    (->>
      candidate-thunks
      (map (fn [f] (f)))
      (filter #(> (count %) 0))
      first
      (map (fn [w] [(get n-words w 1) w]))
      (reduce (partial max-key first))
      second)))
```

Let's see how it works:

```
user=> (correct "deete")
"delete"
user=> (correct "editr")
"editor"
user=> (correct "tranpsose")
"tranpsose"
user=> (correct "eidtor")
"editor"
```

```
user=> (correct "eidtr")
"elder"
```

It doesn't recognize *transpose*, and it miscorrects *eidtr* as *elder*. Let's take a look at the training data to see why:

```
user=> (n-words "transpose")
nil
user=> (n-words "elder")
40
user=> (n-words "editor")
17
```

That explains it. *Transpose* doesn't occur in the training set, and *elder* is there more than twice as often as *editor*, so it's the more likely correction.

## How it works...

The heart of this are the `edits-1` and `known-edits-2` functions. They perform a search over the space between strings, looking for all of the known words that are one or two edits away from the word to be checked. Before the operations are applied, the words are split into two by the `split-word` function. The operations that constitute one edit are defined in a series of functions:

- ▶ `delete-char`: This removes one character from the word (*word* to *wod*)
- ▶ `transpose-char`: This transposes two characters (*word* to *wrod*)
- ▶ `replace-split`: This replaces one letter by another character from the alphabet (*word* to *wobd*)
- ▶ `insert-split`: This inserts a character into the word (*word* to *wobrd*)

The `correct` function looks at all of the edits returned that are in the training set and picks the one that is seen most frequently.

## There's more...

If you want more information on the statistics that make this work (and you should—it's quite interesting), see Norvig's explanation in his article at `http://norvig.com/spell-correct.html`.

# Parsing custom data formats

If you work with data for long enough, you'll eventually come across data that you can't find a library for, and you'll need to write your own parser. Some formats might be simple enough for regular expressions, but if you need to balance syntactic structures in the input, or handle anything too complicated, you're probably better off creating a custom parser. Sometimes, custom parsers can be slower than regular expressions for very large inputs, but sometimes they're still your best option.

Clojure, and most functional languages, are great for parsing, and many have *parser-combinator* libraries that make writing parsers extremely simple.

For this recipe, as an example of a data format that needs parsing, we'll work with some FASTA data (`http://en.wikipedia.org/wiki/FASTA_format`). FASTA is a file format that's used in bioinformatics to exchange nucleotide and peptide sequences. Of course, there are parsers already for this, but it's a simple, yet non-trivial format, which makes a good example case for this recipe.

The first line of FASTA data starts with a > character followed by a unique identifier. This line often contains other information about the specimen described, the database it came from, and more. After this line comes one or more lines that list the sequence information. A more detailed explanation of the FASTA format is available at `http://www.ncbi.nlm.nih.gov/BLAST/blastcgihelp.shtml`. This is how an example FASTA record looks:

```
>gi|5524211|gb|AAD44166.1| cytochrome b [Elephas maximus maximus]
LCLYTHIGRNIYYGSYLYSETWNTGIMLLLITMATAFMGYVLPWGQMSFWGATVITNLFSAIPY
IGTNLVEWIWGGFSVDKATLNRFFAFHFILPFTMVALAGVHLTFLHETGSNNPLGLTSDSDKIP
FHPYYTIKDFLGLLILILLLLLALLSPDMLGDPDNHMPADPLNTPLHIKPEWYFLFAYAILRS
VPNKLGGVLALFLSIVILGLMPFLHTSKHRSMMLRPLSQALFWTLTMDLLTLTWIGSQPVEYPY
TIIGQMASILYFSIILAFLPIAGXIENY
```

We'll use the **parse-ez** library (`https://github.com/protoflex/parse-ez`) to build the parser.

## Getting ready

We need to make sure that `parse-ez` is listed in our Leiningen `project.clj` file:

```
(defproject cleaning-data "0.1.0-SNAPSHOT"
  :dependencies [[org.clojure/clojure "1.6.0"]
                 [parse-ez "0.3.6"]])
```

We also need to make it available to our script or REPL:

```
(use 'protoflex.parse)
```

## How to do it...

To define a parser, we just define functions that parse the different parts of the input and then combine them to parse larger structures:

1.  It would be useful to have a way to parse two things and throw away the results of the second. This function will do that:

```
(defn <| [l r]
  (let [l-output (l)]
    (r)
    l-output))
```

2.  Also, we'll define a parser for the end of a line. It matches either a carriage return or a new line:

```
(defn nl []
  (chr-in #{\newline \return}))
```

3.  Let's start putting the pieces together. The first function parses the sequence definition line by accepting a > character, followed by anything up to the end of the line:

```
(defn defline []
  (chr \>)
  (<| #(read-to-re #"[\n\r]+") nl))
```

4.  We parse a sequence of amino acid or nucleic acid codes by defining a parser for a single code and then building on that to create a parser for a line of code:

```
(defn acid-code []
  (chr-in #{\A \B \C \D \E \F \G \H \I \K \L \M
            \N \P \Q \R \S \T \U \V \W \X \Y \Z
            \- \*}))

(defn acid-code-line []
  (<| #(multi+ acid-code) #(attempt nl)))
```

5.  Next, we combine these parsers into one that parses an entire FASTA record and populates a map with our data. Moreover, we define a combinator that parses multiple FASTA records:

```
(defn fasta []
  (ws?)
  (let [dl (defline)
        gls (apply str (flatten
                        (multi+ acid-code-line)))]
    {:defline dl, :gene-seq gls}))
(defn multi-fasta []
  (<| #(multi+ fasta)
      ws?))
```

6.  Finally, we create a wrapper function that passes our parser to parse-ez and configures the parsing engine the way we need it:

```
(defn parse-fasta [input]
  (parse multi-fasta input
         :eof false :auto-trim false))
```

Now, we can use this function to parse the example record, provided at the beginning of this recipe:

```
user=> parse-fasta test-data)
{:defline
 "gi|5524211|gb|AAD44166.1| cytochrome b [Elephas maximus maximus]",
 :gene-seq
 "LCLYTHIGRNIYYGSYLYSETWNTGIMLLLITMATAFMGYVLPWGQMSFWGATVITNLFSAIPYIGTN
  LVEWIWGGFSVDKATLNRFFAFHFILPFTMVALAGVHLTFLHETGSNNPLGLTSDSDKIPFHPYYTI
  KDFLGLLILILLLLLLALLSPDMLGDPDNHMPADPLNTPLHIKPEWYFLFAYAILRSVPNKLGGVLALF
  LSIVILGLMPFLHTSKHRSMMLRPLSQALFWTLTMDLLTLTWIGSQPVEYPYTIIGQMASILYFSII
  LAFLPIAGXIENY"}
```

## How it works...

At the most abstract level, parsers are functions. They take a string as input and return a data structure. More complex, advanced parsers are built by combining simpler elements.

The `<|` function is a good example of this. It does not parse anything by itself. However, this function makes it possible to combine two other parsers in a useful way: it parses both parts and throws away the results of the second.

The `acid-code` function is an example of how to create a parser from a basic component. It matches any of the characters in the set.

`acid-code-line` then combines the `acid-code` parser. It has to match one or more `acid-code` characters, optionally followed by a `newline`. It uses the `<|` combinator to throw away the `newline` and return the sequence of `acid-codes`.

This entire parser is built up in this way, by composing complex structures from simple parts. While this is a very basic parser, it's possible to create quite complex parsers in this way, leveraging the full power of Clojure while keeping the code readable and maintainable.

# Validating data with Valip

Validating data happens so often that it's good to have an EDSL to express the validation rules that our data has to pass. This makes the rules easier to create, understand, and maintain.

Valip (`https://github.com/weavejester/valip`) provides this. It's aimed at validating input from web forms, so it expects to validate maps with string values. We'll need to work around this expectation a time or two, but it isn't difficult.

## Getting ready

We need to make sure that the **Valip** library is in our Leiningen `project.clj` file:

```
(defproject cleaning-data "0.1.0-SNAPSHOT"
  :dependencies [[org.clojure/clojure "1.6.0"]
                 [org.clojure/data.xml "0.0.8"]
                 [valip "0.2.0"]]])
```

Also, we need to load it into our script or REPL:

```
(use 'valip.core
     'valip.predicates)
```

## How to do it...

To validate some data, we have to define predicates to test the data fields against, then define the fields and predicates to validate, plus validate error messages.

1. First, we need data to validate:

```
(def user
  {:given-name "Fox"
   :surname "Mulder"
   :age 51
   :badge "JTT047101111"})
```

2. We also need to define a predicate to determine whether a number is present or not. The `present?` predicate defined by Valip fails if its input isn't a string:

```
(defn number-present? [x]
  (and (present? (str x))
       (or (instance? Integer x)
           (instance? Long x))))
```

3. We'd also like to validate the badge numbers. Taking this one as a template, let's say they begin with three uppercase letters followed by one or more digits. We can express this using this predicate:

```
(defn valid-badge [n]
  (not (nil? (re-find #"[A-Z]{3}\d+" n))))
```

4.  Now, we can start defining some validation rules. Rules are vector triples, each listing a field, a predicate, and an error message:

```
(defn validate-user [user]
  (validate user
    [:given-name present? "Given name required."]
    [:surname present? "Surname required."]
    [:age number-present? "Age required."]
    [:age (over 0) "Age should be positive."]
    [:age (under 150) "Age should be under 150."]
    [:badge present?
     "The badge number is required."]
    [:badge valid-badge
     "The badge number is invalid."]))
```

Now, we can easily validate data against this set of rules:

```
user=> (validate-user (assoc user :age -42))
{:age ["Age should be positive."]}
user=> (validate-user (assoc user :age -42 :surname nil))
{:age ["Age should be positive."],
 :surname ["Surname required."]}
```

## How it works...

Valip provides an easy-to-use DSL to define validation rules. It then breaks the incoming map structures and validates each field against the rules given. Finally, it returns error messages for any problem data. This system is simple to integrate into a data processing workflow.

# 3
# Managing Complexity with Concurrent Programming

In this chapter, we will cover:

- ▶ Managing program complexity with STM
- ▶ Managing program complexity with agents
- ▶ Getting better performance with commute
- ▶ Combining agents and STM
- ▶ Maintaining consistency with ensure
- ▶ Introducing safe side effects into the STM
- ▶ Maintaining data consistency with validators
- ▶ Monitoring processing with watchers
- ▶ Debugging concurrent programs with watchers
- ▶ Recovering from errors in agents
- ▶ Managing large inputs with sized queues

# Introduction

In general, designing and creating a computer system is a balancing act. We're constantly trying to add features and capabilities while keeping the code simple and the system's performance reasonable. In this respect, data analysis systems are no different. In fact, they may be worse. Often data is only partially consistent, and we need to employ a variety of strategies to extract usable data before we can even begin its analysis. Each added strategy adds a little more complexity, weight, and bloat to the code, each of which makes it a little harder to maintain. This can get out of hand.

Clojure has a number of libraries to help us manage our systems' complexity. One of the most powerful of these is **concurrent programming**. This allows us to conceptualize our programs differently and in ways that can help manage the complexity. Instead of having monolithic blocks of code that do many things and have direct, tight dependencies, we can structure our program more modularly by composing many independent modules together, each of them doing one thing. These communicate using simple, well-defined protocols, but they all work independently and concurrently (that is, at the same time).

> Clojure's concurrency features are built upon its **Software Transactional Memory** (**STM**) system, which is described at `http://clojure.org/refs`. This system takes the semantics of the database's transactions, which most developers are familiar with, and applies it to the computer's memory.

Clojure also has a concurrent message processing system (its agents) built on top of the STM. Agents contain state information and we send them function messages to update that state concurrently. Together, the STM and agents provide a way to structure programs to make them maintainable and easy to understand.

Both of these work well because all native Clojure data structures are **immutable**. They cannot be changed. Because it's working with immutable data, the STM can provide guarantees about the consistency and safety of its transactions, even in a highly concurrent environment. These guarantees are good for us because they help us think and reason about our data and our program, and they help us manage the complexity of the systems we're building.

Note that **concurrent** describes how a program is structured to work that will hopefully result in some speedup. Each thread may be doing different things, but concurrency is often just a good way to organize your program. It separates out and decouples the different parts of your program that are engaged in different tasks but still are coordinating with each other or interacting in some way. If you're doing the same thing over and over, where everything is independent of all the other things, and you want to do it faster, that's **parallelism**. We'll look at recipes related to about that in *Chapter 4, Improving Performance with Parallel Programming*.

# Managing program complexity with STM

The basis of Clojure's concurrency is its STM system. Basically, this extends the semantics of database transactions to the computer's memory.

For this recipe, we'll use the STM to calculate the families per housing unit from a piece of U.S. census data. We'll use `future-call` to perform the calculations in the thread pool and spread the execution over multiple cores. Afterwards, we'll go into more detail about how the STM works in general, and how it's applied in this particular recipe.

## Getting ready

To prepare for this recipe, we first need to list our dependencies in the Leiningen `project.clj` file:

```
(defproject concurrent-data "0.1.0-SNAPSHOT"
  :dependencies [[org.clojure/clojure "1.6.0"]
                 [org.clojure/data.csv "0.1.2"]])
```

We also need to import these dependencies to our script or REPL:

```
(require '[clojure.java.io :as io]
         '[clojure.data.csv :as csv])
```

Finally, we need to have our data file. I downloaded one of the bulk data files from the Investigative Reporters and Editors' U.S. census site at http://census.ire.org/data/bulkdata.html. The data in this recipe will use the family census data for Virginia. I've also uploaded this data at http://www.ericrochester.com/clj-data-analysis/data/all_160_in_51.P35.csv. You can easily download it from here and save it to a directory named `data`. Let's bind the filename to a variable for easy access:

```
(def data-file "data/all_160_in_51.P35.csv")
```

Here's the data file, opened in a spreadsheet, and showing the first few rows:

| | A | B | C | D | E | F | G | H | I | J | K |
|---|---|---|---|---|---|---|---|---|---|---|---|
| 1 | GEOID | SUMLEV | STATE | COUNTY | CBSA | CSA | NECTA | CNECTA | NAME | POP100 | HU100 |
| 2 | 5100148 | 160 | 51 | | | | | | Abingdon town | 8191 | 4271 |
| 3 | 5100180 | 160 | 51 | | | | | | Accomac town | 519 | 229 |
| 4 | 5100724 | 160 | 51 | | | | | | Alberta town | 298 | 163 |
| 5 | 5101000 | 160 | 51 | | | | | | Alexandria city | 139966 | 72376 |
| 6 | 5101256 | 160 | 51 | | | | | | Allisonia CDP | 117 | 107 |

## How to do it...

For this recipe, we'll read in the data, break it into chunks, and use separate threads to total the number of housing units and the number of families in each chunk. Each chunk will add its totals to some global references:

1. We need to define two references that the STM will manipulate: one for the total of housing units and one for families:

```
(def total-hu (ref 0))
(def total-fams (ref 0))
```

2. Now, we'll need a couple of utility functions to safely read a CSV file to a lazy sequence. The first is `lazy-read-csv` from the *Lazily processing very large data sets* recipe in *Chapter 2, Cleaning and Validating Data*. We'll also define a new function, `with-header`, that uses the first row to create maps from the rest of the rows in the dataset:

```
(defn with-header [coll]
  (let [headers (map keyword (first coll))]
    (map (partial zipmap headers) (next coll))))
```

3. Next, we'll define some utility functions. One (`->int`) will convert a string into an integer. Another (`sum-item`) will calculate the running totals for the fields we're interested in. A third function (`sum-items`) will calculate the sums from a collection of data maps:

```
(defn ->int [i] (Integer. i))

(defn sum-item
  ([fields] (partial sum-item fields))
  ([fields accum item]
   (mapv + accum (map ->int (map item fields)))))

(defn sum-items [accum fields coll]
  (reduce (sum-item fields) accum coll))
```

4. We can now define the function that will actually interact with the STM. The `update-totals` function takes a list of fields that contains the housing unit and family data and a collection of items. It will total the fields in the parameter with the items passed into the function and update the STM references with them:

```
(defn update-totals [fields items]
  (let [mzero (mapv (constantly 0) fields)
```

```
     [sum-hu sum-fams] (sum-items
                mzero fields items)]
    (dosync
      (alter total-hu #(+ sum-hu %))
      (alter total-fams #(+ sum-fams %)))))
```

5. In order to call this function with `future-call`, we'll write a function to create a **thunk** (a function created to assist in calling another function). It will just call `update-totals` with the parameters we give:

```
(defn thunk-update-totals-for [fields data-chunk]
  (fn [] (update-totals fields data-chunk)))
```

6. With all this in place, we can define a main function that controls the entire process and returns the ratio of families to housing units:

```
(defn main
  ([data-file] (main data-file [:HU100 :P035001] 5))
  ([data-file fields chunk-count]
   (doall
     (->>
       (lazy-read-csv data-file)
       with-header
       (partition-all chunk-count)
       (map (partial thunk-update-totals-for fields))
       (map future-call)
       (map deref)))
   (float (/ @total-fams @total-hu))))
```

## How it works...

In general, the way the STM works is as follows. First, we mark memory locations to be controlled by the STM using the `ref` function. We can then dereference them anywhere using the `deref` function or the `@` macro, but we can only change the values of a reference inside a `dosync` block. Then, when the point of execution gets to the end of a transaction, the STM performs a check. If any of the references that the transaction altered have been changed by another transaction, the current transaction fails and it's queued to be tried again. However, if none of the references have changed, then the transaction succeeds and is committed.

While we're in the transaction, those values don't appear to have changed to the code outside it. Once the transaction is committed, then any changes we make to those locations with `ref-set` or `alter` will be visible outside that block, as shown in the following diagram:

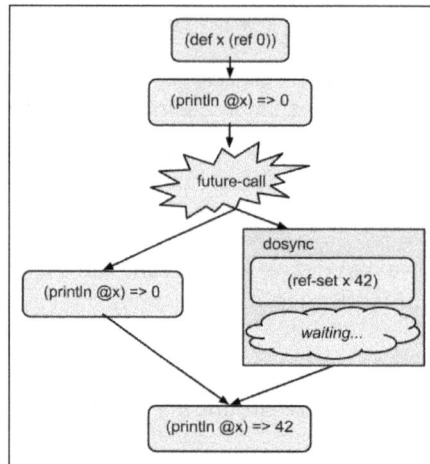

Note the following warnings:

> ▶ With the STM, we should use only Clojure's native, immutable data types. This sounds restrictive, but in practice, it isn't a big deal. Clojure has a rich and flexible collection of data types.

> ▶ We should also limit how much we try to do in each transaction. We only want to bundle together operations that truly must pass or fail as a collection. This keeps transactions from being retried too much, which can hurt performance.

The STM helps us manage complexity by allowing us to divide our processing in a way that makes the most sense to us, and then to run those processes concurrently. The STM, together with the immutable state, keeps this system simple and easy to reason about.

In this particular recipe, the first reference to the STM is in the definitions of `total-hu` and `total-fams`. Each of these is a reference, initially set to zero.

The `update-totals` function contains the `dosync` that updates the references. It uses `alter`, which takes the reference and a function that updates the value. Because of the `dosync`, if either of these values is changed in another thread that is summing another chunk of data, the call to `dosync` is repeated. That's why we calculate the items' totals before we enter that block.

Finally, in `main`, we partition the data into chunks, then package the calls to `update-totals` for each chunk of data into a thunk, and run it in Clojure's thread pool using `future-call`, calling `deref` on future blocks until the value is returned from the thread pool.

We wrap this process in a call to `doall` to make sure that all of the processing is completed. Remember that sequences are lazy by default, so without `doall`, the sequence started by `lazy-read-csv` and ending in the series of `map` calls would be garbage collected before any work would be done. The `future-call` and `deref` functions would never actually be called. The `@` macros in the last line would return the values of these references as originally set in the `def` calls (both zero). The `doall` simply forces all of the processing to be done before we get to the last line.

As this recipe shows, Clojure provides a lot of easy concurrency without having to worry about synchronizing values, locks, monitors, semaphores, or any of the other things that make threads and concurrency difficult and painful.

## See also

We'll approach this problem again with agents, another of Clojure's concurrency tools, in the next recipe, *Managing program complexity with agents*.

# Managing program complexity with agents

Agents build on the STM, and each agent acts a lot like a reference. References allow you to coordinate multiple pieces of the state, but if you only have one piece of the state that you're updating, then that's a good use for agents. You use agents by sending them messages (functions that manipulate the agent's state) and these are run in the thread pool, although each agent only processes one task at a time.

We create agents with the `agent` function, and we send messages to them with `send` and `send-off`. Whatever the function returns is the agent's new state value. This figure illustrates this process:

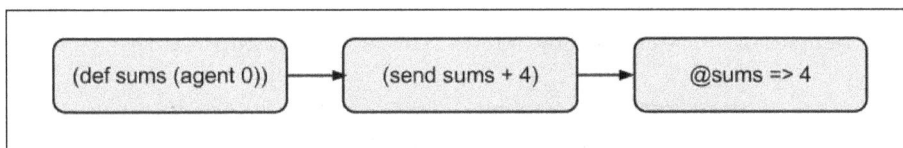

```
(def sums (agent 0))  →  (send sums + 4)  →  @sums => 4
```

For this recipe, we'll again solve the same problem we did in the last recipe, *Managing program complexity with STM*.

## Getting ready

We will include the same references in the `project.clj` file and the same requirements in the REPL as we did in the *Managing program complexity with STM recipe*.

For this recipe, I'm going to use the U.S. political campaign finance data from Open Secrets (http://www.opensecrets.org/). You have to register with the site, but once you do that, the data is free to download. Once you've logged in, look for the **Bulk Data** link. For this, I downloaded the cycles tables for the **Campaign Finance Data**. I unzipped them to the data/campaign-fin directory. For this recipe, we'll focus on the **Political Action Committee (PAC)** data. In this case, we'll just find the total amount of campaign contributions per candidate.

We'll use several utility functions from the last recipe: lazy-read-csv and ->int.

## How to do it...

To use agents, we just need to add a few functions to the ones from the last recipe:

1. The first pair is get-cid and get-amount. These take a row from the data file and return the data fields that we're interested in:

   ```
   (defn get-cid [row] (nth row 3))
   (defn get-amount [row] (->int (nth row 4)))
   ```

2. We'll now add a function that takes those two values and wraps them into a vector pair:

   ```
   (defn get-cid-amount [row]
     [(get-cid row) (get-amount row)])
   ```

3. Now, we'll need a function that indexes those values in a hash map, adding them:

   ```
   (defn add-amount-by [m cid amount]
     (assoc m cid (+ amount (get m cid 0))))
   ```

4. Next, we'll define a function that reads the data from a file and accumulates it in an existing hash map:

   ```
   (defn read-file-amounts [m filename]
     (reduce #(add-amount-by %1 (first %2) (second %2))
             m
             (map get-cid-amount
                  (lazy-read-csv filename))))
   ```

5. Finally, we'll need a function to make working with agents easier—force-val. It takes an agent and uses await to block all of the messages currently in its queue to be processed. Then it dereferences the agent. This function will allow us to thread a series of operations on the agents:

   ```
   (defn force-val
     [a]
     (await a)
     @a)
   ```

6. Now that everything's in place, here is the function that controls the process:

```
(defn main [data-files agent-count]
  (let [agents (map agent (repeat agent-count {}))]
    (dorun
      (map #(send %1 read-file-amounts %2)
           (cycle agents)
           data-files))
    (apply merge-with + (map force-val agents)))))
```

And we can see this in action:

```
User=> (def data-files ["data/campaign-fin/pacs90.txt"
                        "data/campaign-fin/pacs92.txt"
                        "data/campaign-fin/pacs94.txt"
                        "data/campaign-fin/pacs96.txt"
                        "data/campaign-fin/pacs98.txt"
                        "data/campaign-fin/pacs00.txt"
                        "data/campaign-fin/pacs02.txt"
                        "data/campaign-fin/pacs04.txt"
                        "data/campaign-fin/pacs06.txt"
                        "data/campaign-fin/pacs08.txt"
                        "data/campaign-fin/pacs10.txt"])
user=> (def contribs (main data-files 5))
user=> (contribs "|N00026349|")
280
user=> (contribs "|N00001845|")
134121
```

## How it works...

Except for `force-val`, all of the agent-related code is in `main`. Let's walk through the lines that are of interest:

▶ We define the number of agents that we want to use. Each agent is initialized to a vector of zeroes of the same length as the number of fields:

```
(let [agents (map agent (repeat agent-count {}))]
```

▶ Next, after reading the input CSV file to a sequence of maps and partitioning them into chunks of equal size, we send each agent the `read-file-amounts` function. We cycle through the agents until all of the files are assigned to an agent:

```
(dorun
  (map #(send %1 read-file-amounts %2)
       (cycle agents)
       data-files))
```

> ▶ Next, we block until each agent is done by calling `await`, and we dereference each to get its value (both of these take place inside `force-val`). Once we have the data from each agent, we merge them all together into one hashmap:

```
(apply merge-with + (map force-val agents))))
```

## See also

> ▶ *Agents and asynchronous actions* in the Clojure documentation (`http://clojure.org/agents`) for more on agents.

# Getting better performance with commute

The STM system we created in the first recipe of this chapter, *Managing program complexity with STM*, has one subtle problem: threads attempting to reference and update `total-hu` and `total-fams` contend for these two values unnecessarily. Since everything comes down to accessing these two resources, a lot of tasks are probably retried.

But they don't need to be. Both are simply updating those values with commutative functions (`#(+ sum-? %)`). The order in which these updates are applied doesn't matter. Since we block until all of the processing is done, we don't have to worry about the two references getting out of sync. They'll get back together eventually, before we access their values, and that's good enough for this situation.

To update references with a commutative function, instead of `alter`, we use `commute`. The `alter` function updates the references on the spot, while `commute` queues the update to happen later, when the reference isn't otherwise engaged. This prevents contentions on those references and can make the system faster too.

For this recipe, we'll again look at the problem we did in the *Managing program complexity with STM* recipe.

## Getting ready

Everything is going to be the same as it was for *Managing program complexity with STM*. We'll use the same dependencies and requirements and even most of the functions as we did for that recipe.

## How to do it...

In fact, the only change will be for the update-totals function, and even that change is minor:

```
(defn update-totals [fields items]
  (let [mzero (mapv (constantly 0) fields)
        [sum-hu sum-fams] (sum-items mzero fields items)]
    (dosync
      (commute total-hu #(+ sum-hu %))
      (commute total-fams #(+ sum-fams %)))))
```

Do you see the difference? We just used commute instead of alter. That's the only change we need to make.

## How it works...

Now the references are updated after the dosync. With alter, the changes happen inside the dosync, within the same transaction. However, with commute, both changes are run separately, and both are scheduled to run when Clojure knows there will be no conflicts. Depending on the use case, this can dramatically cut down on the number of retries and speed up the overall program.

# Combining agents and STM

Agents by themselves are pretty useful. However, if we want to still use the agent task queuing and concurrency framework, even though an agent function needs to coordinate the state beyond the agent's own data, we'll need to use both agents and the STM: send or send-off to coordinate the agent's state. This will need to be combined with dosync, ref-set, alter, or commute inside the agent function to coordinate with the other state.

This combination provides simplicity over complex state and data coordination problems. This is a huge help in managing the complexity of a data processing and analysis system.

For this recipe, we'll look at the same problem we did in the *Managing program complexity with agents* recipe. However, this time we'll structure it a little differently. The final result will be stored in a shared reference, and the agents will update it as they go.

## Getting ready

We'll need to use the same dependencies as we did for *Managing program complexity with agents*, and we'll use two values and functions from that recipe: `data-files` and `read-file-amounts`.

## How to do it...

For this recipe, we need to define a few functions to work through a queue of input chunks and then block until all of the processing is complete:

1. Most of what we use will be from the previous recipe, including `read-file-amounts`. However, we'll wrap it in another function that takes its output and uses `commute` to update the shared-count hashmap with the counts it has just read:

```
(defn read-update-amounts [m filename count-ref]
  (dosync
    (let [file-amounts (read-file-amounts m filename)]
      (commute count-ref
               #(merge-with + % file-amounts)))))
```

2. We're now ready for the `main` function. This creates the agents and the shared reference, sends tasks to the agents, and waits for the results before returning them:

```
(defn main [data-files agent-count]
  (let [counts (ref {})
        agents (map agent (repeat agent-count {}))]
    (dorun
      (map #(send %1 read-update-amounts %2 counts)
           (cycle agents)
           data-files))
    (doseq [a agents]
      (await a))
    @counts))
```

## How it works...

Using this code looks exactly like how we'd expect:

```
user=> (def amounts (main data-files 8))
user=> (take 5 amounts)
(["" 106549]
 ["|N00032245|" 22750]
 ["|N00027812|" 150]
```

```
["|N00030973|" 9900]
["|N00005656|" 11598514])
```

This solution uses agents to handle the work, and it uses the STM to manage shared data structures. The `main` function first assigns each input file to an agent. Each agent then reads the input file and totals the amount of contributions for each candidate. It takes those totals and uses the STM to update the shared counts.

# Maintaining consistency with ensure

When we use the STM, we are trying to coordinate and maintain consistency between several values, all of which keep changing. However, we'll sometimes want to maintain consistency with those references that won't change and therefore won't be included in the transaction. We can signal that the STM should include these other references in the transaction by using the `ensure` function.

This helps simplify the data processing system by ensuring that the data structures stay synchronized and consistent. The `ensure` function allows us to have more control over what gets managed by the STM.

For this recipe, we'll use a slightly contrived example. We'll process a set of text files and compute the frequency of a term as well as the total number of words. We'll do this concurrently, and we'll be able to watch the results get updated as we progress.

For the set of text files, we'll use the Brown corpus. Constructed in the 1960s, this was one of the first digital collections of texts (or corpora) assembled for linguists to use to study language. At that time, its size (one million words) was huge. Today, similar corpora contain 100 million words or more.

## Getting ready

We'll need to include the `clojure.string` library and have easy access to the `File` class:

```
(require '[clojure.string :as string])
(import '[java.io File])
```

We'll also need to download the Brown corpus. We can download it at http://www.nltk.org/nltk_data/. Actually, you can use any large collection of texts, but the Brown corpus has each word's part of speech listed in the file, so we'll need to parse it specially. If you use a different corpus, you can just change the `tokenize-brown` function, as explained in the next section, to work with your texts.

## How to do it...

For this recipe, we'll go from preprocessing the data to performing the counts in parallel and looking at the results.

1.  Let's get a sequence of the files to process:

    ```
    (def input-files
      (filter #(.isFile %)
              (file-seq (File. "./data/brown"))))
    ```

2.  Now, we'll define some references: `finished` will indicate whether processing is done or not, `total-docs` and `total-words` will keep running totals, `freqs` will map the tokens to their frequencies as a whole, and `running-report` is an agent that contains the current state of the report for the term we're interested in:

    ```
    (def finished (ref false))
    (def total-docs (ref 0))
    (def total-words (ref 0))
    (def freqs (ref {}))
    (def running-report
        (agent {:term nil,
      :frequency 0,
      :ratio 0.0}))
    ```

3.  Let's write the tokenizer. The text in the Brown corpus files look like this:

    ```
    The/at Fulton/np-tl County/nn-tl Grand/jj-tl Jury/nn-tl said/vbd
    Friday/nr an/at investigation/nn of/in Atlanta's/np$ recent/jj
    primary/nn election/nn produced/vbd ``/`` no/at evidence/nn ''/''
    that/cs any/dti irregularities/nns took/vbd place/nn ./.
    ```

    We're not interested in the parts of speech, so our tokenizer will remove them and covert each token to a lowercase keyword:

    ```
    (defn tokenize-brown [input-str]
      (->> (string/split input-str #"\s+")
           (map #(first (string/split % #"/" 2)))
           (filter #(> (count %) 0))
           (map string/lower-case)
           (map keyword)))
    ```

4.  Now, let's write a utility function that increments the frequency map for a token:

    ```
    (defn accum-freq [m token]
      (assoc m token (inc (m token 0))))
    ```

5. We'll use that function in `compute-file`, which does the primary processing for each file. It also uses `send-off` to safely queue the next task for this agent:

```
(defn compute-file [fs]
  (dosync
    (if-let [[s & ss] (seq fs)]
      (let [tokens (tokenize-brown (slurp s))
            tc (count tokens)
            fq (reduce accum-freq {} tokens)]
        (commute total-docs inc)
        (commute total-words #(+ tc %))
        (commute freqs #(merge-with + % fq))
        (send-off *agent* compute-file)
        ss)
      (do (alter finished (constantly true))
          '()))))
```

6. Another function will update the report in parallel:

```
(defn compute-report [{term :term, :as report}]
  (dosync
    (when-not @finished
      (send *agent* compute-report))
    (let [term-freq (term (ensure freqs) 0)
          tc (ensure total-words)
          r (if (zero? tc)
              nil
              (float (/ term-freq tc)))]
      (assoc report
             :frequency term-freq
             :ratio r))))
```

7. Finally, `compute-frequencies` gets the entire thing started:

```
(defn compute-frequencies [inputs term]
  (let [a (agent inputs)]
    (send running-report #(assoc % :term term))
    (send running-report compute-report)
    (send-off a compute-file)))
```

8. To use this, we just call `compute-frequencies` with the inputs and a term, and then we poll `finished` and `running-report` to see how processing is going:

```
user=> (compute-frequencies input-files :committee)
#<Agent@1830f455: (…)>
```

```
user=> [@finished @running-report]
[false {:frequency 79, :ratio 6.933839E-4, :term :committee}]
user=> [@finished @running-report]
[false {:frequency 105, :ratio 2.5916903E-4, :term :committee}]
user=> [@finished @running-report]
[false {:frequency 164, :ratio 1.845714E-4, :term :committee}]
user=> [@finished @running-report]
[true {:frequency 168, :ratio 1.4468178E-4, :term :committee}]
```

We can see from the ratio of the `committee` frequency to the total frequency that initially the word `committee` occurred relatively often (0.07 percent, which is approximately the frequency of other common words in the overall corpus). However, by the end of processing, its frequency had settled down to about 0.014 percent of the total number of words, which is closer to what we would expect.

## How it works...

In this recipe, `compute-frequencies` triggers everything. It creates a new agent that processes the input files one-by-one and updates most of the references in the `compute-file` function.

The `compute-report` function handles the updating of the running report. It bases that report on the frequency map and the total words. However, it doesn't change either of the two. But to keep everything synchronized, it calls `ensure` on both. Otherwise, there's a chance that the count of total words comes from one set of documents and the term frequency from another set. This isn't likely given that only one agent is updating those values, but if we decided to have more than one agent processing the files, that would be a possibility. To generate a report for a new term without reading all of the files again, we can define this function:

```
(defn get-report [term]
  (send running-report #(assoc % :term term))
  (send running-report compute-report)
  (await running-report)
  @running-report)
```

# Introducing safe side effects into the STM

The STM isn't safe as far as side effects are concerned. Since a `dosync` block may get retried, possibly more than once, any side effects will be executed again and again, whether they should be or not. Values may get written to the screen or logfile multiple times. Worse, values may be written to the database more than once.

However, all programs must produce side effects. The trick is adding them while getting a handle on complexity. The easiest way to do that is to keep side effects out of transactions.

For this recipe, to illustrate what can happen, we'll simulate **thread starvation**. That sounds serious, but it just means that one thread isn't able to access the resources it needs, so it can't do its job. We'll also use an **atom** (a reference that isn't controlled by the STM) to keep track of the number of times the STM retries a call to an agent. That way, we can see what happens that creates the problem, and what we need to do to fix it.

## Getting ready

To prepare, we'll need access to `java.lang.Thread` in our REPL:

```
(import [java.lang Thread])
```

## How to do it...

For this recipe, we'll walk through a couple of experiments to simulate thread starvation:

1. For these experiments, we'll use one reference and two agents. The agents will try to read and increment the `counter` reference simultaneously, but they will wait for different amounts of time in the transaction, so one thread will starve the other:

```
(def counter (ref 0))
(def a1 (agent :a1))
(def a2 (agent :a2))
```

2. Now, we'll define a utility to start both agents on the same message function, with different sleep periods:

```
(defn start-agents [msg a1-sleep a2-sleep]
  (send a1 msg a1-sleep)
  (send a2 msg a2-sleep))
```

3. For the first experiment, we'll use a `debug` function for the side effect. It just prints the message and flushes the output stream:

```
(defn debug [msg]
  (print (str msg \newline))
  (flush))
```

4. The first message function will `starve-out` anything:

```
(defn starve-out [tag sleep-for]
  (let [retries (atom 0)]
    (dosync
      (let [c @counter]
        (when-not (zero? @retries)
          (debug (str ":starve-out " tag
                      ", :try " @retries
                      ", :counter " c)))
```

```
(swap! retries inc)
(Thread/sleep sleep-for)
(ref-set counter (inc c))
(send *agent* starve-out sleep-for)
tag))))
```

5.  If we send `starve-out` to both agents with very different sleep periods and look at the output, we'll see that `:a2` is consistently getting starvedout. (You can stop the agents by calling `shutdown-agents`):

```
user=> (start-agents starve-out 50 1000)
:starve-out :a2, :try 1, :counter 19
:starve-out :a2, :try 2, :counter 39
:starve-out :a2, :try 3, :counter 59
:starve-out :a2, :try 4, :counter 78
```

6.  In order to make this safe, we have to move all of the side effects out of the `dosync` block. This means that we'll move the `debug` call out of the STM. While we're at it, we'll move the `send` call since it's theoretically a side effect, even though it should be safe enough here. To be safer, we'll use a new output function, one that uses `io!` (highlighted). The `io!` block will throw an exception if it is executed inside a transaction:

```
(defn debug! [msg] (io! (debug msg)))

(defn starve-safe [tag sleep-for]
  (let [retries (atom 0)]
    (dosync
      (let [c @counter]
        (swap! retries inc)
        (Thread/sleep sleep-for)
        (ref-set counter (inc c))))
    (when-not (zero? @retries)
      (debug! (str ":safe-starve " tag
                   ", :try " @retries
                   ", " @counter)))
    (send *agent* starve-safe sleep-for)
    tag))
```

This version safely handles the I/O in the STM. Moreover, if we forget and refactor the call to `debug!` back inside the transaction, our code will stop working.

# Maintaining data consistency with validators

Clojure has a number of tools to work with agents. One of them is validators. When an agent's message function returns a value, any validator functions assigned to that agent receive the agent's data before it does. If the validators return true, all is well. The agent is updated and processing continues. However, if any validator returns false or raises an error, an error is raised on the agent.

This can be a handy tool to make sure that the data assigned to your agent conforms to your expectations, and it can be an important check on the consistency and validity of your data.

For this recipe, we'll read data from a CSV file and convert the values in some of the columns to integers. We'll use a validator to ensure that this actually happens.

## Getting ready

For this recipe, we'll use the dependencies and requirements that we did from the *Managing program complexity with STM* recipe. We'll also use the `lazy-read-csv` and `with-header` functions from that recipe, and we'll use the data file that we used in that recipe. We'll keep that filename bound to `data-file`.

## How to do it...

This recipe will be built from a number of shorter functions:

1. Let's define a list of the rows that will need to be converted to integers. Looking at the data file, we can come up with this:

```
(def int-rows
  [:GEOID :SUMLEV :STATE :POP100 :HU100 :POP100.2000
    :HU100.2000 :P035001 :P035001.2000])
```

2. Now, we'll define a predicate function to check whether a value is an integer or not:

```
(defn int? [x]
  (or (instance? Integer x) (instance? Long x)))
```

3. We'll create a function that attempts to read a string to an integer, but silently returns the original value if there's an exception:

```
(defn try-read-string [x]
  (try
    (read-string x)
    (catch Exception ex
      x)))
```

4. This system will have three agents, each performing a different task. Here is the function for the agent that converts all whole number fields to integer values. It sends the output to another agent and uses that output as its own new value so it can be validated:

```
(defn coerce-row [_ row sink]
  (let [cast-row
          (apply assoc row
                 (mapcat
                   (fn [k]
                     [k (try-read-string (k row))])
                   int-rows))]
    (send sink conj cast-row)
    cast-row))
```

5. Here is the function for the agent that reads the input. It sends an item of the input to the `coerce-row` agent, queues itself to read another item of the input, and sets its value to the rest of the input:

```
(defn read-row  [rows caster sink]
  (when-let [[item & items] (seq rows)]
    (send caster coerce-row item sink)
    (send *agent* read-row caster sink)
    items))
```

6. Here is the validator for the `coerce-row` agent. It checks that the integer fields are either integers or empty strings:

```
(defn int-val? [x] (or (int? x) (empty? x)))
(defn validate [row]
  (or (nil? row)
      (reduce #(and %1 (int-val? (%2 row)))
              true int-rows)))
```

7. Finally, we'll define a function that defines the agents, starts processing them, and returns them:

```
(defn agent-ints [input-file]
  (let [reader (agent (seque
                        (with-header
                          (lazy-read-csv
                            input-file))))
        caster (agent nil)
        sink (agent [])]
    (set-validator! caster validate)
    (send reader read-row caster sink)
    {:reader reader
     :caster caster
     :sink sink}))
```

8. If we run this, we get a map containing the agents. We can get the output data by dereferencing the `:sink` agent:

```
user=> (def ags (agent-ints data-file))
#'user/ags
user=> (first @(:sink ags))
{:SUMLEV 160, :P035001 2056, :HU100.2000 3788, :HU100 4271, :NAME
"Abingdon town", :GEOID 5100148, :NECTA "", :CBSA "", :CSA "",
:P035001.2000 2091, :POP100.2000 7780, :CNECTA "", :POP100 8191,
:COUNTY "", :STATE 51}
```

## How it works...

The `agent-ints` function is pretty busy. It defines the agents, sets everything up, and returns the map containing the agents.

Let's break it down:

```
(let [reader (agent (seque
                       (with-header
                         (lazy-read-csv input-file))))
      caster (agent nil)
      sink (agent [])]
```

These lines define the agents. One reads in the data, one converts it to integers, and one accumulates the results. This figure illustrates that process:

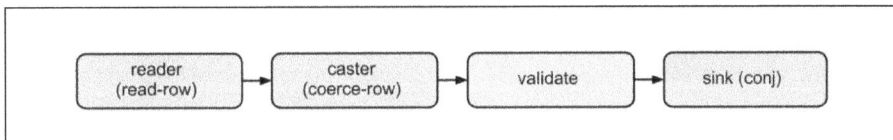

Next, `read-row` simply gets the first item of the input and sends it to the `caster` agent. The `coerce-row` function tries to change the data in the columns listed in `int-rows` to integers. It then passes the results to the `sink` agent. Before it's completely done, however, its new state is passed to its validator function, `validate`.

The validator allows `nil` rows (for the agent's initial state) or integer fields that contain either integers or empty strings. Finally, the `sink` agent is called with `conj`. It accumulates the converted results.

## See also

▶ To learn how to use a nice DSL to validate data, see *Validating data with Valip*, in *Chapter 2, Cleaning and Validating Data*.

# Monitoring processing with watchers

Another tool that Clojure provides for working with agents is **watchers**. These are just functions that get a chance to peek at the agent's data. This happens after the validators have successfully run and the new data is set as the agent's state. Because of the way it's handled, the state may have changed again since then, but watchers give you the chance to look at the data and track it separately.

This can help us keep an eye on the data as it's being processed. We can use it to log progress, sample the data for manual validation, or a number of other tasks.

## Getting ready

We'll need these dependencies:

```clojure
(require '[clojure.java.io :as io]
         '[clojure.data.csv :as csv]
         '[clojure.string :as str])
(import '[java.lang Thread])
```

Also, we'll use the data files from the *Managing program complexity with agents* recipe, along with the binding to the list of those files, `data-files`.

From *Managing program complexity with STM*, we'll use the `lazy-read-csv` and `->int` functions.

## How to do it...

In this recipe, we'll add a watcher to keep track of the number of rows that are converted, and we'll add a flag that lets us know when processing is finished:

1. In order to convert the appropriate fields into rows, we'll need a couple of functions. First, we'll have, `row-ints`, a data binding to indicate which fields need to be converted to integers. Then, we'll define `try->int`, which will normalize the input and attempt to convert it to an integer. If it fails, it will return the original value. Finally, `coerce-row-ints` will take a row, attempt to convert the rows with integers, and send the results to the next agent:

```clojure
(def row-ints [0 4])
(defn try->int [v]
  (try
    (->int (str/trim (str/replace v \| \space)))
    (catch Exception ex
      v)))
(defn coerce-row-ints [_ row indices sink]
```

```
(let [cast-row
      (->> indices
           (mapcat #(vector
                     % (try->int (nth row %))))
           (apply assoc row))]
  (send sink conj cast-row)
  cast-row))
```

2. The agent that reads the data will use the function `read-row`. This is mostly similar to the `read-row` that we saw in the *Maintaining data consistency with validators* recipe. The differences are highlighted here:

```
(defn read-row [rows caster sink done]
  (if-let [[item & items] (seq rows)]
    (do
      (send caster coerce-row-ints
            item row-ints sink)
      (send *agent* read-row caster sink done)
      items)
    (do
      (dosync (commute done (constantly true)))
      '())))
```

3. The function that watches the agent that coerces the data will just update a counter:

```
(defn watch-caster
  [counter watch-key watch-agent old-state new-state]
  (when-not (nil? new-state)
    (dosync (commute counter inc))))
```

4. We'll define a function that polls until processing is finished:

```
(defn wait-for-it [sleep-for ref-var]
  (loop []
    (when-not @ref-var
      (Thread/sleep sleep-for)
      (recur))))
```

5. The last function creates all of the agents and references and dispatches their functions. Finally, it blocks until they are all finished, when it returns the results. Again, I've highlighted the differences from `agent-ints` in the *Maintaining Data consistency with validators* recipe, which is very similar:

```
(defn watch-processing [input-files]
  (let [reader (agent (seque
                        (mapcat
                          lazy-read-csv
                          input-files)))
        caster (agent nil)
```

```
            sink (agent [])
            counter (ref 0)
            done (ref false)]
        (add-watch caster :counter
                (partial watch-caster counter))
        (send reader read-row caster sink done)
        (wait-for-it 250 done)
        {:results @sink
         :count-watcher @counter}))
```

6. When we run the preceding code, we get the data about counts from the watcher:

```
user=> (:count-watcher (watch-processing (take 2 data-files)))
118095
```

## How it works...

This time, instead of associating a validator with the agent that coerces the integers, we called add-watch on it. Each time the agent is updated, the watch function is called with four parameters: a key, the agent, the old state, and the new state. Our watch function first needs a counter reference, which we will supply by partially applying its parameters when we call add-watch.

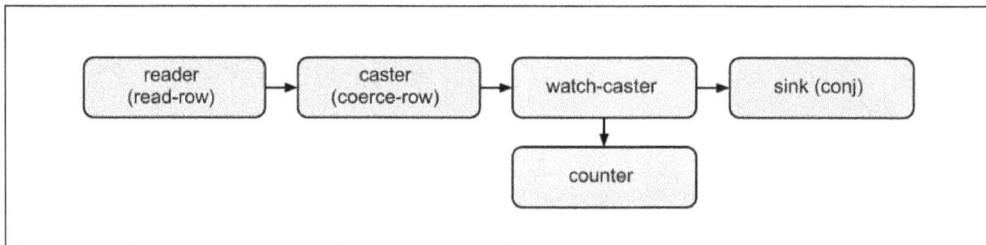

Once everything has been created, watch-processing just sends the input agent the first message, and then it waits for the processing to finish.

# Debugging concurrent programs with watchers

Watchers are not only good for logging and counting, but they are also useful for debugging. If an agent or reference is not getting updated the way we expect, we can temporarily add a watcher to track what's happening so we can see what's going on.

For this recipe, we'll continue the theme we've been working with for the last few recipes. This time, instead of counting the data, the watch function will print the change of state to the console.

## Getting ready

We'll use the dependencies and requirements that we did in the *Monitoring processing with watchers* recipe. For this recipe, we just need to add a two more functions to them.

## How to do it...

1. The main difference from the last recipe is the `watch` function. Here's the new one:

```
(defn debug-watch [watch-key watch-agent old-state new-state]
  (let [output (str watch-key
                    ": "
                    (pr-str old-state)
                    " => "
                    (pr-str new-state)
                    \newline)]
    (print output))))
```

2. Of course, the main function that creates the system and runs it is different. I've highlighted the changes:

```
(defn watch-debugging
  [input-file]
  (let [reader (agent
                 (seque
                   (mapcat
                     lazy-read-csv
                     input-files)))
        caster (agent nil)
        sink (agent [])
        counter (ref 0)
        done (ref false)]
    (add-watch caster :counter
               (partial watch-caster counter))
    (add-watch caster :debug debug-watch)
    (send reader read-row caster sink done)
    (wait-for-it 250 done)
    {:results @sink
     :count-watcher @counter}))
```

3. Now, when we run this processing system, we get a lot of debugging output:

```
user=> (:count-watcher (watch-debugging (take 2 data-files)))
:debug: [1990 "|0028670|" "|C00186288|" "|N00001783|" 1000
"06/15/1990" "|C4100|" "|24K|" "|D|" "|H6MI16034|"] => [1990
"|0028677|" "|C00186288|" "|N00007967|" 2000 "06/15/1990"
"|C4100|" "|24K|" "|D|" "|H6WA05023|"]
```

```
:debug: [1990 "|0028677|" "|C00186288|" "|N00007967|" 2000
"06/15/1990" "|C4100|" "|24K|" "|D|" "|H6WA05023|"] => [1990
"|0028687|" "|C00186288|" "|N00002497|" 500 "07/18/1990" "|C4100|"
"|24K|" "|D|" "|H6SC03025|"]
:debug: [1990 "|0028687|" "|C00186288|" "|N00002497|" 500
"07/18/1990" "|C4100|" "|24K|" "|D|" "|H6SC03025|"] => [1990
"|0028706|" "|C00186288|" "|N00007763|" 1000 "09/28/1990"
"|C4100|" "|24K|" "|D|" "|S8OR00017|"]
```

## There's more...

This is a good option to debug output if you need a lot of flexibility. However, if all you need is to track function calls, arguments, and outputs, `clojure.tools.trace` (`https://github.com/clojure/tools.trace`) is better. It does this and only this, and it's also less intrusive on your program's structure.

# Recovering from errors in agents

Since agents run in a thread pool, the way exceptions are signaled and handled becomes an issue. Does the offending message function simply stop running? Does the agent stop? What happens to the `Exception` instance?

Clojure has several mechanisms to deal with errors in agent functions. We'll walk through them in this recipe.

## How to do it...

The agent's **error mode** and **error handler** determine how it handles errors. The error mode can be set when the agent is created or with the function `set-error-mode!`, and the error handler is set with `set-error-handler!`.

### Failing on errors

The default error mode is `:fail`. If we don't specify an error mode when we create an agent, this is what it gets. With this error mode, when one of the agent's message functions throws an exception, the agent stops processing any more messages and stores the exception. We can retrieve the exception with `agent-error`, and we can start processing it again with `restart-agent`:

```
user=> (def agent-99 (agent 0))
#'user/agent-99
user=> (send agent-99 #(/ 100 %))
#<Agent@aa711 FAILED: 0>
user=> (agent-error agent-99)
#<ArithmeticExceptionjava.lang.ArithmeticException: Divide by zero>
```

```
user=> @agent-99
0
user=> (restart-agent agent-99 0)
0
```

## Continuing on errors

The other option for an error mode is :continue. With this error mode, when an agent throws an exception, the exception and the message that caused it are silently swallowed. The agent continues processing as if nothing has happened:

```
user=> (def agent-99 (agent 0 :error-mode :continue))
#'user/agent-99
user=> (send agent-99 #(/ 100 %))
#<Agent@f1b6fa6: 0>
user=> (agent-error agent-99)
nil
user=> @agent-99
0
```

## Using a custom error handler

If the agent's error handler is set, that is used instead of the error mode. The error handler is just a function that is called with the agent and the exception that was thrown. In this example, the new error handler will simply print the exception:

```
user=> (def agent-99 (agent 0 :error-handler #(prn %2)))
#'user/agent-99
user=> (send agent-99 #(/ 100 %))
#<ArithmeticExceptionjava.lang.ArithmeticException: Divide by zero>
#<Agent@2da13aa9: 0>
user=> (agent-error agent-99)
nil
user=> @agent-99
0
```

Once an error has been caught using a custom error handler, the agent is free to continue processing. If we send agent-99 a new message, it will process it as if nothing has happened.

## There's more...

The canonical source of information about Clojure's agent system and how it handles errors is the *Agents and Asynchronous Actions* page in the Clojure documentation at http://clojure.org/agents.

# Managing large inputs with sized queues

When we work with very large datasets, we often talk about structuring our program concurrently. One big problem when dealing with very large datasets concurrently is coordinating and managing the flow of data between different parts of our program. If one part produces data too quickly, or another part processes it too slowly (depending on how you look at it), the message queue between the two can get backed up. If that happens, the memory will fill up with messages and data waiting to be processed.

## How to do it...

The solution for this in Clojure is quite simple: use `seque`. This uses an instance of `java.util.concurrent.LinkedBlockingQueue` to pull values from a lazy sequence. It works ahead of where we're pulling values out of the queue, but not too far ahead. And once we've wrapped a sequence with `seque`, we can treat it just like any other sequence:

```
user=> (take 20 (seque 5 (range Integer/MAX_VALUE)))
(0 1 2 3 4 5 6 7 8 9 10 11 12 13 14 15 16 17 18 19)
```

## How it works...

The `seque` function reads ahead a bit (usually a little more than we specify). It then waits until some of the items that it has read have been consumed, and then it reads ahead a little more. This ensures that the rest of our system always has input to process, but its memory won't get filled by input waiting to be processed. This is an easy solution to balancing input and processing, and this function's simplicity helps keep an often complex problem from introducing incidental complexity into our processing system.

# 4
# Improving Performance with Parallel Programming

In this chapter, we will cover the following topics:

- ▶ Parallelizing processing with pmap
- ▶ Parallelizing processing with Incanter
- ▶ Partitioning Monte Carlo simulations for better pmap performance
- ▶ Finding the optimal partition size with simulated annealing
- ▶ Combining function calls with reducers
- ▶ Parallelizing with reducers
- ▶ Generating online summary statistics for data streams with reducers
- ▶ Using type hints
- ▶ Benchmarking with Criterium

# Introduction

If concurrent processing has performance implications when structuring programs, parallel processing is a way to get better performance that has implications on how we structure our programs. Although they are often conflated, concurrent processing and parallel processing are different solutions to different problems. Concurrency is good for expressing programs that involve different tasks that can be, or must be, carried out at the same time. Parallelization is a good option if you want to perform the same task many times, all at once. Parallelization is not necessary, but it can help tremendously with your program's performance.

Earlier, the easiest, and often best, strategy to improve performance was to go on a vacation. Moore's law implies that processor speed will double approximately every 18 months, so in the 1990s, we could go on vacation, return, buy a new computer, and our programs were faster. This was magic.

Today, we're no longer under Moore's law, instead, as the saying goes, *the free lunch is over*. Now, processor speeds have plateaued or even declined. Instead, computers are made faster by packing more processors into them. To make use of these processors, we have to employ **parallel programming**.

Of course, the processor isn't always the slowest part of the program (that is, our programs aren't always CPU bound). Sometimes, it's the disk or network that limits how fast our programs run. If that's the case, we have to read from multiple disks or network connections simultaneously in order to see any improvement in speed. For example, reading from a single file from different processors might even be slower, but if you can copy the file onto different disks and read each file from a separate processor, it will be faster in all likelihood.

The recipes in this chapter focus on leveraging multiple cores by showing different ways to parallelize Clojure programs. It also includes a few recipes on related topics. For instance, consider the *Using type hints* recipe, which talks about how to optimize our code, and the *Benchmarking with Criterium* recipe, which discusses how to get good data for optimizing our code.

# Parallelizing processing with pmap

The easiest way to parallelize data is to take a loop that you already have and handle each item in it in a thread.

This is essentially what `pmap` does. If you replace a call to `map` with `pmap`, it takes each call to the function's argument and executes it in a thread pool. `pmap` is not completely lazy, but it's not completely strict either. Instead, it stays just ahead of the output consumed. So, if the output is never used, it won't be fully realized.

For this recipe, we'll calculate the **Mandelbrot** set. Each point in the output takes enough time that this is a good candidate to parallelize. We can just swap map for pmap and immediately see a speedup.

## How to do it...

The Mandelbrot set can be found by feeding a point into a function and then feeding the results of this back into the function. The point will either settle on a value or it will take off. The Mandelbrot set contains the points that don't settle that is, points whose values explode after repeatedly being feed into the function.

1. We need a function that takes a point and the maximum number of iterations in order to return the iteration it escapes on. This just means that the value goes above four:

```
(defn get-escape-point
  [scaled-x scaled-y max-iterations]
  (loop [x 0, y 0, iteration 0]
    (let [x2 (* x x)
      y2 (* y y)]
      (if (and (< (+ x2 y2) 4)
               (< iteration max-iterations))
        (recur (+ (- x2 y2) scaled-x)
               (+ (* 2 x y) scaled-y)
               (inc iteration))
        iteration)))))
```

2. The scaled points are the pixel points in the output. These are scaled to relative positions in the Mandelbrot set. Here are the functions that handle the scaling. Along with a particular x-y coordinate in the output, they're given the range of the set and the number of pixels in each direction:

```
(defn scale-to [pixel maximum [lower upper]]
  (+ (* (/ pixel maximum)
        (Math/abs (- upper lower))) lower))

(defn scale-point
  [pixel-x pixel-y max-x max-y set-range]
  [(scale-to pixel-x max-x (:x set-range))
   (scale-to pixel-y max-y (:y set-range))])
```

3. The output-points function returns a sequence of X, Y values for each of the pixels in the final output:

```
(defn output-points [max-x max-y]
  (let [range-y (range max-y)]
    (mapcat (fn [x] (map #(vector x %) range-y))
            (range max-x))))
```

4. For each output pixel, we need to scale it to a location in the range of the Mandelbrot set and then get the escape point for this location:

```
(defn mandelbrot-pixel
  ([max-x max-y max-iterations set-range]
   (partial mandelbrot-pixel
            max-x max-y max-iterations set-range))
  ([max-x max-y max-iterations set-range
    [pixel-x pixel-y]]
   (let [[x y] (scale-point pixel-x pixel-y
                            max-x max-y
                            set-range)]
     (get-escape-point x y max-iterations))))
```

5. At this point, we can simply map `mandelbrot-pixel` over the results of `output-points`. We'll also pass in the function to be used (`map` or `pmap`):

```
(defn mandelbrot
  [mapper max-iterations max-x max-y set-range]
  (doall
    (mapper (mandelbrot-pixel
              max-x max-y max-iterations set-range)
            (output-points max-x max-y))))
```

6. Finally, we have to define the range that the Mandelbrot set covers:

```
(def mandelbrot-range
  {:x [-2.5, 1.0], :y [-1.0, 1.0]})
```

How does running this with `map` and `pmap` compare? A lot depends on the other parameters we pass them. (For more precise and robust times, we use Criterium. See the *Benchmarking with Criterium* recipe for more information on this library and how to use it.) The following is an example output from timing `map` using Criterium:

```
user=> (quick-bench
          (mandelbrot map 500 1000 1000 mandelbrot-range))
WARNING: Final GC required 1.788622983983204 % of runtime
Evaluation count : 6 in 6 samples of 1 calls.
             Execution time mean : 20.993891 sec
    Execution time std-deviation : 38.107942 ms
   Execution time lower quantile : 20.971178 sec ( 2.5%)
   Execution time upper quantile : 21.059463 sec (97.5%)
                   Overhead used : 1.817165 ns

Found 1 outliers in 6 samples (16.6667 %)
        low-severe        1 (16.6667 %)
 Variance from outliers : 13.8889 % Variance is moderately inflated by
outliers
```

**Timings for map and pmap**

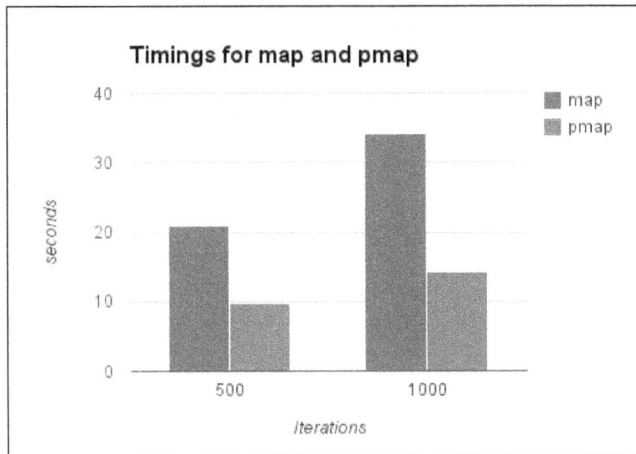

In both the cases, `pmap` is more than twice as fast when running it on a machine with eight cores.

## How it works...

Parallelization is a balancing act. If each separate work item is small, the overhead of creating threads, coordinating between them, and passing data back and forth takes more time than doing the work itself. However, when each thread has enough to do, we can get nice speedups just by using `pmap`.

Behind the scenes, `pmap` takes each item and uses `future` to run it in a thread pool. It forces only a couple of more items than the number of processors, so it keeps your machine busy without generating more work or data than you need.

## There's more...

For an in-depth, excellent discussion on the nuts and bolts of `pmap`, along with pointers about things to watch out for, check out David Liebke's talk, *From Concurrency to Parallelism* (`http://youtu.be/ZampUP6PdQA`).

## See also

> ▶ In the *Partitioning Monte Carlo simulations for better pmap performance* recipe, later in this chapter, we'll take a look at a trick to make smaller tasks more suitable for parallelization using `pmap`

# Parallelizing processing with Incanter

In the upcoming chapters, many recipes will feature Incanter. One of its good features is that it uses the Parallel Colt Java library (http://sourceforge.net/projects/parallelcolt/) to actually handle its processing. So when you use a lot of matrix, statistical, or other functions, they're automatically executed on multiple threads.

For this, we'll revisit the Virginia housing-unit census data from the *Managing program complexity with STM* recipe in *Chapter 3, Managing Complexity with Concurrent Programming*. This time, we'll fit it to a linear regression.

## Getting ready

We need to add Incanter to our list of dependencies in our Leiningen project.clj file:

```
(defproject parallel-data "0.1.0"
  :dependencies [[org.clojure/clojure "1.6.0"]
                 [incanter "1.5.5"]])
```

We also need to pull these libraries into our REPL or script:

```
(use '(incanter core datasets io optimize charts stats))
```

We'll use the data file from the *Managing program complexity with STM* recipe in *Chapter 3, Managing Complexity with Concurrent Programming*. We can bind that filename to the name data-file, just as we did in that recipe:

```
(def data-file "data/all_160_in_51.P35.csv")
```

## How to do it...

For this recipe, we'll extract the data to be analyzed and perform a linear regression. We'll then graph the data.

1. First, we'll read in the data and pull the population and housing-unit columns into their own matrices:

   ```
   (def data (to-matrix
                 (sel (read-dataset data-file :header true)
                      :cols [:POP100 :HU100])))
   ```

2. From this matrix, we can bind the population and the housing-unit data to their own names:

   ```
   (def population (sel data :cols 0))
   (def housing-units (sel data :cols 1))
   ```

3. Now that we have these, we can use Incanter to fit the data:

```
(def lm (linear-model housing-units population))
```

4. We'll talk more about graphing and plotting in a later chapter, but Incanter makes it so easy that it's difficult *not* to look at it:

```
(def plot (scatter-plot population housing-units
            :legend true))
(add-lines plot population (:fitted lm))
(view plot)
```

Here, you can see that the graph of housing units to families is a straight line:

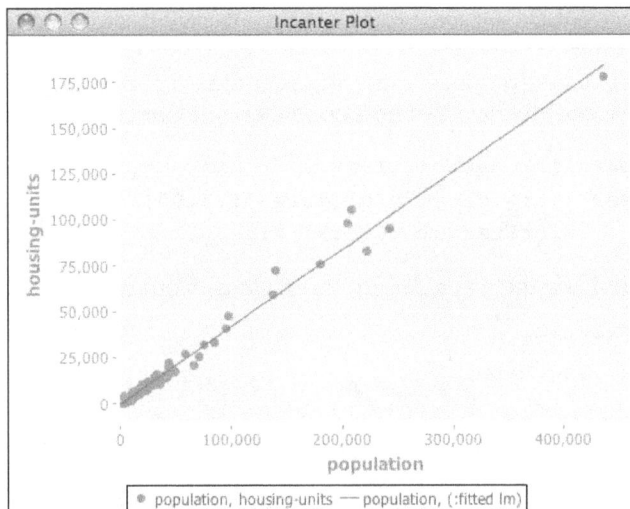

## How it works...

Under the hood, Incanter takes the data matrix and partitions it into chunks. It then spreads those over the available CPUs to speed up processing. Of course, you don't have to worry about this. This just works. That's part of what makes Incanter so powerful.

# Partitioning Monte Carlo simulations for better pmap performance

In the *Parallelizing processing with pmap* recipe we found that while using pmap is easy enough, knowing when to use it is more complicated. Processing each task in the collection has to take enough time to make the costs of threading, coordinating processing, and communicating the data worth it. Otherwise, the program will spend more time with *how* the parallelization is done and not enough time with *what* the task is.

A way to get around this is to make sure that `pmap` has enough to do at each step it parallelizes. The easiest way to do this is to partition the input collection into chunks and run `pmap` on groups of the input.

For this recipe, we'll use Monte Carlo methods to approximate *pi*. We'll compare a serial version against a naïve parallel version as well as a version that uses parallelization and partitions.

Monte Carlo methods work by attacking a deterministic problem, such as computing pi, nondeterministically. That is, we'll take a nonrandom problem and throw random data at it in order to compute the results. We'll see how this works and go into more detail on what this means toward the end of this recipe.

## Getting ready

We'll use Criterium (`https://github.com/hugoduncan/criterium`) to handle benchmarking, so we'll need to include it as a dependency in our Leiningen `project.clj` file:

```
(defproject parallel-data "0.1.0"
  :dependencies [[org.clojure/clojure "1.6.0"]
                 [criterium "0.4.3"]])
```

We'll also use Criterium and the `java.lang.Math` class in our script or REPL:

```
(use 'criterium.core)
(import [java.lang Math])
```

## How to do it...

To implement this, we'll define some core functions and then implement a Monte Carlo method that uses `pmap` to estimate pi.

1.  We need to define the functions that are necessary for the simulation. We'll have one function that generates a random two-dimensional point, which will fall somewhere in the unit square:

    ```
    (defn rand-point [] [(rand) (rand)])
    ```

2.  Now, we need a function to return a point's distance from the origin:

    ```
    (defn center-dist [[x y]]
      (Math/sqrt (+ (* x x) (* y y))))
    ```

3.  Next, we'll define a function that takes a number of points to process and creates that many random points. It will return the number of points that fall inside a circle:

    ```
    (defn count-in-circle [n]
      (->> (repeatedly n rand-point)
           (map center-dist)
    ```

```
      (filter #(<= % 1.0))
      count))
```

4. This simplifies our definition of the base (serial) version. This calls `count-in-circle` to get the proportion of random points in a unit square that fall inside a circle. It multiplies this by `4`, which should approximate pi:

```
(defn mc-pi [n]
   (* 4.0 (/ (count-in-circle n) n)))
```

5. We'll use a different approach for the simple `pmap` version. The function that we'll parallelize will take a point and either return `1` if it's in the circle, or it will return `0` if it is not. Then, we can add these up to find the number in the circle:

```
(defn in-circle-flag [p]
   (if (<= (center-dist p) 1.0) 1 0))

(defn mc-pi-pmap [n]
   (let [in-circle (->> (repeatedly n rand-point)
                        (pmap in-circle-flag)
                        (reduce + 0))]
      (* 4.0 (/ in-circle n))))
```

6. Moreover, for the version that chunks the input, we'll do something different again. Instead of creating a sequence of random points and partitioning it, we'll have a sequence that tells us how large each partition should be and have `pmap` walk across it, calling `count-in-circle`. This means that the creation of larger sequences is also parallelized:

```
(defn mc-pi-part
   ([n] (mc-pi-part 512 n))
   ([chunk-size n]
    (let [step (int
                  (Math/floor (float (/ n chunk-size))))
          remainder (mod n chunk-size)
          parts (lazy-seq
                  (cons remainder
                        (repeat step chunk-size)))
          in-circle (reduce + 0
                            (pmap count-in-circle
                                  parts))]
       (* 4.0 (/ in-circle n)))))
```

Now, how well do these work? We'll bind our parameters to names, and then we'll run one set of benchmarks before we take a look at a table of all of them. We'll discuss the results in the next section.

```
user=> (def chunk-size 4096)
#'user/chunk-size
```

```
user=> (def input-size 1000000)
#'user/input-size
user=> (quick-bench (mc-pi input-size))
WARNING: Final GC required 3.825293394551939 % of runtime
Evaluation count : 6 in 6 samples of 1 calls.
             Execution time mean : 354.953166 ms
    Execution time std-deviation : 13.118006 ms
   Execution time lower quantile : 345.135999 ms ( 2.5%)
   Execution time upper quantile : 375.628874 ms (97.5%)
                   Overhead used : 1.871847 ns

Found 1 outliers in 6 samples (16.6667 %)
        low-severe        1 (16.6667 %)
 Variance from outliers : 13.8889 % Variance is moderately inflated by
outliers
nil
```

The following table shows the timings of each way of running the program, along with the parameters given, if applicable:

| Function | Input size | Chunk size | Mean | Std deviation | GC time |
|----------|-----------|-----------|------|--------------|---------|
| mc-pi | 1,000,000 | NA | 354.953ms | 13.118ms | 3.825% |
| mc-pi-pmap | 1,000,000 | NA | 944.230ms | 7.363ms | 1.588% |
| mc-pi-part | 1,000,000 | 4,096 | 430.404ms | 8.952ms | 3.303% |

Here's a chart with the same information:

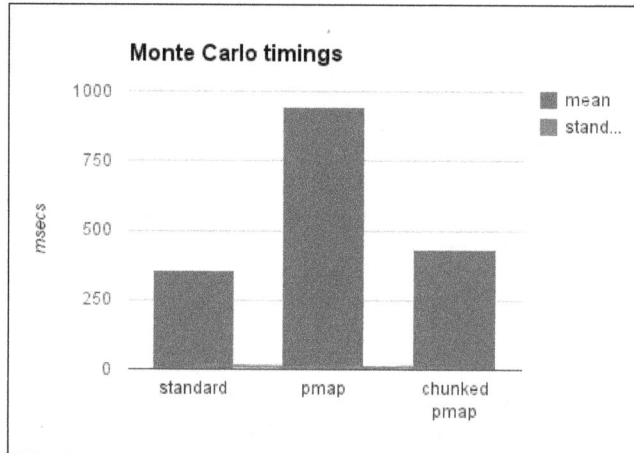

## How it works...

There are a couple of things we should talk about here. Primarily, we need to look at chunking the inputs for `pmap`, but we should also discuss Monte Carlo methods.

### Estimating with Monte Carlo simulations

Monte Carlo simulations work by throwing random data at a problem that is fundamentally deterministic and when it's practically infeasible to attempt a more straightforward solution. Calculating pi is one example of this. By randomly filling in points in a unit square, π/4 will be approximately the ratio of the points that fall within a circle centered at 0, 0. The more random points we use, the better the approximation is.

Note that this is a good demonstration of Monte Carlo methods, but it's a terrible way to calculate pi. It tends to be both slower and less accurate than other methods.

Although not good for this task, Monte Carlo methods are used for designing heat shields, simulating pollution, ray tracing, financial option pricing, evaluating business or financial products, and many other things.

> For a more in-depth discussion, you can refer to Wikipedia, which has a good introduction to Monte Carlo methods, at http://en.wikipedia.org/wiki/Monte_Carlo_method.

### Chunking data for pmap

The table present in this section makes it clear that partitioning helps. The partitioned version took roughly the same amount of time as the serial version, while the naïve parallel version took almost three times longer.

The speedup between the naïve and chunked parallel versions is because each thread is able to spend longer on each task. There is a performance penalty on spreading the work over multiple threads. Context switching (that is, switching between threads) costs time as does coordinating between threads. However, we expect to be able to make that time (and more) by doing more things at once.

However, if each task itself doesn't take long enough, then the benefit won't outweigh the costs. Chunking the input, and effectively creating larger individual tasks for each thread, gets around this by giving each thread more to do, thereby spending less time in context switching and coordinating, relative to the overall time spent in running.

# Finding the optimal partition size with simulated annealing

In the previous recipe, *Partitioning Monte Carlo simulations for better pmap performance*, we more or less guessed what will make a good partition size. We tried a few different values and saw what gives us the best results. However, it's still largely guesswork since just making the partitions larger or smaller doesn't give consistently better or worse results.

This is the type of task that computers are good at. Namely, searching a complex space to find the function parameters that result in an optimal output value. For this recipe, we'll use a fairly simple optimization algorithm called **simulated annealing**. Similar to many optimization algorithms, this is based on a natural process: the way molecules settle into low-energy configurations as the temperature drops to freezing. This is what allows water to form efficient crystal lattices as it freezes.

In simulated annealing, we feed a state to a cost function. At each point, we evaluate a random neighboring state and possibly move to it. As the energy in the system (the temperature) goes down, we are less likely to jump to a new state, especially if that state is worse than the current one according to the cost function. Finally, after either reaching a target output or iterating through a set number of steps, we take the best match found. Similar to many optimization algorithms, this doesn't guarantee that the result will be the absolute best match, but it should be a good one.

For this recipe, we'll use the Monte Carlo pi approximation function that we did in the *Partitioning Monte Carlo simulations for better pmap performance* recipe, and we'll use simulated annealing to find a better partition size.

## Getting ready

We need to use the same dependencies, uses, imports, and functions as we did in the *Partitioning Monte Carlo simulations for better pmap performance* recipe. In addition, we'll also need the `mc-pi-part` function from that recipe.

## How to do it...

1.  For this recipe, we'll first define a generic simulated annealing system. Then, we'll define some functions to pass them as parameters. Everything will be driven by the simulated `annealing` function that takes all of the function parameters for the process as arguments (we'll discuss them in more detail in a minute):

```
(defn annealing
  [initial max-iter max-cost
    neighbor-fn cost-fn p-fn temp-fn]
    (let [get-cost (memoize cost-fn)
```

```
              cost (get-cost initial)]
      (loop [state initial
             cost cost
             k 1
             best-seq [{:state state, :cost cost}]]
        (println '>>> 'sa k \. state \$ cost)
        (if (and (< k max-iter)
                 (or (nil? max-cost)
                     (> cost max-cost)))
          (let [t (temp-fn (/ k max-iter))
                next-state (neighbor-fn state)
                next-cost (get-cost next-state)
                next-place {:state next-state,
                            :cost next-cost}]
            (if (> (p-fn cost next-cost t) (rand))
              (recur next-state next-cost (inc k)
                     (conj best-seq next-place))
              (recur state cost (inc k) best-seq)))
          best-seq))))
```

2. For parameters, `annealing` takes an initial state, a limit to the number of iterations, a target output value, and a series of functions. The first function takes the current state and returns a new neighboring state.

   To write this function, we have to decide how best to handle the state for this problem. Namely, since the function to be evaluated has multiple parameters, we will use a vector and randomly slide one value in that around. However, for this problem, we only have one input value: the partition size.

   So, for this problem, we'll use an integer between 0 and 20 instead. The actual partition size will be 2 raised to that power. To find a neighbor, we just randomly slide the state's value up or down at most by five units, within the range of 0 to 20:

```
(defn get-neighbor [state]
    (max 0 (min 20 (+ state (- (rand-int 11) 5)))))
```

3. The next function parameter used for `annealing` is the `cost` function. This will take the state and return the value that we're trying to minimize. In this case, we benchmark `mc-pi-part` with the given partition size (2 raised to the power) and return the average time:

```
(defn get-pi-cost [n state]
    (let [chunk-size (long (Math/pow 2 state))]
      (first (:mean (quick-benchmark
                      (mc-pi-part chunk-size n)
                      {})))))
```

4. The next function takes the current state's cost, a potential new state's cost, and the current energy in the system (from 0 to 1). It returns the odds that the new state should be used. Currently, this will always skip to an improved state or a worse state 25 percent of the time (both of these are prorated by the temperature):

```
(defn should-move [c0 c1 t]
  (* t (if (< c0 c1) 0.25 1.0)))
```

5. The final function parameter takes the current percent through the iteration count and returns the energy or temperature as a number from 0 to 1. This can use a number of easing functions, but for this, we'll just use a simple linear one:

```
(defn get-temp [r] (- 1.0 (float r)))
```

That's it. We can let this find a good partition size. We'll start with the value that we used in the *Partitioning Monte Carlo simulations for better pmap performance* recipe. We'll only allow 10 iterations since the search space is relatively small:

```
user=> (annealing 12 10 nil get-neighbor
                  (partial get-pi-cost 1000000)
                  should-move get-temp)
>>> sa 1 . 12 $ 0.5805938333333334
>>> sa 2 . 8 $ 0.38975950000000004
>>> sa 3 . 8 $ 0.38975950000000004
>>> sa 4 . 8 $ 0.38975950000000004
>>> sa 5 . 8 $ 0.38975950000000004
>>> sa 6 . 8 $ 0.38975950000000004
>>> sa 7 . 6 $ 0.357514
>>> sa 8 . 6 $ 0.357514
>>> sa 9 . 6 $ 0.357514
>>> sa 10 . 6 $ 0.357514
[{:state 12, :cost 0.5805938333333334}
 {:state 8, :cost 0.38975950000000004}
 {:state 6, :cost 0.357514}]
```

We can see that a partition size of 64 (26) is the best time, and rerunning the benchmarks verifies this.

## How it works...

In practice, this algorithm won't help if we run it over the full input data. However, if we can get a large enough sample, this can help us process the full dataset more efficiently by taking a lot of the guesswork out of picking the right partition size for the full evaluation.

1. What we did was kind of interesting. Let's take the `annealing` function apart to see how it works. The process is handled by a `loop` inside the `annealing` function. Its parameters are a snapshot of the state of the annealing process:

```
(loop [state initial
       cost cost
       k 1
       best-seq [{:state state, :cost cost}]]
```

2. We only continue if we need more iterations or if we haven't bested the maximum cost:

```
(if (and (< k max-iter)
         (or (nil? max-cost)
             (> cost max-cost)))
```

3. If we continue, we calculate the next energy and get a potential state and cost to evaluate:

```
(let [t (temp-fn (/ k max-iter))
      next-state (neighbor-fn state)
      next-cost (get-cost-cache next-state)
      next-place {:state next-state, :cost next-cost}]
```

4. If the probability function (in this case, `should-move`) indicates so, we move to the next state and loop. Otherwise, we stay at the current state and loop:

```
(if (> (p-fn cost next-cost t) (rand))
  (recur next-state next-cost (inc k)
         (conj best-seq next-place))
  (recur state cost (inc k) best-seq)))
```

5. If we're done, we return the sequence of the best states and costs seen:

```
best-seq)))))
```

This provides a systematic way to explore the problem area. In this case, it was to find a better partition size for this problem.

## There's more...

Simulated annealing is one of a class of algorithms known as **metaheuristic**. This is a class of algorithms that are widely applicable to search a result space but that do not guarantee a globally optimal solution. Instead, they often approach the problem stochastically, randomly searching for the best solution that they can find within a reasonable amount of time. All of these take a function (the `cost-fn` function mentioned previously) and try to find the largest or smallest value for it.

Other optimization algorithms include genetic algorithms, ant colony optimization, particle swarm optimization, and many others. This is a broad and interesting field, and being familiar with these algorithms can be helpful for anyone who does data analysis.

# Combining function calls with reducers

Clojure 1.5 introduced the `clojure.core.reducers` library. This library provides a lot of interesting and exciting features. It allows you to compose multiple calls to `map` and other sequence-processing, high-order functions. This also makes it possible to abstract `map` and other functions for different types of collections while maintaining the collection type.

Looking at the following chart, initial operations on individual data items such as `map` and `filter` operate on items of the original dataset. Then, the outputs of the operations on the items are combined using a reduce function. Finally, the outputs of the reduction step are progressively combined until the final result is produced. This might involve a reduce-type operation (such as addition), or an accumulation (such as the `into` function).

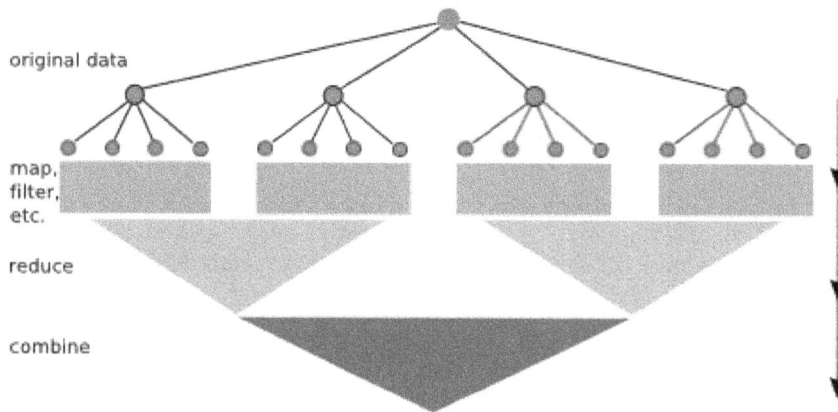

In this recipe, we'll take a look at how we can use reducers to minimize the number of sequences that Clojure creates and immediately throws away.

## Getting ready

The primary dependency that we'll need for this is the `reducers` library, but we'll also use the `clojure.string` library:

```
(require '[clojure.string :as str]
         '[clojure.core.reducers :as r])
```

## How to do it...

To illustrate this feature of reducers, we'll take a sequence of words and run them through a series of transformations. We'll take a look at how Clojure handles these both with and without the `reducers` library.

The data that we'll work on will be a sequence of strings that contain words and numbers. We'll convert all of the letters to lowercase and all of the numbers to integers. Based on this specification, the first step of the processing pipeline will be `str/lower-case`. The second step will be the `->int` function:

```
(defn ->int [x]
  (try
    (Long/parseLong x)
    (catch Exception e
      x)))
```

The data that we'll work on will be this list:

```
(def data
  (str/split (str "This is a small list. It contains 42 "
                  "items. Or less.")
             #"\s+"))
```

If you run this using `clojure.core/map`, you will get the results that you had expected:

```
user=> (map ->int
           (map str/lower-case
                data))
("this" "is" "a" "small" "list." "it" "contains" 42 "items." "or"
"less.")
```

The problem with this approach isn't the results; it's what Clojure is doing between the two calls to `map`. In this case, the first `map` creates an entirely new lazy sequence. The second `map` walks over it again before throwing it and its contents away. Repeatedly allocating lists and immediately throwing them away is wasteful. It takes more time, and can potentially consume more memory, than you have available. In this case, this isn't really a problem, but for longer pipelines of the `map` calls (potentially processing long sequences) this can be a performance problem.

This is a problem that reducers address. Let's change our calls to `map` into calls to `clojure.reducers/map` and see what happens:

```
user=> (r/map ->int
           (r/map str/lower-case
                data))
#<reducers$folder$reify__1529 clojure.core.reducers$folder$reify__152
9@37577fd6>
```

## What happened here?

Actually, this is exactly what the `reducers` library is supposed to do. Instead of actually processing the input, the stacked calls to `r/map` compose the two functions into one. When results are needed, the `reducers` library processes the input sequence through the combined functions. It, thereby, accomplishes the processing without creating an intermediate, throwaway sequence.

So, how do we get the output? We simply tell Clojure to feed it into a vector or other data structure:

```
user=> (into []
             (r/map ->int
                    (r/map str/lower-case
                           data)))
["this" "is" "a" "small" "list." "it" "contains" 42 "items." "or"
"less."]
```

## There's more...

For more information on reducers, see Rich Hickey's blog posts at `http://clojure.com/blog/2012/05/08/reducers-a-library-and-model-for-collection-processing.html` and `http://clojure.com/blog/2012/05/15/anatomy-of-reducer.html`. Also, his presentation on reducers for EuroClojure 2012 (`http://vimeo.com/45561411`) has a lot of good information.

## See also

We'll take a look at another feature of reducers in the next recipe, *Parallelizing with reducers*.

# Parallelizing with reducers

In the last recipe, *Combining function calls with reducers*, we looked at the ability of reducers to compose multiple sequence processing functions into one function. This saves the effort of creating intermediate data structures.

Another feature of reducers is that they can automatically partition and parallelize the processing of tree-based data structures. This includes Clojure's native vectors and hash maps.

For this recipe, we'll continue the Monte Carlo simulation example that we started in the *Partitioning Monte Carlo simulations for better pmap performance* recipe. In this case, we'll write a version that uses reducers and see how it performs.

## Getting ready

From the *Partitioning Monte Carlo simulations for better pmap performance* recipe, we'll use the same imports, as well as the `rand-point`, `center-dist`, and `mc-pi` functions. Along with these, we also need to `require` the reducers and Criterium libraries:

```
(require '[clojure.core.reducers :as r])
(use 'criterium.core)
```

Also, if you're using Java 1.6, you'll need the ForkJoin library, which you can get by adding this to your `project.clj` dependencies:

```
[org.codehaus.jsr166-mirror/jsr166y ""1.7.0""]
```

## How to do it...

1. This version of the Monte Carlo pi approximation algorithm will be structured in a similar manner to how `mc-pi` was structured in the *Partitioning Monte Carlo simulations for better pmap performance* recipe. First, we'll define a `count-in-circle-r` function that uses the reducers library to compose the processing and spread it over the available cores:

```
(defn count-items [c _] (inc c))
(defn count-in-circle-r [n]
  (->> (repeatedly n rand-point)
       vec
       (r/map center-dist)
       (r/filter #(<= % 1.0))
       (r/fold + count-items)))

(defn mc-pi-r [n]
  (* 4.0 (/ (count-in-circle-r n) n)))
```

2. Now, we can use Criterium to compare the two functions:

```
user=> (quick-bench (mc-pi 1000000))
WARNING: Final GC required 1.5511109061811519 % of runtime
WARNING: Final GC required 1.3658615618441179 % of runtime
Evaluation count : 6 in 6 samples of 1 calls.
             Execution time mean : 983.603832 ms
   Execution time std-deviation : 16.553276 ms
  Execution time lower quantile : 964.015999 ms ( 2.5%)
  Execution time upper quantile : 1.007418 sec (97.5%)
```

```
                    Overhead used : 1.875845 ns

    Found 1 outliers in 6 samples (16.6667 %)
            low-severe        1 (16.6667 %)
     Variance from outliers : 13.8889 % Variance is moderately
    inflated by outliers
    nil
    user=> (quick-bench (mc-pi-r 1000000))
    WARNING: Final GC required 8.023979507099268 % of runtime
    Evaluation count : 6 in 6 samples of 1 calls.
                Execution time mean : 168.998166 ms
        Execution time std-deviation : 3.615209 ms
       Execution time lower quantile : 164.074999 ms ( 2.5%)
       Execution time upper quantile : 173.148749 ms (97.5%)
                    Overhead used : 1.875845 ns
    nil
```

Not bad. On eight cores, the version without reducers is almost six times slower. This is more impressive because we made relatively minor changes to the original code, especially when compared to the version of this algorithm that partitioned the input before passing it to pmap, which we also saw in the *Partitioning Monte Carlo simulations for better pmap performance* recipe.

## How it works...

The reducers library does a couple of things in this recipe. Let's take a look at some lines from count-in-circle-r. Converting the input to a vector was important, because vectors can be parallelized, but generic sequences cannot.

Next, these two lines are combined into one reducer function that doesn't create an extra sequence between the call to r/map and r/filter. This is a small, but important, optimization, especially if we stacked more functions into this stage of the process:

```
(r/map center-dist)
(r/filter #(<= % 1.0))
```

The bigger optimization is in the line for r/fold. r/reduce always processes serially, but if the input is a tree-based data structure, r/fold will employ a fork-join pattern to parallelize it. This line takes the place of a call to count by incrementing a counter function for every item in the sequence so far:

```
(r/fold + count-items))))
```

Graphically, this process looks something similar to this chart:

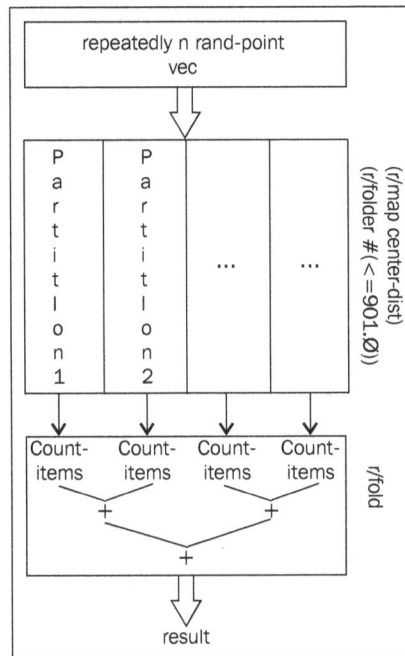

The reducers library has a lot of promise to automatically parallelize structured operations with a level of control and simplicity that we haven't seen elsewhere.

## See also

▶   We'll see another example with reducers in the next recipe, *Generating online summary statistics for data streams with reducers*

# Generating online summary statistics for data streams with reducers

We can use reducers in a lot of different situations, but sometimes we need to change how we process data to do so.

For this example, we'll show you how to compute summary statistics with reducers. We'll use some algorithms and formulas, first proposed by Tony F. Chan, Gene H. Golub, and Randall J. LeVeque in 1979, and later extended by Timothy B. Terriberry in 2007. These allow you to approximate the mean, standard deviation, and skew for online data (that is, to stream data that we might only see once). So, we will need to compute all of the statistics on one pass without holding the full collection in memory.

The following formulas are a little complicated and difficult to read in lisp notation. However, there's a good overview of this process, with formulas, on the Wikipedia page for Algorithms to calculate variance (`http://en.wikipedia.org/wiki/Algorithms_for_calculating_variance`). In order to somewhat simplify this example, we'll only calculate the mean and variance.

## Getting ready

For this, we'll need to have easy access to the `reducers` library and the Java `Math` class:

```
(require '[clojure.core.reducers :as r])
(import '[java.lang Math])
```

## How to do it...

For this recipe, we'll first define the accumulator data structures and then the accumulator functions. Finally, we'll put it all together.

1. We need to define a data structure to store all of the data that we want to accumulate and keep track of:

   ```
   (def zero-counts {:n (long 0), :s 0.0,
                     :mean 0.0, :m2 0.0})
   ```

2. Now, we'll need some way to add data to the counts and accumulation. The `accum-counts` function will take care of this:

   ```
   (defn accum-counts
     ([] zero-counts)
     ([{:keys [n mean m2 s] :as accum} x]
      (let [new-n (long (inc n))
            delta (- x mean)
            delta-n (/ delta new-n)
            term-1 (* delta delta-n n)
            new-mean (+ mean delta-n)]
        {:n new-n
         :mean new-mean
         :s (+ s x)
         :m2 (+ m2 term-1)})))
   ```

3. Next, we'll need a way to combine two accumulators. This has the complete, unsimplified versions of the formulae from `accum-counts`. Because some of the numbers can get very large and can overflow the range of the primitive Java types, we'll use `*'`. This is a variant of the multiplication operator that automatically promotes values into Java's `BigInteger` types instead of overflowing:

```
(defn op-fields
  "A utility function that calls a function on
  the values of a field from two maps."
  [op field item1 item2]
  (op (field item1) (field item2)))

(defn combine-counts
  ([] zero-counts)
  ([xa xb]
   (let [n (long (op-fields + :n xa xb))
         delta (op-fields - :mean xb xa)
         nxa*xb (*' (:n xa) (:n xb))]
     {:n n
      :mean (+ (:mean xa) (* delta (/ (:n xb) n)))
      :s (op-fields + :s xa xb)
      :m2 (+ (:m2 xa) (:m2 xb)
             (* delta delta (/ nxa*xb n)))})))
```

4. Now, we need a way to take the accumulated counts and values and turn them into the final statistics:

```
(defn stats-from-sums [{:keys [n mean m2 s] :as sums}]
  {:mean (double (/ s n))
   :variance (/ m2 (dec n))})
```

5. Finally, we can combine all of these functions to produce results:

```
(defn summary-statistics [coll]
  (stats-from-sums
    (r/fold combine-counts accum-counts coll)))
```

For a pointless example, we can use this to find summary statistics on 1,000,000 random numbers:

```
user=> (summary-statistics (repeatedly 1000000 rand))
{:mean 0.5004908831693459, :variance 0.08346136740444697}
```

# Using type hints

Most problems that are good targets for parallelization involve doing calculations in tight loops. These places are good for all kinds of performance optimizations, from hoisting conditionals out of them to fine-tuning compiler hints, which we will do here.

Being a dynamic language, Clojure doesn't require type declarations. However, if we know what types we are using, we can get better performance by including **type hints** in our code. This is helpful for object types, where Clojure can then resolve method calls at compile time, and also for primitive types, where Clojure can generate well-tuned code that doesn't include boxing or wrapping the primitive type in a heavier Java object.

> For more information about type hints and working with Java primitives, see the documentation on interacting with Java from Clojure at `http://clojure.org/java_interop`.

Type hints are expressed as metadata tags for return types and object types. We'll see examples of both in this recipe. For this recipe, we'll revisit the Monte Carlo simulation to estimate the value of pi. We first saw this in the *Paritioning Monte Carlo simulations for better pmap performance* recipe. This example has enough low-level math which makes it a good candidate for this kind of optimization.

## Getting ready

We'll use the Criterium library for benchmarking, so include these in our Leiningen `project.clj` file:

```
(defproject parallel-data ""0.1.0""
  :dependencies [[org.clojure/clojure ""1.6.0""]
                 [criterium ""0.4.3""]])
```

Use it and the `java.lang.Math` class in our script or REPL:

```
(use 'criterium.core)
(import [java.lang Math])
```

From the *Partitioning Monte Carlo simulations for better pmap performance* recipe, we'll use the `rand-point` and `center-dist` functions.

## How to do it...

We'll implement the Monte Carlo simulation without type hints, benchmark it, and then reimplement it with type hints to see whether we can get better performance.

1. The simulation itself places n random points in the unit square and tests how many of them fall within the upper-right quadrant of a circle centered at 0, 0. The ratio of those that fall within the circle, multiplied by 4, should approximate the value of pi:

```
(defn mc-pi [n]
  (let [in-circle (->> (repeatedly n rand-point)
                       (map center-dist)
                       (filter #(<= % 1.0))
                       count)]
    (* 4.0 (/ in-circle n))))
```

2. If we benchmark the existing implementation with Criterium, it will give us something to shoot for. This shows us that the average runtime is 45.7 milliseconds:

```
user=> (bench (mc-pi 100000))
WARNING: Final GC required 1.476534955514225 % of runtime
Evaluation count : 1320 in 60 samples of 22 calls.
             Execution time mean : 45.774244 ms
    Execution time std-deviation : 621.709776 µs
   Execution time lower quantile : 44.878862 ms ( 2.5%)
   Execution time upper quantile : 46.787552 ms (97.5%)
                   Overhead used : 1.780493 ns

Found 3 outliers in 60 samples (5.0000 %)
        low-severe      2 (3.3333 %)
        low-mild        1 (1.6667 %)
 Variance from outliers : 1.6389 % Variance is slightly inflated
by outliers
nil
```

3. Now, we'll add casts for the primitive doubles in center-dist and add type hint metadata for the return type too:

```
(defn center-dist-hint
  (^double [[x y]]
    (Math/sqrt (+ (Math/pow (double x) (double 2.0))
                  (Math/pow (double y)
                            (double 2.0))))))
```

4. Next, change `mc-pi` to call `center-dist-hint` and add a type hint to it:

```
(defn mc-pi-hint
  (^double [n]
    (let [in-circle (double
                      (->>
                        (repeatedly n rand-point)
                        (map center-dist-hint)
                        (filter #(<= % (double 1.0)))
                        count))]
      (double
        (* (double 4.0) (/ in-circle (double n)))))))
```

Finally, let's see if this helps:

```
user=> (bench (mc-pi-hint 100000))
Evaluation count : 1380 in 60 samples of 23 calls.
             Execution time mean : 46.317966 ms
    Execution time std-deviation : 1.237294 ms
   Execution time lower quantile : 44.981042 ms ( 2.5%)
   Execution time upper quantile : 49.716563 ms (97.5%)
                   Overhead used : 1.780493 ns

Found 5 outliers in 60 samples (8.3333 %)
        low-severe      2 (3.3333 %)
        low-mild        3 (5.0000 %)
 Variance from outliers : 14.1789 % Variance is moderately inflated by
outliers
nil
```

In this case, it resulted in a slight slowdown. However, I have seen simple changes such as this result in good performance improvements for a minimal amount of work.

## How it works...

The first type hint we used is the `^double`, which indicates the functions' return types and parameters. These allow the Clojure compiler to generate a bytecode that's well-optimized for these return types and for working with the Java primitives.

The other use of type hints allow the Clojure compiler to resolve methods at compile time. The `clojure.string` namespace has a good example of this:

```
user=> (require '[clojure.string :as string])
user=> (source string/trim)
(defn ^String trim
  "Removes whitespace from both ends of string."
```

```
  {:added ""1.2""}
  [^CharSequence s]
(.. s toString trim))
nil
```

We can see that the parameter to the `string/trim` function is a `CharSequence`, and the compiler can use this information to know which `toString` to dispatch to.

## See also

> ▸ For more information on the pros and cons of different methods of benchmarking and what the Criterium library does, see the *Benchmarking with Criterium* recipe

> ▸ For more information on Monte Carlo methods, see the *Partitioning Monte Carlo simulations for Better pmap Performance* recipe

# Benchmarking with Criterium

Benchmarking can be an important part of the data analysis process. Especially when faced with very large datasets that need to be processed in multiple ways, choosing algorithms that will finish in a reasonable amount of time is important. Benchmarking gives us an empirical basis on which to make these decisions.

For some of the recipes in this chapter, we've used the Criterium library (https://github.com/hugoduncan/criterium). Why will we want to go to the trouble of using an entire library just to see how fast our code is?

Generally, when we want to benchmark our code, we often start by using something similar to the `time` macro. This means:

1. Get the start time.
2. Execute the code.
3. Get the end time.

If you've done this often, you will realize that this has a number of problems, especially for benchmarking small functions that execute quickly. The times are often inconsistent, and they can be dependent on a number of factors that are external to your program, such as the memory or disk cache. Using this benchmarking method often ends up being an exercise in frustration.

Fortunately, Criterium takes care of all of this. It makes sure that the caches are warmed up, runs your code multiple times, and presents a statistical look at the execution times.

This presents more information than just a single raw time. It also presents a lot of other useful information, such as how much time is spent in garbage collection.

For this recipe, we'll take the functions that we created to do the Monte Carlo pi estimates in the *Using type hints* recipe, and compare the timings we get with the `time` macro against those we get from Criterium.

## Getting ready

To use Criterium, we just need to add it to the list of dependencies in our `project.clj` file:

```
(defproject parallel-data ""0.1.0""
  :dependencies [[org.clojure/clojure ""1.6.0""]
                 [criterium ""0.4.3""]])
```

We need to use it in our script or REPL:

```
(use 'criterium.core)
```

We'll also need the code the benchmark, which means the `mc-pi` and `mc-pi-hint` functions from the *Using type hints* recipe along with their dependencies.

## How to do it...

First, let's look at the results of running the `time` macro several times on each function. Here's how we do it once:

```
user=> (time (mc-pi 1000000))
""Elapsed time: 1304.007 msecs""
3.14148
```

The following chart shows the results of all five calls on each:

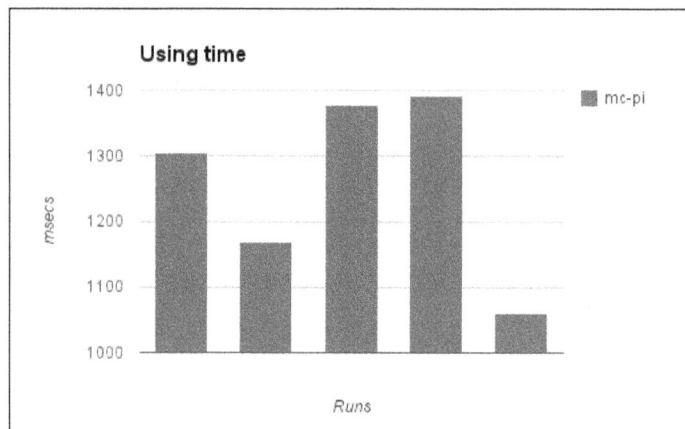

You can see that the results are all over the map. It's difficult to say how to synthesize these results without losing some information that might be important.

For comparison, here are the results with Criterium:

```
user=> (bench (mc-pi 1000000))
WARNING: Final GC required 1.6577782102371632 % of runtime
Evaluation count : 120 in 60 samples of 2 calls.
             Execution time mean : 1.059337 sec
    Execution time std-deviation : 61.159841 ms
   Execution time lower quantile : 963.110499 ms ( 2.5%)
   Execution time upper quantile : 1.132513 sec (97.5%)
                   Overhead used : 1.788607 ns

Found 1 outliers in 60 samples (1.6667 %)
        low-severe        1 (1.6667 %)
 Variance from outliers : 43.4179 % Variance is moderately inflated by
outliers
```

The results are immediately clear (without having to type them into a spreadsheet, which I did to create the chart), and there's a lot more information given.

## How it works...

So, how does Criterium help us? First, it runs the code several times, and just throws away the results. This means that we don't have to worry about initial inconsistencies while the JVM, memory cache, and disk cache get settled.

Second, it runs the code a lot more than five times. Quick benchmarking runs it six times. Standard benchmarking runs it sixty times. This gives us a lot more data and a lot more confidence in our interpretation.

Third, it provides us with a lot more information about the runs. With `time`, we have to eyeball the results and go with our gut instinct for what all those numbers mean. If we want to be more precise, we can retype all of the numbers into a spreadsheet and generate some statistics. Criterium does that for us. It also analyzes the results to tell us whether some outliers are throwing off the statistics. For instance, in the results mentioned previously, we can see that there was one low outlier.

Criterium gives us a much better basis on which to make decisions about how best to optimize our code and improve its performance.

## See also

We've really just touched the surface of the functionality that Criterium provides and the functions it exports. For more information about this fantastic library, see the documentation at `https://github.com/hugoduncan/criterium`.

# 5
# Distributed Data Processing with Cascalog

In this chapter, we will cover the following recipes:

- ▶ Initializing Cascalog and Hadoop for distributed processing
- ▶ Querying data with Cascalog
- ▶ Distributing data with Apache HDFS
- ▶ Parsing CSV files with Cascalog
- ▶ Executing complex queries with Cascalog
- ▶ Aggregating data with Cascalog
- ▶ Defining new Cascalog operators
- ▶ Composing Cascalog queries
- ▶ Transforming data with Cascalog

## Introduction

Over the course of the last few chapters, we've been progressively moving outward. We started with the assumption that everything will run on one processor, probably in a single thread. Then we looked at how to structure our program without this assumption, performing different tasks on many threads. We then tried to speed up processing by getting multiple threads and cores working on the same task. Now we've pulled back about as far as we can, and we're going to take a look at how to break up work in order to execute it on multiple computers. For large amounts of data, this can be especially useful.

In fact, big data has become more and more common. The definition of big data is a moving target as disk sizes grow, but you're working with big data if you have trouble processing it in memory or even storing it on disk. There's a lot of information locked in that much data, but getting it out can be a real problem. The recipes in this chapter will help address these issues.

Currently, the most common way to distribute computation in production is to use the **MapReduce** algorithm, which was originally described in a research paper by Google, although the company has moved away from using this algorithm (`http://research.google.com/archive/mapreduce.html`). The MapReduce process should be familiar to anyone who uses Clojure, as MapReduce is directly inspired by functional programming. Data is partitioned over all the computers in the cluster. An operation is mapped across the input data, with each computer in the cluster performing part of the processing. The outputs of the map function are then accumulated using a **Reduce** operation. Conceptually, this is very similar to the `reducers` library that we discussed in some of the recipes in *Chapter 4, Improving Performance with Parallel Programming*. The following diagram illustrates the three stages of processing:

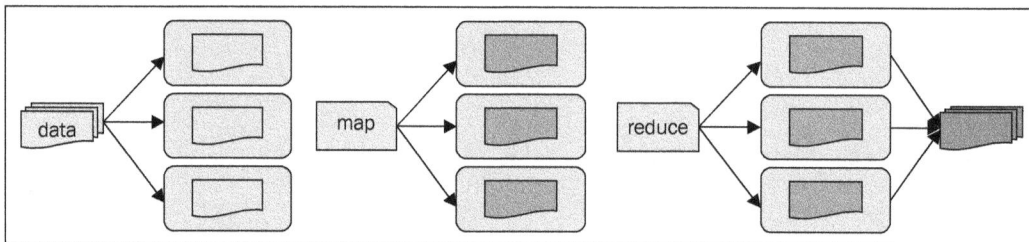

Clojure itself doesn't have any features for distributed processing. However, it has an excellent interoperability with the Java Virtual Machine, and Java has a number of libraries and systems for creating and using distributed systems. In the recipes of this chapter, we'll primarily use **Hadoop** (`http://hadoop.apache.org/`), and we'll especially focus on **Cascading** (`http://www.cascading.org/`) and the Clojure wrapper for this library, **Cascalog** (`https://github.com/nathanmarz/cascalog`). This toolchain makes distributed processing simple.

All these systems also work using just a single server, such as a developer's working computer. This is what we'll use in most of the recipes in this chapter. The code should work in a multiserver, cluster environment too.

# Initializing Cascalog and Hadoop for distributed processing

Hadoop was developed by Yahoo! to implement Google's MapReduce algorithm, and then it was open sourced. Since then, it's become one of the most widely tested and used systems for creating distributed processing.

The central part of this ecosystem is Hadoop, but it's also complemented by a range of other tools, including the **Hadoop Distributed File System** (**HDFS**) and **Pig**, a language used to write jobs in order to run them on Hadoop.

One tool that makes working with Hadoop easier is Cascading. This provides a workflow-like layer on top of Hadoop that can make the expression of some data processing and analysis tasks much easier. Cascalog is a Clojure-idiomatic interface to Cascading and, ultimately, Hadoop.

This recipe will show you how to access and query data in Clojure sequences using Cascalog.

## Getting ready

First, we have to list our dependencies in the Leiningen `project.clj` file:

```
(defproject distrib-data "0.1.0"
  :dependencies [[org.clojure/clojure "1.6.0"]
                 [cascalog "2.1.1"]
                 [org.slf4j/slf4j-api "1.7.7"]]
  :profiles {:dev
             {:dependencies
              [[org.apache.hadoop/hadoop-core "1.1.1"]]}})
```

Finally, we'll require the packages that we'll use, including the `clojure.string` library:

```
(require '[clojure.string :as string])
(require '[cascalog.logic.ops :as c])
(use 'cascalog.api)
```

## How to do it...

Most part of this recipe will define the data we'll query. For this, we will use a list of companions and actors from the British television program *Doctor Who*. The data is in a sequence of maps, so we'll need to transform it into several sequences of vectors, which is what Cascalog can access. In one sequence there will be a list of the companions' lowercased names, for which we'll use keys in other data tables. One will be the name key and the full name, and the final one will be a table of the companions' keys to a doctor they tagged along with. We'll also define a list of the actors who played the role of doctors and the years in which they played them.

1. At the time of writing this book, there are about 50 companions. I've only listed 10 here, but the examples might show the other companions. The full data is available in the source code. You can also download just the code to create this dataset from http://www.ericrochester.com/clj-data-analysis/data/companions.clj:

```clojure
(def input-data
  [{:given-name "Susan", :surname "Forman", :doctors [1]}
   {:given-name "Katarina", :surname nil, :doctors [1]}
   {:given-name "Victoria", :surname "Waterfield", :doctors [2]}
   {:given-name "Sarah Jane", :surname "Smith", :doctors [3 4 10]}
   {:given-name "Romana", :surname nil, :doctors [4]}
   {:given-name "Kamelion", :surname nil, :doctors [5]}
   {:given-name "Rose", :surname "Tyler", :doctors [9 10]}
   {:given-name "Martha", :surname "Jones", :doctors [10]}
   {:given-name "Adelaide", :surname "Brooke", :doctors [10]}
   {:given-name "Craig", :surname "Owens", :doctors [11]}])

(def companion (map string/lower-case
                    (map :given-name input-data)))
(def full-name
  (map (fn [{:keys [given-name surname]}]
         [(string/lower-case given-name)
          (string/trim
            (string/join \space [given-name surname]))])
       input-data))
(def doctor
  (mapcat #(map (fn [d] [(string/lower-case (:given-name %)) d])
                (:doctors %))
          input-data))
```

```
(def actor
  [[1 "William Hartnell" "1963-66"]
   [2 "Patrick Troughton" "1966-69"]
   [3 "Jon Pertwee" "1970-74"]
   [4 "Tom Baker" "1974-81"]
   [5 "Peter Davison" "1981-84"]
   [6 "Colin Baker" "1984-86"]
   [7 "Sylvester McCoy" "1987-89, 1996"]
   [8 "Paul McGann" "1996"]
   [9 "Christopher Eccleston" "2005"]
   [10 "David Tennant" "2005-10"]
   [11 "Matt Smith" "2010-present"]])
```

2.  We'll explain the syntax for the query in more detail in the *How it works...* section. In the meantime, let's just dive in:

    ```
    (?<- (stdout) [?companion] (companion ?companion))
    ```

3.  When you execute this, you might see a lot of logging messages from Hadoop. Towards the end, you should see this:

    ```
    RESULTS
    --------------------
    susan
    barbara
    ian
    vicki
    steven
    ...
    ```

4.  You can also query the other tables, as follows:

    ```
    (?<- (stdout) [?name] (full-name _ ?name))
    ...
    RESULTS
    --------------------
    Susan Forman
    Barbara Wright
    Ian Chesterton
    Vicki
    Steven Taylor
    ...
    ```

## How it works...

The structure of query statements is not hard to understand. Let's break one query statement apart:

```
(?<- (stdout) [?name] (full-name _ ?name))
```

The ?<- operator creates a query and executes it. It's a combination of the <- macro, which creates a query from output variables and predicates, and the ?- function, which executes a query to a sink.

```
(?<- (stdout) [?name] (full-name _ ?name))
```

The first parameter is a Cascading **tap** sink. This is a destination for the data. Obviously, if there's a lot of data being output, just dumping it in the console won't be a good idea. In that case, you can send it to a file. Since there's not much data, we'll just write it to the screen.

```
(?<- (stdout) [?name] (full-name _ ?name))
```

The preceding is a vector of output variables. The names here must occur in the predicates that follow.

```
(?<- (stdout) [?name] (full-name _ ?name))
```

This is a list of predicates. In this example, there's only one predicate. It queries the full-name table. It doesn't care about the values in the first column, so it just uses an underscore as a placeholder (_). Using underscore as a variable name in this way is a convention in Clojure and similar languages for values that you want to ignore. The values in the second column are bound to the name ?name, which is also found in the vector of output columns.

Of course, working with in-memory data isn't that useful. It's good for development and debugging, though. Later, we'll see how to connect to a datafile, and the query syntax is exactly the same.

## See also

For information on how to access data that's not held in memory check out the following recipes:

▶ *Distributing data with Apache HDFS*
▶ *Parsing CSV files with Cascalog*

# Querying data with Cascalog

In the *Initializing Cascalog and Hadoop for distributed processing* recipe, we looked at how to query data in Cascalog with a couple of small examples. However, Cascalog's query language is much more powerful than what we saw here. We'll dive in further in this recipe and start looking at some of the logical predicates available. Recipes in the later part of this chapter will have still more examples of querying with Cascalog.

## Getting ready

For this recipe, we'll need the `project.clj` dependencies and imports from the *Initializing Cascalog and Hadoop for distributed processing* recipe. We'll also use the data from that recipe: the sequences of information about the companions and actors from the British television program *Doctor Who*.

## How to do it...

1. For the first example, we'll get the first five actors who played the role of the doctor:

```
(?<- (stdout) [?n ?actor ?period]
     (actor ?n ?actor ?period) (<= ?n 5))
...
RESULTS
----------------------
1        William Hartnell        1963-66
2        Patrick Troughton       1966-69
3        Jon Pertwee     1970-74
4        Tom Baker       1974-81
5        Peter Davison   1981-84
```

2. For the next example, we'll get all the companions of the tenth Doctor (David Tennant):

```
(?<- (stdout) [?companion] (doctor ?companion ?n) (= ?n 10))
...
RESULTS
----------------------
sarahjane
rose
jack
mickey
donna
```

```
martha
astrid
jackson
rosita
christina
adelaide
wilfred
```

Well, he's a popular guy.

## How it works...

Let's take a look at the second example in a little more detail.

```
(?<- (stdout) [?companion] (doctor ?companion ?n) (= ?n 10))
```

The predicates are evaluated once for each row in the input data. Once a name has been bound to one predicate, it will keep that value throughout all the predicates. Moreover, a row is only output when *all* the predicates pass.

```
(?<- (stdout) [?companion] (doctor ?companion ?n) (= ?n 10))
```

This predicate only passes where ?n is bound to 10. Since all the predicates have to pass successfully, this only returns the companions for Doctor number 10.

## There's more

**Variable binding**, which we saw in this recipe, is a well-known feature of data-oriented systems. Prolog (http://www.learnprolognow.org/), for example, uses it extensively.

# Distributing data with Apache HDFS

One of the best features of Hadoop is the Hadoop Distributed File System. This creates a network of computers that automatically synchronize their data, making our input data available to all the computers. Not having to worry about how the data gets distributed makes our lives much easier.

For this recipe, we'll put a file into HDFS and read it back out using Cascalog, line by line.

## Getting ready

The previous recipes in this chapter used the version of Hadoop that Leiningen downloaded as one of Cascalog's dependencies. For this recipe, however, we'll need to have Hadoop installed and running separately. Go to `http://hadoop.apache.org/` and download and install it. You might also be able to use your operating system's package manager. Alternatively, Cloudera has a VM with a 1-node Hadoop cluster that you can download and use (`https://ccp.cloudera.com/display/SUPPORT/CDH+Downloads#CDHDownloads-CDH4PackagesandDownloads`).

You'll still need to configure everything. Take a look at the Hadoop website for the **Getting Started** documentation of your version. Get a single node setup working.

Once it's installed and configured, go ahead and start the servers. There's a script in the `bin` directory to do this:

```
$ ./bin/start-dfsdfs.sh
```

We still need to have everything working with Clojure, however. For this, we just use the same dependencies and references as we did in the *Initializing Cascalog and Hadoop for distributed processing* recipe. However, this time, don't worry about the REPL. We'll take care of that separately.

For data, we'll use a dataset of the U.S. domestic flights from 1990–2009. You can download this dataset yourself from Infochimps at `http://www.ericrochester.com/clj-data-analysis/data/flights_with_colnames.csv.gz`. I've unzipped it into the data directory.

## How to do it...

For this recipe, we'll insert a file into the distributed file system, run the Clojure REPL inside Hadoop, and read the data back out.

1. First, the data file must be in HDFS. We'll use the `data/16285/flights_with_colnames.csv` file. We can insert it into HDFS with this command:

```
$ hadoop fs -put \
    datadata/16285/flights_with_colnames.csv \
    flights_with_colnames.csv
```

2. Now, in order to run our code in the Hadoop environment, we have to use the `hadoop` command on a JAR file created from our project. Create an empty namespace to give the JAR file a little content. For example, I created a file named `src/distrib_data/cascalog_setup.clj` with this content:

```
(ns distrib-data.cascalog-setup
  (:require [cascalog.logic.ops :as c]
            [clojure.string :as string])
  (:use cascalog.api))
```

3.  Once this is in place, we create a JAR file containing this file and all of its dependencies:

    ```
    $ lein uberjar
    Created /Users/err8n/p/cljbook/distrib-data/target/distrib-data-
    0.1.0.jar
    Created /Users/err8n/p/cljbook/distrib-data/target/distrib-data-
    0.1.0-standalone.jarjar
    ```

> If you're using Windows, Mac, or another OS with a case-insensitive
> filesystem, you'll need to remove the LICENSE file, because it will clash
> with a license directory. To do this, you can use this command:
>
> ```
> $ zip -d target/distrib-data-0.1.0-standalone.jar \
> META-INF/LICENSE
> deleting: META-INF/LICENSE
> ```

4.  Now, we can start the Clojure REPL from within the Hadoop-controlled grid of computers, using the hadoop command on the JAR file we just created:

    ```
    $ hadoop jar target/distrib-data-0.1.0-standalone.jar
    Clojure 1.66.0
    user=>
    ```

5.  Inside the REPL that just started, we need to import the libraries that we're going to use:

    ```
    user=> (require '[clojure.string :as string]
               '[cascalog.logic.ops :as c])
    nil
    user=> (use 'cascalog.api)
    nil
    ```

6.  Finally, once this is in place, we can execute the Cascalog query to read the companions.txt file:

    ```
    user=> (?<- (stdout) [?line]
      ((hfs-textline "hdfs:///user/err8n/flights_with_colnames.csv")
      :> ?line))
    ...
    RESULTS
    origin_airport,destin_airport,passengers,flights,month
    MHK,AMW,21,1,200810
    EUG,RDM,41,22,199011
    EUG,RDM,88,19,199012
    EUG,RDM,11,4,199010
    ...
    ```

## How it works...

There are several moving parts to this recipe. The primary one is Hadoop. It has its own configuration, environment variables, and libraries that the process executing the Cascalog queries must access. The easiest way to manage this is to run everything through the `hadoop` command, so that's what we did.

The `hadoop` command has an `fs` task, which provides access to a whole range of operations to work with HDFS. In this case, we used its `-put` option to move a data file into HDFS.

Once there, we can refer to the file using the `hdfs:` URI scheme. Hadoop knows how to find these URIs.

In the Cascalog query, `hfs-textline` reads the file line by line. We use the `:>` operator to bind each line to the `?line` name, which is returned as the output of the query.

# Parsing CSV files with Cascalog

In the previous recipe, the file we read was a CSV file, but we read it line by line. That's not optimal. Cascading provides a number of taps—sources of data or sinks to send data to—including one for CSV and other delimited data formats. Also, Cascalog has some good wrappers for several of these taps, but not for the CSV one.

In truth, creating a wrapper that exposes all the functionality of the delimited text format tap will be complex. There are options for delimiter characters, quote characters, including a header row, the types of columns, and other things. That's a lot of options, and dispatching to the right method can be tricky.

We won't worry about how to handle all the options right here. For this recipe, we will create a simple wrapper around the delimited text file tap that includes some of the more common options to read CSV files.

## Getting ready

First, we'll need to use some of the same dependencies as the ones we've been using as well as some new ones. Here are the full dependencies that we'll need in our `project.clj` file:

```
(defproject distrib-data "0.1.0"
  :dependencies [[org.clojure/clojure "1.6.0"]
                 [cascalog "2.1.1"]
                 [org.slf4j/slf4j-api "1.7.7"]]
  :profiles {:dev
              {:dependencies
               [[org.apache.hadoop/hadoop-core "1.2.1"]]}})
```

Also, we'll need to import a number of namespaces from these libraries into our script or REPL:

```
(require '[cascalog.logic.ops :as c]
         '[cascalog.cascading.tap :as tap]
         '[cascalog.cascading.util :as u])
(use 'cascalog.api)
(import [cascading.tuple Fields]
        [cascading.scheme.hadoop.TextDelimited])
```

We'll also use the data file that we did in the *Distributing data with Apache HDFS* recipe. You can access it either locally or through HDFS, as we did earlier. I'll access it locally for this recipe.

## How to do it...

1.  We just need to write a function that creates a `cascading.scheme.hadoop.TextDelimited` tap scheme with the correct options and then calls the `cascalog.tap/hfs-tap` Cascalog function with it. That will handle the rest, as shown here:

```
(defn hfs-text-delim
  [path & {:keys [fields has-header delim quote-str]
           :as opts
           :or {fields Fields/ALL, has-header false, delim ",",
                quote-str "\""}}]
  (let [scheme (TextDelimited. (w/fields fields) has-header delim
                               quote-str)
        tap-opts (select-keys opts [:scascalog :sinkmode
                                    :sinkparts
                                    :source-pattern
                                    :sink-template
                                    :templatefields])]
    (apply tap/hfs-tap scheme path tap-opts)))
```

2.  Now, let's try this out:

```
user=> (?<- (stdout)
       [?origin_airport ?destin_airport]
       ((hfs-text-delim "data/16285/flights_with_colnames.csv"
                        :has-header true)
        ?origin_airport ?destin_airport ?passengers ?flights
?month))
…
RESULTS
-----------------------
MHK     AMW
EUG     RDM
EUG     RDM
EUG     RDM
…
```

## How it works...

This function takes a number of options, such as `fields, has-header, delim`, and `quote-str`. The defaults are for CSV files, but they can be easily overridden for a variety of other formats. We saw the use of the `:has-header` option in the previous example.

With the options in hand, it creates a `TextDelimited` scheme object. And finally passes it to the `hfs-tap` function, which wraps the scheme object in a tap. The tap serves as a data generator, and we bind the values from it to the names in our query.

## There's more

Hadoop can consume a number of different file formats. Avro (`http://avro.apache.org/`) uses JSON schemas to store data in a fast, compact, and binary data format. Sequence files (`http://wiki.apache.org/hadoop/SequenceFile`) contain a binary key-value store. XML and JSON are also common data formats.

If we want to parse our own data formats in Cascading or Cascalog, we'll need to write our own source tap (`http://docs.cascading.org/cascading/2.5/userguide/html/ch03s05.html`). If it's a delimited text format, such as CSV or TSV, we can base the new tap on `cascading.scheme.hadoop.TextDelimited`, just as we did in this recipe. See the JavaDocs for this class at `http://docs.cascading.org/cascading/2.5/cascading-hadoop/cascading/scheme/hadoop/TextDelimited.html` for more information on this.

# Executing complex queries with Cascalog

So far, we've seen basic Cascalog predicates and queries. We saw queries that pull data from one source generator and maybe include one predicate test. In this recipe, we'll see several more complex queries.

## Getting ready

For this recipe, we'll need the same `project.clj` file and dependencies from the *Initializing Cascalog and Hadoop for distributed processing* recipe. We'll also use the *Doctor Who* companion data that we defined in that recipe. The source code for this data is available in the code for the book, and you can also download just the code from `http://www.ericrochester.com/clj-data-analysis/data/companions.clj` to create this dataset.

## How to do it...

We'll start with simple queries and build up from there:

1. First, let's take a look at a simple join:

```
user=> (?<- (stdout) [?name ?dr]
       (full-name ?c ?name) (doctor ?c ?dr))
...
RESULTS
-----------------------
Ace        7
Adam Mitchell    9
Adelaide Brooke 10
Adric    4
Adric    5
Amy Pond        11
Astrid Peth     10
...
```

This pulls each companion's full name from one table and the numbers of Doctors they accompanied from another table. The binding for the companion's key, ?c, stays the same across all the generators and predicates for each row of the output. Also, notice that the second predicate (doctor ?c ?dr) can generate more than one row of output for each value of ?c, as it did for Adric.

2. Let's take a look at one that's slightly more complex:

```
user=> (?<- (stdout)
          [?name ?dr ?actor ?tenure]
          (full-name ?c ?name) (doctor ?c ?dr)
          (actor ?dr ?actor ?tenure))
...
RESULTS
-----------------------
Ace        7        Sylvester McCoy 1987-89, 1996
Adam Mitchell    9        Christopher Eccleston    2005
Adelaide Brooke 10        David Tennant    2005-10
Adric    4        Tom Baker        1974-81
Adric    5        Peter Davison    1981-84
Amy Pond        11        Matt Smith        2010-present
Astrid Peth     10        David Tennant    2005-10
...
```

This time, we've reused the same query as the preceding one, but we've also included the table of actors who've played *Doctor Who*.

3. Even with more than one generator, we can still include one or more test predicates. Here's a query that only returns companions for the modern-era Doctors:

```
user=> (?<- (stdout) [?name]
            (full-name ?c ?name) (doctor ?c ?dr)
            (>= ?dr 9))
...
RESULTS
----------------------
Adelaide Brooke
Amy Pond
Astrid Peth
Christina de Souza
Craig Owens
Donna Noble
...
```

4. Test predicates can be used to do more than just filter data. We can also use them to generate data. For example, in the next query, we add a `modern` flag to each row in order to indicate whether they are from the modern era or not. We do this by assigning the test predicate's output to a variable binding using the : > operator:

```
user=> (?<- (stdout)
            [?name ?modern]
            (full-name ?c ?name) (doctor ?c ?dr)
            (>= ?dr 9 :> ?modern))
...
RESULTS
----------------------
Ace         false
Adam Mitchell    true
Adelaide Brooke  true
Adric       false
Adric       false
Amy Pond         true
Astrid Peth      true
...
```

Out of the simple building blocks of generator and predicates, Cascalog makes it easy to build complex queries in an intuitive way. We'll see even more complex queries in the upcoming recipes, but composing generators and predicates and sharing bindings are the basis of all of them.

# Aggregating data with Cascalog

So far, the Cascalog queries you saw have all returned tables of results. However, sometimes you'll want to aggregate the tables in order to boil them down to a single value or into a table where groups from the original data are aggregated.

Cascalog also makes this easy to do, and it includes a number of aggregate functions. For this recipe, we'll only use two—`cascalog.logic.opts/distinct-count` and `cascalog.logic.ops/sumsum`—but you can find more easily in the API documentation on the Cascalog website (`http://nathanmarz.github.io/cascalog/cascalog.logic.ops.html`).

## Getting ready

We'll use the same dependencies and imports as we did in *Parsing CSV Files with Cascalog*. We'll also use the same data that we defined in that recipe.

## How to do it...

We'll take a look at a couple of examples on how to aggregate data with the `count` function:

1.  First, we'll query how many:

    ```
    user=> (?<- (stdout)
        [?count]
        ((hfs-text-delim "data/16285/flights_with_colnames.csv"
                        :has-header true)
         ?origin_airport _ _ _ _)
        (:distinct true)
        (c/distinct-count ?origin_airport :> ?count))
    ...
    RESULTS
    ---------------------
    683
    683
    ---------------------
    ```

    For this, we need to specify that we want to have distinct results for entire rows (the default). Then specify that we just include the aggregate operator as a predicate and give its results to a new name binding (`?count`). We use this binding—and only this binding—in the results. The other predicates in the query are used to select the data that we want aggregated.

2. Now let's try something more complicated. We'll find out how many flights leave each airport. To do this, we first need to define a mapping function in order to convert the values in a column to `longs`, using `defmapfn`. We'll use this to convert the flights column to numbers, and we'll use the `c/sum` function to aggregate those by airport:

```
user=> (defmapfn ->long
  "Converts a value to a long."
  [value]
  (Long/parseLong value))
user=> (?<- (stdout)
    [?origin_airport ?count]
    ((hfs-text-delim "data/16285/flights_with_colnames.csv"
                     :has-header true)
     ?origin_airport _ _ ?flights _)
    (:distinct true)
    (->long ?flights :> ?f)
    (c/sum ?f :> ?count))
...
RESULTS
---------------------
1B11B1    1
ABE       197049
ABI       50043
ABQ       758168
ABR       30832
ABY       34298
...
```

This query is very similar. We use the `map` function to prepare the column that we want aggregated. We also include an aggregator predicate. Next, in the output bindings, we include both the value that we want the data grouped on (`?origin_airport`) and the aggregated binding (`?count`).

It's this simple. Cascalog takes care of the rest.

## There's more

Cascalog provides a number of other aggregator functions as well. Some functions that you'll want to use regularly include `count`, `max`, `min`, `sum`, and `avg`. See the documentation for the build-in operations (`https://github.com/nathanmarz/cascalog/wiki/Built-in-operations`) for a more complete list.

We'll also talk more about `defmapfn` in the next recipe, *Defining new Cascalog operators*.

# Defining new Cascalog operators

Cascalog comes with a number of operators; however, you'll often need to define your own, as we saw in the *Aggregating data in Cascalog* recipe.

For different uses, Cascalog defines a number of different categories of operators, each with different properties. Some are run in the map phase of processing, and some are run in the reduce phase. The ones in the map phase can use a number of extra optimizations, so if you can push some of your processing into that stage, you'll get better performance. In this recipe, you'll see which categories of operators are on the map side and which are on the reduce side. We'll also provide an example of each and see how they fit into the larger processing model.

## Getting ready

For this recipe, we'll use the same dependencies and inclusions that we did in the *Initializing Cascalog and Hadoop for distributed processing* recipe. We'll also use the *Doctor Who* companion data from that recipe.

## How to do it...

As I mentioned, Cascalog allows you to specify a number of different operator types. Each type is used in a different situation and with different classes of problems and operations. Let's take a look at each type of operator.

### Creating map operators

Map operators transform data in the map phase, with one input row being mapped to one output row. A simple example of a custom map operator is an operator that triples all the numbers that pass through it:

```
(defmapfn triple-value [x] (* 3 x))
```

Something similar to this can be used to rescale all the values in a field.

### Creating map concatenation operators

Map concatenation operators transform data in the map phase, but each input row can map to one output row, many output rows, or none. These operators return a sequence, and each item in the sequence is a new output row. For example, this operator splits a string in whitespace, and each token is a new output row. We'll use this in the following predicate to count the number of names that each companion had:

```
(defmapcatfn split [string] (string/split string #"\s+"))
(?<- (stdout)
     [?name ?count]
     (full-name _ ?name) (split ?name :> ?token) (c/count ?count))
```

# Creating filter operators

Filter operators remove rows from the output in the map phase. They take one item, and they return a Boolean. If true, the item should be included in the results; if false, then the item should be held back. For example, this filter returns true if the input is an even number, and we use it in a query to return only the companions who accompanied an even number of doctors:

```
(deffilterfn is-even? [x] (even? x))
(?<- (stdout)
[?companion ?dr-count]
     (doctor ?companion _)
     (c/count ?dr-count)
     (is-even? ?dr-count))
```

# Creating buffer operators

Buffers operators work in the reduce phase. They process a group of rows as a single input. They take an entire list of input rows to process and return one or more items for the output. For example, this buffer operator takes rows of strings and returns the total number of characters in all the strings. We use it in the query to count the characters in the full names of the companions for each doctor:

```
(defbufferfn count-chars [strings]
  [(reduce + 0 (mapcat #(map count %) strings))])
(?<- (stdout)
[?dr ?companion-chars]
     (doctor ?c ?dr)
     (full-name ?c ?name)
     (count-chars ?name :> ?companion-chars))
```

# Creating aggregate operators

Aggregate functions work in the reduce phase to combine input rows into one value. Compared to buffer operators, aggregate operators are in some ways more flexible—they can be used with other aggregators—but are more restricted in other ways.

Each aggregator function has to be able to be called with no parameters, one parameter, or two parameters. The call with no parameters returns the initial value, while the call with one parameter takes the aggregator's state and returns the final value. Moreover, the call with two parameters takes the state and a new value and folds the two together into a new state.

For example, this returns the average length of the names of each doctor's companions:

```
(defaggregatefn mean-count
  ([] [0 0])
  ([[n total] string]
```

```
            [(inc n) (+ total (count string)))])
         ([[n total]] [(float (/ total n))]]))
(?<- (stdout)
[?dr ?companion-chars]
        (doctor ?c ?dr)
        (full-name ?c ?name)
        (mean-count ?name :> ?companion-chars))
```

## Creating parallel aggregate operators

Parallel aggregate operators are the most restricted, but they also give the best performance. Unlike the rest, they can be run in the map phase of the computation. These aggregators are defined by two functions. One function is called on each row, and one is called to combine the results of calling the first function on two rows.

This example returns the average length of the name of each doctor's companions:

1.  First, you have to define the aggregator functions as named functions. Cascalog serializes them as names, so you can't use anonymous functions:

    ```
    (defn mean-init [x] [1 (count x)])
    (defn mean-step [n1 t1 n2 t2] [(+ n1 n2) (+ t1 t2)])
    ```

2.  Then use these variables to define the parallel aggregator:

    ```
    (defparallelagg
    mean-count-p
      :init-var #'mean-init
      :combine-var #'mean-step)
    ```

3.  The aggregator returns both the item count and the total number of characters, so you have to divide the two in the query that calls the aggregator:

    ```
    (?<- (stdout) [?dr ?companion-chars]
         (doctor ?c ?dr)
         (full-name ?c ?name)
         (mean-count-p ?name :> ?n ?total)
         (div ?total ?n :> ?companion-chars))
    ```

Having so many options to build operators provides us with a lot of flexibility and power in how we define and create queries and transformations in Cascalog. This allows you to create powerful, custom workflows.

# Composing Cascalog queries

One of the best things about Cascalog queries is that they can be composed together. Similar to composing functions, this can be a good way to build a complex process from smaller, easy-to-understand parts.

In this recipe, we'll parse the Virginia census data we first used in the *Managing program complexity with STM* recipe in *Chapter 3, Managing Complexity with Concurrent Programming*. You can download this data from `http://www.ericrochester.com/clj-data-analysis/data/all_160_in_51.P35.csv`. We'll also use a new census datafile that contains the race data. You can download it from `http://www.ericrochester.com/clj-data-analysis/data/all_160_in_51.P3.csv`.

## Getting ready

Since we're reading CSV, we'll need to use the dependencies and imports from the *Parsing CSV files with Cascalog* recipe.

We'll also use the `hfs-text-delim` function from that recipe and `->long` from the *Aggregating data with Cascalog* recipe.

Also, we'll need the data files from `http://www.ericrochester.com/clj-data-analysis/data/all_160_in_51.P35.csv` and `http://www.ericrochester.com/clj-data-analysis/data/all_160_in_51.P3.csv`. We'll put them into the `data` directory, as follows:

```
(def families-file "data/all_160_in_51.P35.csv")
(def race-file "data/all_160_in_51.P3.csv")
```

## How to do it...

We'll read these datasets and convert some of the fields in each to integers. Then we'll join the two together and select only a few of the fields.

1.  We'll define a query that reads the `families` data file and converts the integer fields to numbers:

    ```
    (def family-data
        (<- [?GEOID ?SUMLEV ?STATE
          ?NAME ?POP100 ?HU100 ?P035001]
          ((hfs-text-delim families-file
    ```

```
                            :has-header true)
            ?GEOID ?SUMLEV ?STATE _ _ _ _ _
            ?NAME ?spop100 ?shu100 _ _ ?sp035001 _)
       (->long ?spop100           :> ?POP100)
       (->long ?shu100            :> ?HU100)
       (->long ?sp035001          :> ?P035001)))
```

2. We also need to read in the `race` data file:

```
(def race-data
  (<- [?GEOID ?SUMLEV ?STATE
       ?NAME ?POP100 ?HU100 ?P003001 ?P003002
       ?P003003 ?P003004 ?P003005 ?P003006 ?P003007
       ?P003008]
      ((hfs-text-delim race-file :has-header true)
          ?GEOID ?SUMLEV ?STATE _ _ _ _ _
          ?NAME ?spop100 ?shu100 _ _
          ?sp003001 _ ?sp003002 _ ?sp003003 _
          ?sp003004 _ ?sp003005 _ ?sp003006 _
          ?sp003007 _ ?sp003008 _)
      (->long ?spop100  :> ?POP100)
      (->long ?shu100   :> ?HU100)
      (->long ?sp003001 :> ?P003001)
      (->long ?sp003002 :> ?P003002)
      (->long ?sp003003 :> ?P003003)
      (->long ?sp003004 :> ?P003004)
      (->long ?sp003005 :> ?P003005)
      (->long ?sp003006 :> ?P003006)
      (->long ?sp003007 :> ?P003007)
      (->long ?sp003008 :> ?P003008)))
```

3. We'll use the preceding queries to build a query that joins them on the `?GEOID` field. It will also rename some of the fields:

```
(def census-joined
  (<- [?name ?pop100 ?hu100 ?families
       ?white ?black ?indian ?asian ?hawaiian ?other
       ?multiple]
      (family-data ?geoid _ _
                   ?name ?pop100 ?hu100 ?families)
      (race-data ?geoid _ _ _ _ _
                 ?white ?black ?indian ?asian
                 ?hawaiian ?other ?multiple)))
```

Now we can run this and send the results to the standard output:

```
user=> (?- (stdout) census-joined)
...
RESULTS
-----------------------

Abingdon town   8191    4271    2056    7681    257    15    86
6
Accomac town    519     229     117     389     106    0     3
1
Adwolf CDP      1530    677     467     1481    17     1     4
0
Alberta town    298     163     77      177     112    4     0
0
Alexandria city 139966  72376   30978   85186   30491  589   8432
141
Altavista town  3450    1669    928     2415    891    5     20
0
Amherst town    2231    1032    550     1571    550    17    14
0
Annandale CDP   41008   14715   9790    20670   3533   212   10103
53
Appalachia town 1754    879     482     1675    52     4     2
0
Appomattox town 1733    849     441     1141    540    8     3
0
Aquia Harbour CDP       6727    2300    1914    5704   521   38
150
...
```

## How it works...

In every recipe so far, we've used the ?<- macro, which is a combination of <- and ?-. The arrow, <-, allows you to create and compose queries. The ?- executes the query and sends the results to a sink. Using the combined ?<- macro is convenient, but using the separate ones can be more powerful.

# Transforming data with Cascalog

Often, simply querying data won't do everything you need to do. The data might not be in a form you can use, for instance. In that case, you'll need to transform the data. You can easily do this in Cascalog.

For this recipe, we'll define a custom operation and use it to split year ranges of the form '2000–2010' into two fields.

## Getting ready

We'll use the same dependencies and inclusions that we used in the *Initializing Cascalog and Hadoop for distributed processing* recipe. We'll also use the *Doctor Who* companion data from that recipe.

## How to do it...

1. We'll define a new, custom operation to take a date range string and split it into two values. In this dataset, we're splitting them on an en-dash (#"\u2013"). If the input isn't a range (that is, it's just a year), then the year is returned for both the start and end of the range:

```
(defmapfn split-range [date-range]
   (let [[from to] (string/split (str date-range) #"\u2013" 2)]
      [from (if (nil? to) from (str (.substring from 0 2) to))]))
```

2. Then we can use this to transform the tenure dates in the actors' data:

```
user=> (?<- (stdout)
            [?n ?name ?from ?to]
            (actor ?n ?name ?range)
            (split-range ?range :> ?from ?to))
...
RESULTS
----------------------
1       William Hartnell        1963    1966
2       Patrick Troughton       1966    1969
3       Jon Pertwee     1970    1974
...
```

## How it works...

In the `split-range` operator, we return a vector containing two years for the output. Then, in the query, we use the `:>` operator to bind the output values from `split-range` to the names `?from` and `?to`. Destructuring makes this especially easy.

# 6
# Working with Incanter Datasets

In this chapter, we will cover the following recipes:

- ► Loading Incanter's sample datasets
- ► Loading Clojure data structures into datasets
- ► Viewing datasets interactively with view
- ► Converting datasets to matrices
- ► Using infix formulas in Incanter
- ► Selecting columns with $
- ► Selecting rows with $
- ► Filtering datasets with $where
- ► Grouping data with $group-by
- ► Saving datasets to CSV and JSON
- ► Projecting from multiple datasets with $join

# Introduction

We've seen Incanter (`http://incanter.org/`) earlier in this book, but we'll spend a lot more time with this library over the next few chapters. Incanter combines the power to do statistics using a fully-featured statistical language such as R (`http://www.r-project.org/`) with the ease and joy of Clojure.

Incanter's core data structure is the dataset, so we'll spend some time in this chapter to look at how to use them effectively. While learning basic tools in this manner is often not the most exciting way to spend your time, it can still be incredibly useful. At its most fundamental level, an Incanter dataset is a table of rows. Each row has the same set of columns, much like a spreadsheet. The data in each cell of an Incanter dataset can be a string or a numeric. However, some operations require the data to only be numeric.

First you'll learn how to populate and view datasets, then you'll learn different ways to query and project the parts of the dataset that you're interested in onto a new dataset. Finally, we'll take a look at how to save datasets and merge multiple datasets together.

# Loading Incanter's sample datasets

Incanter comes with a set of default datasets that are useful for exploring Incanter's functions. I haven't made use of them in this book, since there is so much data available in other places, but they're a great way to get a feel of what you can do with Incanter. Some of these datasets—for instance, the Iris dataset—are widely used to teach and test statistical algorithms. It contains the species and petal and sepal dimensions for 50 irises. This is the dataset that we'll access today.

In this recipe, we'll load a dataset and see what it contains.

## Getting ready

We'll need to include Incanter in our Leiningen `project.clj` file:

```
(defproject inc-dsets "0.1.0"
  :dependencies [[org.clojure/clojure "1.6.0"]
                 [incanter "1.5.5"]])
```

We'll also need to include the right Incanter namespaces into our script or REPL:

```
(use '(incanter core datasets))
```

## How to do it...

Once the namespaces are available, we can access the datasets easily:

```
user=> (def iris (get-dataset :iris))
#'user/iris
user=> (col-names iris)
[:Sepal.Length :Sepal.Width :Petal.Length :Petal.Width :Species]
user=> (nrow iris)
150
user=> (set ($ :Species iris))
#{"versicolor" "virginica" "setosa"}
```

## How it works...

We use the `get-dataset` function to access the built-in datasets. In this case, we're loading the Fisher's Iris dataset, sometimes called Anderson's dataset. This is a multivariate dataset for discriminant analysis. It gives petal and sepal measurements for 150 different Irises of three different species.

Incanter's sample datasets cover a wide variety of topics—from U.S. arrests to plant growth and ultrasonic calibration. They can be used to test different algorithms and analyses and to work with different types of data.

By the way, the names of functions should be familiar to you if you've previously used R. Incanter often uses the names of R's functions instead of using the Clojure names for the same functions. For example, the preceding code sample used `nrow` instead of `count`.

## There's more...

Incanter's API documentation for `get-dataset` (`http://liebke.github.com/incanter/datasets-api.html#incanter.datasets/get-dataset`) lists more sample datasets, and you can refer to it for the latest information about the data that Incanter bundles.

# Loading Clojure data structures into datasets

While they are good for learning, Incanter's built-in datasets probably won't be that useful for your work (unless you work with irises). Other recipes cover ways to get data from CSV files and other sources into Incanter (see *Chapter 1, Importing Data for Analysis*). Incanter also accepts native Clojure data structures in a number of formats. We'll take look at a couple of these in this recipe.

## Getting ready

We'll just need Incanter listed in our `project.clj` file:

```
(defproject inc-dsets "0.1.0"
  :dependencies [[org.clojure/clojure "1.6.0"]
                 [incanter "1.5.5"]])
```

We'll also need to include this in our script or REPL:

```
(use 'incanter.core)
```

## How to do it...

The primary function used to convert data into a dataset is `to-dataset`. While it can convert single, scalar values into a dataset, we'll start with slightly more complicated inputs.

1. Generally, you'll be working with at least a matrix. If you pass this to `to-dataset`, what do you get?

   ```
   user=> (def matrix-set (to-dataset [[1 2 3] [4 5 6]]))
   #'user/matrix-set
   user=> (nrow matrix-set)
   2
   user=> (col-names matrix-set)
   [:col-0 :col-1 :col-2]
   ```

2. All the data's here, but it can be labeled in a better way. Does `to-dataset` handle maps?

   ```
   user=> (def map-set (to-dataset {:a 1, :b 2, :c 3}))
   #'user/map-set
   user=> (nrow map-set)
   1
   user=> (col-names map-set)
   [:a :c :b]
   ```

3. So, map keys become the column labels. That's much more intuitive. Let's throw a sequence of maps at it:

   ```
   user=> (def maps-set (to-dataset [{:a 1, :b 2, :c 3},
                                      {:a 4, :b 5, :c 6}]))
   #'user/maps-set
   user=> (nrow maps-set)
   2
   user=> (col-names maps-set)
   [:a :c :b]
   ```

4. This is much more useful. We can also create a dataset by passing the column vector and the row matrix separately to `dataset`:

```
user=> (def matrix-set-2
          (dataset [:a :b :c]
                      [[1 2 3] [4 5 6]]))
#'user/matrix-set-2
user=> (nrow matrix-set-2)
2
user=> (col-names matrix-set-2)
[:c :b :a]
```

## How it works...

The `to-dataset` function looks at the input and tries to process it intelligently. If given a sequence of maps, the column names are taken from the keys of the first map in the sequence.

Ultimately, it uses the `dataset` constructor to create the dataset. When you want the most control, you should also use the dataset. It requires the dataset to be passed in as a column vector and a row matrix. When the data is in this format or when we need the most control—to rename the columns, for instance—we can use `dataset`.

## See also...

Several recipes in *Chapter 1, Importing Data for Analysis*, look at how to load data from different external sources into Incanter datasets.

# Viewing datasets interactively with view

Being able to interact with our data programmatically is important, but sometimes it's also helpful to be able to look at it. This can be especially useful when you do data exploration.

## Getting ready

We'll need to have Incanter in our `project.clj` file and script or REPL, so we'll use the same setup as we did for the *Loading Incanter's sample datasets* recipe, as follows. We'll also use the Iris dataset from that recipe.

```
(use '(incanter core datasets))
```

## How to do it...

Incanter makes this very easy. Let's take a look at just how simple it is:

1.  First, we need to load the dataset, as follows:

    ```
    user=> (def iris (get-dataset :iris))
    #'user/iris
    ```

2.  Then we just call `view` on the dataset:

    ```
    user=> (view iris)
    ```

This function returns the Swing window frame, which contains our data, as shown in the following screenshot. This window should also be open on your desktop, although for me, it's usually hiding behind another window:

| :Sepal.Leng... | :Sepal.Width | :Petal.Length | :Petal.Width | :Species |
|---|---|---|---|---|
| 5.1 | 3.5 | 1.4 | 0.2 | setosa |
| 4.9 | 3.0 | 1.4 | 0.2 | setosa |
| 4.7 | 3.2 | 1.3 | 0.2 | setosa |
| 4.6 | 3.1 | 1.5 | 0.2 | setosa |
| 5.0 | 3.6 | 1.4 | 0.2 | setosa |
| 5.4 | 3.9 | 1.7 | 0.4 | setosa |
| 4.6 | 3.4 | 1.4 | 0.3 | setosa |
| 5.0 | 3.4 | 1.5 | 0.2 | setosa |
| 4.4 | 2.9 | 1.4 | 0.2 | setosa |

*Incanter Dataset*

## How it works...

Incanter's `view` function takes any object and tries to display it graphically. In this case, it simply displays the raw data as a table. We'll use this function a lot in *Chapter 11, Graphing in Incanter*, when we talk about Incanter's graphing functionality.

## See also...

▶   *Chapter 11, Graphing in Incanter*, for more sophisticated and exciting ways to visualize Incanter datasets

# Converting datasets to matrices

Although datasets are often convenient, many times we'll want to treat our data as a matrix from linear algebra. In Incanter, matrices store a table of doubles. This provides good performance in a compact data structure. Moreover, we'll need matrices many times because some of Incanter's functions, such as `trans`, only operate on a matrix. Plus, it implements Clojure's ISeq interface, so interacting with matrices is also convenient.

## Getting ready

For this recipe, we'll need the Incanter libraries, so we'll use this `project.clj` file:

```
(defproject inc-dsets "0.1.0"
  :dependencies [[org.clojure/clojure "1.6.0"]
                 [incanter "1.5.5"]]])
```

We'll use the `core` and `io` namespaces, so we'll load these into our script or REPL:

```
(use '(incanter core io))
```

We'll use the Virginia census data that we've used periodically throughout the book. See the *Managing program complexity with STM* recipe from *Chapter 3, Managing Complexity with Concurrent Programming*, for information on how to get this dataset. You can also download it from http://www.ericrochester.com/clj-data-analysis/data/all_160_in_51.P35.csv.

This line binds the file name to the identifier `data-file`:

```
(def data-file "data/all_160_in_51.P35.csv")
```

## How to do it...

For this recipe, we'll create a dataset, convert it to a matrix, and then perform some operations on it:

1.  First, we need to read the data into a dataset, as follows:

    ```
    (def va-data (read-dataset data-file :header true))
    ```

2.  Then, in order to convert it to a matrix, we just pass it to the `to-matrix` function. Before we do this, we'll pull out a few of the columns since matrixes can only contain floating-point numbers:

    ```
    (def va-matrix
        (to-matrix ($ [:POP100 :HU100 :P035001] va-data)))
    ```

3. Now that it's a matrix, we can treat it like a sequence of rows. Here, we pass it to `first` in order to get the first row, `take` in order to get a subset of the matrix, and `count` in order to get the number of rows in the matrix:

```
user=> (first va-matrix)
 A 1x3 matrix
 -------------
 8.19e+03   4.27e+03   2.06e+03

user=> (count va-matrix)
591
```

4. We can also use Incanter's matrix operators to get the sum of each column, for instance. The `plus` function takes each row and sums each column separately:

```
user=> (reduce plus va-matrix)
 A 1x3 matrix
 -------------
 5.43e+06   2.26e+06   1.33e+06
```

## How it works...

The `to-matrix` function takes a dataset of floating-point values and returns a compact matrix. Matrices are used by many of Incanter's more sophisticated analysis functions, as they're easy to work with.

## There's more...

In this recipe, we saw the `plus` matrix operator. Incanter defines a full suite of these. You can learn more about matrices and see what operators are available at `https://github.com/liebke/incanter/wiki/matrices`.

## See also...

▶ The *Selecting columns with $* recipe in this chapter has more information on how to select specific columns from a dataset

# Using infix formulas in Incanter

There's a lot to like about lisp: macros, the simple syntax, and the rapid development cycle. Most of the time, it is fine if you treat math operators as functions and use prefix notations, which is a consistent, function-first syntax. This allows you to treat math operators in the same way as everything else so that you can pass them to `reduce`, or anything else you want to do.

However, we're not taught to read math expressions using prefix notations (with the operator first). And especially when formulas get even a little complicated, tracing out exactly what's happening can get hairy.

## Getting ready

For this recipe we'll just need Incanter in our `project.clj` file, so we'll use the dependencies statement—as well as the `use` statement—from the *Loading Clojure data structures into datasets* recipe.

For data, we'll use the matrix that we created in the *Converting datasets to matrices* recipe.

## How to do it...

Incanter has a macro that converts a standard math notation to a lisp notation. We'll explore that in this recipe:

1. The `$=` macro changes its contents to use an infix notation, which is what we're used to from math class:

   ```
   user=> ($= 7 * 4)
   28
   user=> ($= 7 * 4 + 3)
   31
   ```

2. We can also work on whole matrixes or just parts of matrixes. In this example, we perform a scalar multiplication of the matrix:

   ```
   user=> ($= va-matrix * 4)
    A 591x3 matrix
    ---------------
    3.28e+04  1.71e+04  8.22e+03
    2.08e+03  9.16e+02  4.68e+02
    1.19e+03  6.52e+02  3.08e+02
    . . .
   ```

```
1.41e+03   7.32e+02   3.72e+02
1.31e+04   6.64e+03   3.49e+03
3.02e+04   9.60e+03   6.90e+03
user=> ($= (first va-matrix) * 4)

A 1x3 matrix
-------------
3.28e+04   1.71e+04   8.22e+03
```

3.  Using this, we can build complex expressions, such as this expression that takes the mean of the values in the first row of the matrix:

```
user=> ($= (sum (first va-matrix)) /
           (count (first va-matrix)))
4839.333333333333
```

4.  Or we can build expressions take the mean of each column, as follows:

```
user=> ($= (reduce plus va-matrix) / (count va-matrix))

A 1x3 matrix
-------------
9.19e+03   3.83e+03   2.25e+03
```

## How it works...

Any time you're working with macros and you wonder how they work, you can always get at their output expressions easily, so you can see what the computer is actually executing. The tool to do this is `macroexpand-1`. This expands the macro one step and returns the result. It's sibling function, `macroexpand`, expands the expression until there is no macro expression left. Usually, this is more than we want, so we just use `macroexpand-1`.

Let's see what these macros expand into:

```
user=> (macroexpand-1 '($= 7 * 4))
(incanter.core/mult 7 4)
user=> (macroexpand-1 '($= 7 * 4 + 3))
(incanter.core/plus (incanter.core/mult 7 4) 3)
user=> (macroexpand-1 '($= 3 + 7 * 4))
(incanter.core/plus 3 (incanter.core/mult 7 4))
```

Here, we can see that the expression doesn't expand into Clojure's * or + functions, but it uses Incanter's matrix functions, `mult` and `plus`, instead. This allows it to handle a variety of input types, including matrices, intelligently.

Otherwise, it switches around the expressions the way we'd expect. Also, we can see by comparing the last two lines of code that it even handles operator precedence correctly.

# Selecting columns with $

Often, you need to cut the data to make it more useful. One common transformation is to pull out all the values from one or more columns into a new dataset. This can be useful for generating summary statistics or aggregating the values of some columns.

The Incanter macro $ slices out parts of a dataset. In this recipe, we'll see this in action.

## Getting ready

For this recipe, we'll need to have Incanter listed in our `project.clj` file:

```
(defproject inc-dsets "0.1.0"
  :dependencies [[org.clojure/clojure "1.6.0"]
                 [incanter "1.5.5"]
                 [org.clojure/data.csv "0.1.2"]])
```

We'll also need to include these libraries in our script or REPL:

```
(require '[clojure.java.io :as io]
         '[clojure.data.csv :as csv]
         '[clojure.string :as str]
         '[incanter.core :as i])
```

Moreover, we'll need some data. This time, we'll use some country data from the World Bank. Point your browser to `http://data.worldbank.org/country` and select a country. I picked China. Under **World Development Indicators**, there is a button labeled **Download Data**. Click on this button and select **CSV**. This will download a ZIP file. I extracted its contents into the `data/chn` directory in my project. I bound the filename for the primary data file to the `data-file` name.

## How to do it...

We'll use the $ macro in several different ways to get different results. First, however, we'll need to load the data into a dataset, which we'll do in steps 1 and 2:

1. Before we start, we'll need a couple of utilities that load the data file into a sequence of maps and makes a dataset out of those:

```
(defn with-header [coll]
  (let [headers (map #(keyword (str/replace % \space \-))
                     (first coll))]
    (map (partial zipmap headers) (next coll))))
```

```
(defn read-country-data [filename]
  (with-open [r (io/reader filename)]
    (i/to-dataset
      (doall (with-header
               (drop 2 (csv/read-csv r)))))))
```

2. Now, using these functions, we can load the data:

```
user=> (def chn-data (read-country-data data-file))
```

3. We can select columns to be pulled out from the dataset by passing the column names or numbers to the $ macro. It returns a sequence of the values in the column:

```
user=> (i/$ :Indicator-Code chn-data)
("AG.AGR.TRAC.NO" "AG.CON.FERT.PT.ZS" "AG.CON.FERT.ZS" …
```

4. We can select more than one column by listing all of them in a vector. This time, the results are in a dataset:

```
user=> (i/$ [:Indicator-Code :1992] chn-data)
```

```
|             :Indicator-Code |               :1992 |
|-----------------------------+---------------------|
|              AG.AGR.TRAC.NO |              770629 |
|           AG.CON.FERT.PT.ZS |                     |
|              AG.CON.FERT.ZS |                     |
|              AG.LND.AGRI.K2 |             5159980 |
…
```

5. We can list as many columns as we want, although the formatting might suffer:

```
user=> (i/$ [:Indicator-Code :1992 :2002] chn-data)
```

```
|             :Indicator-Code |               :1992 |
:2002 |
|-----------------------------+---------------------+---------------
------|
|              AG.AGR.TRAC.NO |              770629 |
|
|           AG.CON.FERT.PT.ZS |                     |
122.73027213719 |
|              AG.CON.FERT.ZS |                     |
373.087159048868 |
|              AG.LND.AGRI.K2 |             5159980 |
5231970 |
…
```

## How it works...

The $ function is just a wrapper over Incanter's `sel` function. It provides a good way to slice columns out of the dataset, so we can focus only on the data that actually pertains to our analysis.

## There's more...

The indicator codes for this dataset are a little cryptic. However, the code descriptions are in the dataset too:

```
user=> (i/$ [0 1 2] [:Indicator-Code :Indicator-Name] chn-data)


|    :Indicator-Code |
:Indicator-Name |
|-------------------+---------------------------------------------------
--------------|
|    AG.AGR.TRAC.NO |                            Agricultural
machinery, tractors |
| AG.CON.FERT.PT.ZS |             Fertilizer consumption (% of
fertilizer production) |
|    AG.CON.FERT.ZS | Fertilizer consumption (kilograms per hectare of
arable land) |
...
```

## See also...

▶    For information on how to pull out specific rows, see the next recipe, *Selecting rows with $*.

# Selecting rows with $

The Incanter macro $ also pulls rows out of a dataset. In this recipe, we'll see this in action.

## Getting ready

For this recipe, we'll use the same dependencies, imports, and data as we did in the *Selecting columns with $* recipe.

## How to do it...

Similar to how we use $ in order to select columns, there are several ways in which we can use it to select rows, shown as follows:

1. We can create a sequence of the values of one row using $, and pass it the index of the row we want as well as passing :all for the columns:

```
user=> (i/$ 0 :all chn-data)
("AG.AGR.TRAC.NO" "684290" "738526" "52661" "" "880859" "" "" ""
"59657" "847916" "862078" "891170" "235524" "126440" "469106"
"282282" "817857" "125442" "703117" "CHN" "66290" "705723"
"824113" "" "151281" "669675" "861364" "559638" "191220" "180772"
"73021" "858031" "734325" "Agricultural machinery, tractors"
"100432" "" "796867" "" "China" "" "" "155602" "" "" "770629"
"747900" "346786" "" "398946" "876470" "" "795713" "" "55360"
"685202" "989139" "798506" "")
```

2. We can also pull out a dataset containing multiple rows by passing more than one index into $ with a vector (There's a lot of data, even for three rows, so I won't show it here):

```
(i/$ (range 3) :all chn-data)
```

3. We can also combine the two ways to slice data in order to pull specific columns and rows. We can either pull out a single row or multiple rows:

```
user=> (i/$ 0 [:Indicator-Code :1992] chn-data)
("AG.AGR.TRAC.NO" "770629")
user=> (i/$ (range 3) [:Indicator-Code :1992] chn-data)
```

```
|    :Indicator-Code |   :1992 |
|--------------------+---------|
|     AG.AGR.TRAC.NO | 770629  |
| AG.CON.FERT.PT.ZS  |         |
|     AG.CON.FERT.ZS |         |
```

## How it works...

The $ macro is the workhorse used to slice rows and project (or select) columns from datasets. When it's called with two indexing parameters, the first is the row or rows and the second is the column or columns.

# Filtering datasets with $where

While we can filter datasets before we import them into Incanter, Incanter makes it easy to filter and create new datasets from the existing ones. We'll take a look at its query language in this recipe.

## Getting ready

We'll use the same dependencies, imports, and data as we did in the *Selecting columns with $* recipe.

## How to do it...

Once we have the data, we query it using the `$where` function:

1. For example, this creates a dataset with a row for the percentage of China's total land area that is used for agriculture:

```
user=> (def land-use
          (i/$where {:Indicator-Code "AG.LND.AGRI.ZS"}
                    chn-data))
user=> (i/nrow land-use)
1
user=> (i/$ [:Indicator-Code :2000] land-use)
("AG.LND.AGRI.ZS" "56.2891584865366")
```

2. The queries can be more complicated too. This expression picks out the data that exists for 1962 by filtering any empty strings in that column:

```
user=> (i/$ (range 5) [:Indicator-Code :1962]
          (i/$where {:1962 {:ne ""}} chn-data))
```

| :Indicator-Code | :1962 |
|-----------------|-------|
| AG.AGR.TRAC.NO | 55360 |
| AG.LND.AGRI.K2 | 3460010 |
| AG.LND.AGRI.ZS | 37.0949187612906 |
| AG.LND.ARBL.HA | 103100000 |
| AG.LND.ARBL.HA.PC | 0.154858284392508 |

Incanter's query language is even more powerful than this, but these examples should show you the basic structure and give you an idea of the possibilities.

## How it works...

To better understand how to use $where, let's break apart the last example:

```
($i/where {:1962 {:ne ""}} chn-data)
```

The query is expressed as a hashmap from fields to values (highlighted). As we saw in the first example, the value can be a raw value, either a literal or an expression. This tests for inequality.

```
($i/where {:1962 {:ne ""}} chn-data)
```

Each test pair is associated with a field in another hashmap (highlighted).

In this example, both the hashmaps shown only contain one key-value pair. However, they might contain multiple pairs, which will all be ANDed together.

Incanter supports a number of test operators. The basic boolean tests are :$gt (greater than), :$lt (less than), :$gte (greater than or equal to), :$lte (less than or equal to), :$eq (equal to), and :$ne (not equal). There are also some operators that take sets as parameters: :$in and :$nin (not in).

The last operator—:$fn—is interesting. It allows you to use any predicate function. For example, this will randomly select approximately half of the dataset:

```
(def random-half
   (i/$where {:Indicator-Code {:$fn (fn [_] (< (rand) 0.5))}}
             chnchn-data))
```

## There's more...

For full details of the query language, see the documentation for incanter.core/query-dataset (http://liebke.github.com/incanter/core-api.html#incanter.core/query-dataset).

# Grouping data with $group-by

Datasets often come with an inherent structure. Two or more rows might have the same value in one column, and we might want to leverage that by grouping those rows together in our analysis.

## Getting ready

First, we'll need to declare a dependency on Incanter in the `project.clj` file:

```
(defproject inc-dsets "0.1.0"
  :dependencies [[org.clojure/clojure "1.6.0"]
                 [incanter "1.5.5"]
                 [org.clojure/data.csv "0.1.2"]])
```

Next, we'll include Incanter `core` and `io` in our script or REPL:

```
(require '[incanter.core :as i]
         '[incanter.io :as i-io])
```

For data, we'll use the census race data for all the states. You can download it from `http://www.ericrochester.com/clj-data-analysis/data/all_160.P3.csv`.

These lines will load the data into the `race-data` name:

```
(def data-file "data/all_160.P3.csv")
(def race-data (i-io/read-dataset data-file :header true))
```

## How to do it...

Incanter lets you group rows for further analysis or to summarize them with the `$group-by` function. All you need to do is pass the data to `$group-by` with the column or function to group on:

```
(def by-state (i/$group-by :STATE race-data))
```

## How it works...

This function returns a map where each key is a map of the fields and values represented by that grouping. For example, this is how the keys look:

```
user=> (take 5 (keys by-state))
({:STATE 29} {:STATE 28} {:STATE 31} {:STATE 30} {:STATE 25})
```

We can get the data for Virginia back out by querying the group map for state 51.

```
user=> (i/$ (range 3) [:GEOID :STATE :NAME :POP100]
            (by-state {:STATE 51}))
```

| :GEOID  | :STATE |         :NAME | :POP100 |
|---------|--------|---------------|---------|
| 5100148 |     51 | Abingdon town |    8191 |
| 5100180 |     51 | Accomac town  |     519 |
| 5100724 |     51 | Alberta town  |     298 |

# Saving datasets to CSV and JSON

Once you've done the work of slicing, dicing, cleaning, and aggregating your datasets, you might want to save them. Incanter by itself doesn't have a good way to do this. However, with the help of some Clojure libraries, it's not difficult at all.

## Getting ready

We'll need to include a number of dependencies in our `project.clj` file:

```
(defproject inc-dsets "0.1.0"
  :dependencies [[org.clojure/clojure "1.6.0"]
                 [incanter "1.5.5"]
                 [org.clojure/data.csv "0.1.2"]
                 [org.clojure/data.json "0.2.5"]])
```

We'll also need to include these libraries in our script or REPL:

```
(require '[incanter.core :as i]
         '[incanter.io :as i-io]
         '[clojure.data.csv :as csv]
         '[clojure.data.json :as json]
         '[clojure.java.io :as io])
```

Also, we'll use the same data that we introduced in the *Selecting columns with $* recipe.

## How to do it...

This process is really as simple as getting the data and saving it. We'll pull out the data for the year 2000 from the larger dataset. We'll use this subset of the data in both the formats here:

```
(def data2000
  (i/$ [:Indicator-Code :Indicator-Name :2000] chn-data))
```

### Saving data as CSV

To save a dataset as a CSV, all in one statement, open a file and use `clojure.data.csv/write-csv` to write the column names and data to it:

```
(with-open [f-out (io/writer "data/chn-2000.csv")]
  (csv/write-csv f-out [(map name (i/col-names data2000))])
  (csv/write-csv f-out (i/to-list data2000)))
```

## Saving data as JSON

To save a dataset as JSON, open a file and use `clojure.data.json/write` to serialize the file:

```
(with-open [f-out (io/writer "data/chn-2000.json")]
  (json/write (:rows data2000) f-out))
```

## How it works...

For CSV and JSON, as well as many other data formats, the process is very similar. Get the data, open the file, and serialize data into it. There will be differences in how the output function wants the data (`to-list` or `:rows`), and there will be differences in how the output function is called (for instance, whether the file handle is the first or second argument). But generally, outputting datasets will be very similar and relatively simple.

## See also...

In *Chapter 1, Importing Data for Analysis*, we talked about how to read CSV files (*Reading CSV data into Incanter datasets* recipe) and JSON files (*Reading JSON data into Incanter datasets* recipe) into Incanter.

# Projecting from multiple datasets with $join

So far, we've been focusing on splitting up datasets, on dividing them into groups of rows or groups of columns with functions and macros such as `$` or `$where`. However, sometimes we'd like to move in the other direction. We might have two related datasets and want to join them together to make a larger one. For example, we might want to join crime data to census data, or take any two related datasets that come from separate sources and analyze them together.

## Getting ready

First, we'll need to include these dependencies in our `project.clj` file:

```
(defproject inc-dsets "0.1.0"
  :dependencies [[org.clojure/clojure "1.6.0"]
                 [incanter "1.5.5"]
                 [org.clojure/data.csv "0.1.2"]])
```

We'll use these statements for inclusions:

```
(require '[clojure.java.io :as io]
         '[clojure.data.csv :as csv]
         '[clojure.string :as str]
         '[incanter.core :as i])
```

For our data file, we'll use the same data that we introduced in the *Selecting columns with $* recipe: China's development dataset from the World Bank.

## How to do it...

In this recipe, we'll take a look at how to join two datasets using Incanter:

1. To begin with, we'll load the data from the `data/chn/chn_Country_en_csv_v2.csv` file. We'll use the `with-header` and `read-country-data` functions that were defined in the *Selecting columns with $* recipe:

```
(def data-file "data/chn/chn_Country_en_csv_v2.csv")
(def chn-data (read-country-data data-file))
```

2. Currently, the data for each row contains the data for one indicator across many years. However, for some analyses, it will be more helpful to have each row contain the data for one indicator for one year. To do this, let's first pull out the data from 2 years into separate datasets. Note that for the second dataset, we'll only include a column to match the first dataset (`:Indicator-Code`) and the data column (`:2000`):

```
(def chn-1990
   (i/$ [:Indicator-Code :Indicator-Name :1990]
        chn-data))
(def chn-2000
   (i/$ [:Indicator-Code :2000] chn-data))
```

3. Now, we'll join these datasets back together. This is contrived, but it's easy to see how we will do this in a more meaningful example. For example, we might want to join the datasets from two different countries:

```
(def chn-decade
   (i/$join [:Indicator-Code :Indicator-Code]
            chn-1990 chn-2000))
```

From this point on, we can use `chn-decade` just as we use any other Incanter dataset.

## How it works...

Let's take a look at this in more detail:

```
(i/$join [:Indicator-Code :Indicator-Code] chn-1990 chn-2000)
```

The pair of column keywords in a vector (`[:Indicator-Code :Indicator-Code]`) are the keys that the datasets will be joined on. In this case, the `:Indicator-Code` column from both the datasets is used, but the keys can be different for the two datasets. The first column that is listed will be from the first dataset (`chn-1990`), and the second column that is listed will be from the second dataset (`chn-2000`).

This returns a new dataset. Each row of this new dataset is a superset of the corresponding rows from the two input datasets.

# 7
# Statistical Data Analysis with Incanter

In this chapter, we will cover the following recipes:

- ▸ Generating summary statistics with `$rollup`
- ▸ Working with changes in values
- ▸ Scaling variables to simplify variable relationships
- ▸ Working with time series data with Incanter Zoo
- ▸ Smoothing variables to decrease variation
- ▸ Validating sample statistics with bootstrapping
- ▸ Modeling linear relationships
- ▸ Modeling non-linear relationships
- ▸ Modeling multinomial Bayesian distributions
- ▸ Finding data errors with Benford's law

## Introduction

So far, we've focused on data and process. We've seen how to get data and how to get it ready to analyze. We've also looked at how to organize and partition our processing to keep things simple and get the best performance.

We'll now look at how to leverage statistics to gain insights into our data. This is a subject that is both broad and deep, and covering statistics in any meaningful way is far beyond the scope of this chapter. For more information about some of the procedures and functions described here, you should refer to a textbook, class, your local statistician, or another resource. For instance, **Coursera** has an online statistics course (`https://www.coursera.org/course/stats1`), and **Harvard** has a course on probability on iTunes (`https://itunes.apple.com/us/course/statistics-110-probability/id502492375`).

Some of the recipes in this chapter will involve generating simple summary statistics. Some will involve further messaging our data to make trends and relationships more clear. We'll then look at different ways to model the relationships in our data. Finally, we'll look at Benford's law, a curious observation about the behavior of naturally occurring sequences of numbers, which we can leverage to discover problems with our data.

# Generating summary statistics with $rollup

One of the basic ways of getting a grip on a dataset is to look at some summary statistics: measures of centrality and variance, such as mean and standard deviation. These provide useful insights into our data, help us know what questions to ask next, and know how best to proceed.

## Getting ready

First, we'll need to make sure Incanter is listed in the dependencies of our Leiningen `project.clj` file:

```
(defproject statim "0.1.0"
  :dependencies [[org.clojure/clojure "1.6.0"]
                 [incanter "1.5.5"]]))
```

And we'll need to require these libraries in our script or REPL:

```
(require '[incanter.core :as i]
         'incanter.io
         '[incanter.stats :as s])
```

Finally, we'll use the dataset of census race data that we compiled for the *Grouping data with $group-by* recipe in *Chapter 6, Working with Incanter Datasets*. We'll bind the file name to the name `data-file`. You can download this from `http://www.ericrochester.com/clj-data-analysis/data/all_160.P3.csv`:

```
(def data-file "data/all_160.P3.csv")
```

## How to do it...

To generate summary statistics in Incanter, we'll use the `$rollup` function.

First, we'll load the dataset and bind it to the name `census`:

```
(def census (incanter.io/read-dataset data-file :header true))
```

Then, we'll use `$rollup` to get the statistics for groups of data:

```
user=> (i/$rollup :mean :POP100 :STATE census)
| :STATE |      :POP100 |
|--------+---------------|
|     34 |    1054049/109 |
|      6 | 35184222/1523 |
|     18 |    4413508/681 |
|      5 |    1941247/541 |
...
user=> (i/$rollup s/sd :POP100 :STATE census)
| :STATE |      :POP100 |
|--------+---------------|
|     34 |    1054049/109 |
|      6 | 35184222/1523 |
|     18 |    4413508/681 |
|      5 |    1941247/541 |||
...
```

## How it works...

The `$rollup` function takes the dataset (the fourth parameter) and groups the rows by the values of the grouping field (the third parameter). It takes the group subsets of the data and extracts the values from the field to aggregate (the second parameter). It passes those values to the aggregate function (the first parameter) to get the final table of values. That's a lot for one small function. Here's a snapshot to make it clearer:

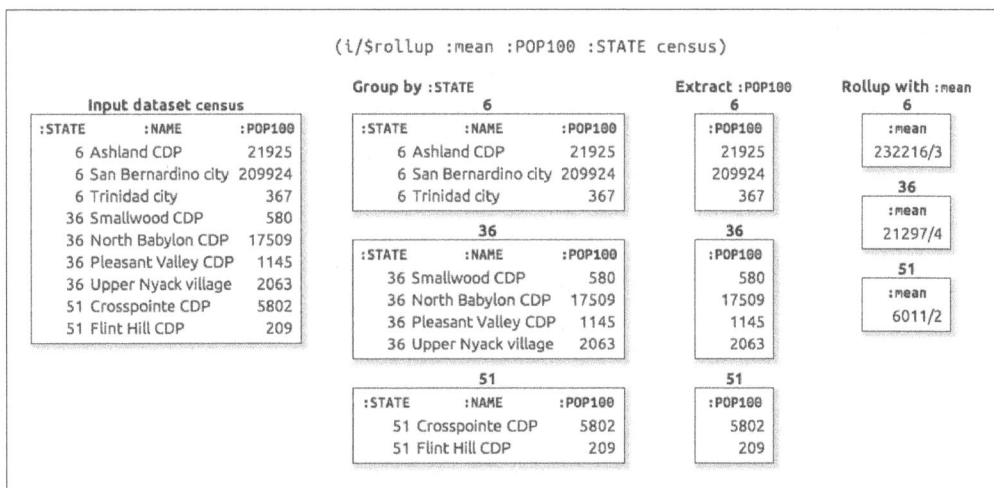

`$rollup` defines some standard aggregation functions (`:count`, `:sum`, `:min`, `:max`, and `:mean`) but we can also use any other function that takes a collection of values and returns a single value. This is what we did with `incanter.stats/sd`. For full details of the `$rollup` function and the aggregate keyword functions it provides, see the documentation at `http://liebke.github.com/incanter/core-api.html#incanter.core/$rollup`.

As an aside, the numbers in the first example, which calculated the mean, are expressed as rational numbers. These are real numbers that are more precise than IEEE floating-point numbers, which is what Clojure uses for its doubles. When Clojure divides two integers, we get rational numbers. If you want to see floating-point numbers, you convert them by passing the values to `float`:

```
user=> (/ 695433 172)
695433/172
user=> (float 695433/172)
4043.215
```

# Working with changes in values

Sometimes, we are more interested in how values change over time, or across some other progression, than we are in the values themselves. This information is latent in the data, but making it explicit makes it easier to work with and visualize.

## Getting ready

First, we'll use these dependencies in our `project.clj`:

```
(defproject statim "0.1.0"
  :dependencies [[org.clojure/clojure "1.6.0"]
                 [incanter "1.5.5"]])
```

We also need to require Incanter in our script or REPL:

```
(require '[incanter.core :as i]
         'incanter.io)
```

Finally, we'll use the Virginia census data. You can download the file from `http://www.ericrochester.com/clj-data-analysis/data/all_160_in_51.P3.csv`:

```
(def data-file "data/all_160_in_51.P3.csv")
```

## How to do it...

For this recipe, we'll take some census data and add a column to show the change in population between the 2000 and 2010 censuses:

1. To begin, we'll need to read in the data:

```
(def data
  (incanter.io/read-dataset data-file
  :header true))
```

2. If we look at the values in the field for the 2000 census population, some of them are empty. This will cause errors, so we'll replace those with zeros. Here's the function to do that:

```
(defn check-int [x] (if (integer? x) x 0)) x 0))
```

3. Now we can get the difference in population between the two censuses:

```
(def growth-rates
  (->> data
    (i/$map check-int :POP100.2000)
    (i/minus (i/sel data :cols :POP100))
    (i/dataset [:POP.DELTA])
    (i/conj-cols data)))
```

4. As we might expect, some places have grown and some have shrunk:

```
user=> (i/sel growth-rates
        :cols [:NAME :POP100 :POP100.2000 :POP.DELTA]
        :rows (range 5))
```

|            :NAME | :POP100 |  :POP100.2000 | :POP.DELTA |
| ---------------- | ------- | ------------- | ---------- |
|    Abingdon town |    8191 |          7780 |      411.0 |
|    Accomac town  |     519 |           547 |      -28.0 |
|    Alberta town  |     298 |           306 |       -8.0 |
| Alexandria city  |  139966 |        128283 |    11683.0 |
|    Allisonia CDP |     117 |               |      117.0 |

## How it works...

This was a pretty straightforward process, but let's look at it line-by-line to make sure everything's clear. We'll follow the steps of the ->> macro.

1. We'll map the values in the 2000 census population column over the `replace-empty` function we defined earlier to get rid of empty values:

   ```
   (->> data
       (i/$map check-int :POP100.2000)
   ```

2. We'll select the 2010 census population and subtract the 2000 values from it:

   ```
   (i/minus (i/sel data :cols :POP100))
   ```

3. We'll take the differences and create a new dataset with one column named `:POP.DELTA`:

   ```
   (i/dataset [:POP.DELTA])
   ```

4. Lastly, we'll merge it back into the original dataset with `incanter.core/conj-cols`. This function takes two datasets with the same number of rows, and it returns a new dataset with the columns from both of the input datasets:

   ```
   (i/conj-cols data))
   ```

# Scaling variables to simplify variable relationships

We don't always work with numbers as they are. For example, population is often given in thousands. In this recipe, we'll scale some values to make them easier to work with. In fact, some algorithms work better with scaled data. For instance, linear regression models are sometimes able to fit the data better after the data has been scaled logarithmically.

## Getting ready

We'll use these dependencies in our `project.clj` file:

```
(defproject statim "0.1.0"
  :dependencies [[org.clojure/clojure "1.6.0"]
                 [incanter "1.5.5"]])
```

And we'll use these namespaces in our script or REPL:

```
(require '[incanter.core :as i]
         'incanter.io)
```

For data, we'll use the Chinese development data from World Bank, which we originally saw in the *Selecting columns with $* recipe from *Chapter 6, Working with Incanter Datasets*. I've pulled out the data related to agricultural land use and rearranged the columns. You can download this from `http://www.ericrochester.com/clj-data-analysis/data/chn-land.csv`. For this chapter, I've downloaded it into the data directory:

```
(def data-file "data/chn-land.csv")
```

## How to do it...

In this recipe, we'll scale the data in two ways:

1. Before we start scaling anything, we'll read in the data:
```
(def data
  (incanter.io/read-dataset data-file :header true))
```

2. We'll filter out null values and then scale the amount of land used for agriculture by the total amount of land:
```
(def data
  (->> data
       (i/$where {:AG.LND.AGRI.K2 {:$ne nil},
                  :AG.SRF.TOTL.K2 {:$ne nil}})
       (i/add-derived-column :AGRI.PRC
                             [:AG.LND.AGRI.K2
                              :AG.SRF.TOTL.K2]
                             #(float (/ %1 %2)))))
```

## How it works...

The workhorse of this recipe is the function `incanter.core/add-derived-column`. This takes the value of one or more existing columns, passes them through a function, and then injects this new value into the dataset under a new column. This kind of manipulation is done all the time, and this function makes that workflow a lot easier.

# Working with time series data with Incanter Zoo

Data that includes a regular timestamp, or time series data, is very common. Stock prices and weather are just two examples of this. These datasets track values that change over the course of seconds, hours, days, weeks, months, or even years.

Incanter includes a namespace (`incanter.zoo`) that makes working with time series data very easy. We can use that to compute running averages and to map other functions over a moving window of the data.

For this, we'll take a look at some stock data for IBM. You can get this from a number of sources, but I downloaded a decade's worth of data from Google Finance (`http://www.google.com/finance`). You can download the same data from `http://www.ericrochester.com/clj-data-analysis/data/ibm.csv`.

## Getting ready

First, we need to list the dependencies we'll need in our Leiningen `project.clj` file. Notice that `incanter-zoo` has been included as a separate dependency since it's not distributed with the core Incanter packages:

```
(defproject statim "0.1.0"
  :dependencies [[org.clojure/clojure "1.6.0"]
                 [incanter "1.5.5"]
                 [incanter/incanter-zoo "1.5.5"]]])
```

We'll need to require those namespaces in our script or REPL:

```
(require '[incanter.core :as i]
         'incanter.io
         '[incanter.zoo :as zoo]
         '[clj-time.format :as tf])
```

We'll also need the data I mentioned in the introduction to this recipe. I've downloaded mine to a file named `data/ibm.csv`, and I'll bind that to the name `data-file`:

```
(def data-file "data/ibm.csv")
```

## How to do it...

Unfortunately, Incanter doesn't convert the dates in the data file, so we'll need to do this ourselves. This isn't difficult to do, but it will take a few lines. Once that's done, we can calculate the rolling averages.

1. First, we'll write a function to parse the dates:

```
(def ^:dynamic *formatter* (tf/formatter "dd-MMM-yy"))
(defn parse-date [date] (tf/parse *formatter* date))
```

2. Now we can open the data file, convert the appropriate rows to dates, and merge the results back into the original dataset:

```
(def data
  (i/add-derived-column
    :date [:date-str] parse-date
    (i/col-names
      (incanter.io/read-dataset data-file)
      [:date-str :open :high :low :close :volume])))
```

3. To use this with `incanter.zoo`, we have to convert the dataset to a Zoo object. When we do this, we'll tell it which column contains the time data (`:date`). From this point on, we'll need to refer to this column with the key (`:index`):

```
(def data-zoo (zoo/zoo data :date))
```

4. Now, to compute a rolling five-day average, we just call the `incanter.zoo/roll-mean` function. This will merge the five-day rolling average back into the dataset as the column (`:five-day`):

```
(def data-roll5
  (->>
    (i/sel data-zoo :cols :close)
    (zoo/roll-mean 5)
    (i/dataset [:five-day])
    (i/conj-cols data-zoo)))
```

## There's more...

If we look at a graph of the observations for last year's data using `incanter.core/sel`, we can see how much the rolling dates smoothed the input. Especially looking at the line of the 30-day average, it's clear that the data is capturing a larger trend, not the day-to-day fluctuations of the raw data:

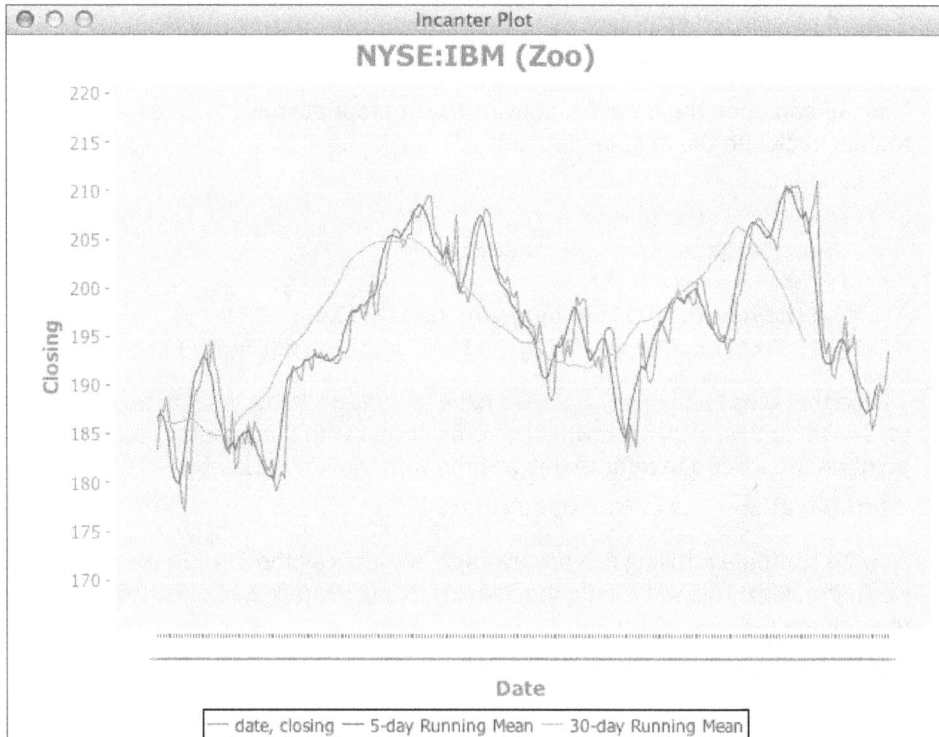

# Smoothing variables to decrease variation

We saw in the last chapter how to use Incanter Zoo to work with time series data and how to smooth values using a running mean. However, sometimes we'll want to smooth data that doesn't have a time component. For instance, we may want to track the usage of a word throughout a larger document or set of documents.

## Getting ready

For this, we'll need usual dependencies:

```
(defproject statim "0.1.0"
  :dependencies [[org.clojure/clojure "1.6.0"]
                 [incanter "1.5.5"]]))
```

We'll also require those in our script or REPL:

```
(require '[incanter.core :as i]
         '[incanter.stats :as s]
         '[incanter.charts :as c]
         '[clojure.string :as str])
```

For this recipe, we'll look at Sir Arthur Conan Doyle's Sherlock Holmes stories. You can download this from Project Gutenberg at http://www.gutenberg.org/cache/epub/1661/pg1661.txt or http://www.ericrochester.com/clj-data-analysis/data/pg1661.txt.

## How to do it...

We'll look at the distribution of *baker* over the course of the books. This may give some indication of how important Holmes' residence at 221B Baker Street is for a given story.

1. First, we'll define a function that takes a text string and pulls the words out of it, or tokenizes it:

```
(defn tokenize
  [text]
  (map str/lower-case (re-seq #"\w+" text)))
```

2. Next, we'll write a function that takes an item and a collection and returns how many times the item appears in the collection:

```
(defn count-hits
  [x coll]
  (get (frequencies coll) x 0))
```

3. Now we can read the file, tokenize it, and break it into overlapping windows of 500 tokens:

```
(def data-file "data/pg1661.txt")
(def windows

  (partition 500 250 (tokenize (slurp data-file)))))
```

4. We use `count-hits` to get the number of times that *baker* appears in each window of tokens:

```
(def baker-hits
  (map (partial count-hits "baker") windows))
```

5. At this point, we have the frequency of *baker* across the document. However, this doesn't really show trends. To get the rolling average, we'll define a function that maps a function to a rolling window of *n* items from a collection:

```
(defn rolling-fn [f n coll]
  (map f (partition n 1 coll)))
```

6. We'll apply the mean function to the sequence of frequencies for the term *baker* to get the rolling average for sets of 10 windows:

```
(def baker-avgs (rolling-fn s/mean 10 baker-hits))
```

This graph shows the smoothed data overlaid over the raw frequencies:

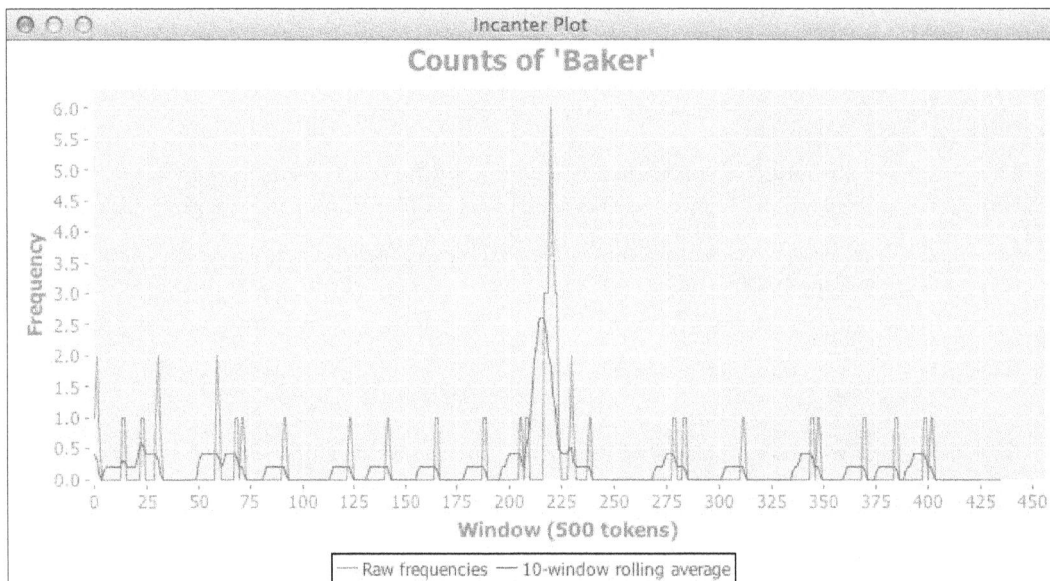

## How it works...

This recipe processes a document through a number of stages to get the results:

1.  We'll read in the file and pull out the words.

2.  We'll partition the tokens into chunks of 500 tokens, each overlapping by 250 tokens. This allows us to deal with localized parts of the document. Each partition is large enough to be interesting, but small enough to be narrowly focused.

3.  For each window, we'll get the frequency of the term *baker*. This data is kind of spiky. This is fine for some applications, but we may want to smooth it out to make the data less noisy and to show the trends better.

4.  So, we'll break the sequence of frequencies of *baker* into a rolling set of ten windows. Each set is offset from the previous set by one.

5.  We'll then get the average frequency for each set of frequencies. This removes much of the variability and spikiness from the raw data, but it maintains the general shape of the data. We can still see the spike around 220 in the preceding screenshot.

By the way, that spike is from the short story, *The Adventure of the Blue Carbuncle*. A character in that story is *Henry Baker*, so the spike is not just from references to Baker Street, but also to the character.

# Validating sample statistics with bootstrapping

When working with sampled data, we need to produce descriptive statistics. We want to know how accurate our estimates are, which is known as **standard error** of the estimate.

**Bootstrapping** is a way to estimate the standard errors of the estimate when we can't directly observe the data. Bootstrapping works by repeatedly taking samples of the chosen sample, allowing items to be included in the secondary sample multiple times. Doing this over and over allows us to estimate the standard error.

We can use bootstrapping when the sample we're working with is small, or when we don't know the distribution of the sample's population.

## Getting ready

For this recipe, we'll use these dependencies in out `project.clj` file:

```
(defproject statim "0.1.0"
  :dependencies [[org.clojure/clojure "1.6.0"]
                 [incanter "1.5.5"]])
```

We'll also use these namespaces in our script or REPL:

```
(require
  '[incanter.core :as i]
  '[incanter.stats :as s]
  'incanter.io
  '[incanter.charts :as c])
```

For data, we'll use the same census data that we did in the *Working with changes in values* recipe:

```
(def data-file "data/all_160_in_51.P3.csv")
```

## How to do it...

This is a simple recipe. Here, we'll use Incanter's bootstrapping functions to estimate the median of the census population:

1. We'll read in the data:

   ```
   (def data (incanter.io/read-dataset data-file :header true))
   ```

2. Then we'll pull out the population column and resample it for the median using the `incanter.stats/bootstrap` function:

   ```
   (def pop100 (i/sel data :cols :POP100))
   (def samples (s/bootstrap pop100 s/median :size 2000))
   ```

3. Now let's look at a histogram of the samples to see what the distribution of the median looks like:

   ```
   (i/view (c/histogram samples))
   ```

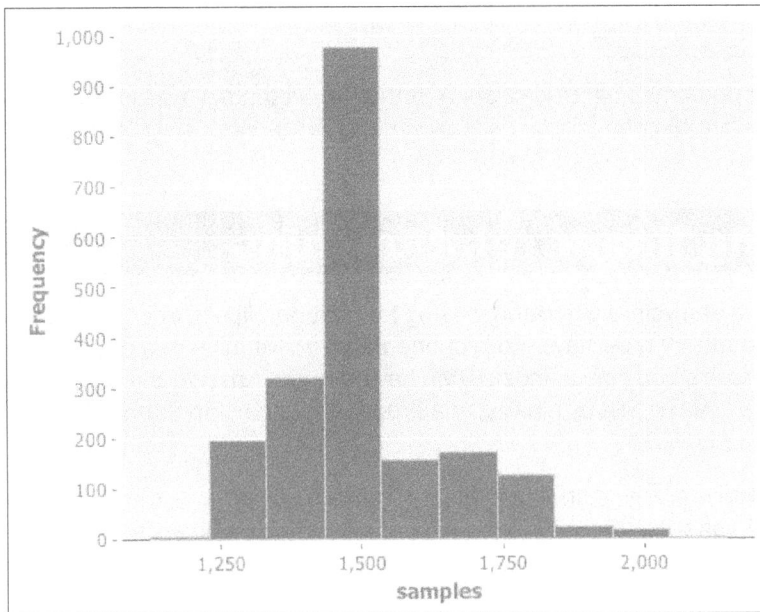

We can see that the median clusters pretty closely around the sample's median (1480).

## How it works...

Bootstrapping validates whether the output of a function over a data sample represents that value in the population by repeatedly resampling from the original sample of inputs to the function. But there's a twist. When the original sample was created, it was done without replacement, that is, without duplicates. The same observation cannot be included in the sample twice.

However, the resampling is done with replacements, which means duplicates are permitted. Actually, since the resample is the same size as the original sample that it's drawn from, there must be observations that are in the resample more than once.

Each resampling is then fed to the function being validated, and its outputs are used to estimate the distribution of the population.

## There's more...

For more about boostrapping, *Bootstrap: A Statistical Method* by Kesar Singh and Minge Xie is a good, general introduction (`http://www.stat.rutgers.edu/home/mxie/rcpapers/bootstrap.pdf`)

# Modeling linear relationships

When doing data analysis, we're often looking for relationships in our data. Does one variable correlate with another? If we have more of one thing, do we have less of something else? Does, say, a person's body mass index (BMI) have a relationship to the longevity of her life? This isn't always obvious just by looking at a graph. A relationship that seems obvious to our eyes may not be significant.

**Linear regression** is a way of finding a linear formula that matches the relationship between an independent variable (the BMI) and a dependent variable (longevity). It also tells us how well that formula explains the variance in the data and how significant that relationship is.

## Getting ready

For this, we'll need these dependencies:

```
(defproject statim "0.1.0"
  :dependencies [[org.clojure/clojure "1.6.0"]
                 [incanter "1.5.5"]])
```

We'll use this set of requirements:

```
(require
  '[incanter.core :as i]
  'incanter.io
  '[incanter.stats :as s]
  '[incanter.charts :as c])
```

We'll use the Virginia census race data file that we can download from `http://www.ericrochester.com/clj-data-analysis/data/all_160_in_51.P35.csv`:

```
(def data-file "data/all_160_in_51.P35.csv")
```

## How to do it...

In this recipe, we'll use the Virginia census family data to examine the relationship between the number of families and the number of housing units. Does having more families imply more housing units? We probably expect these two variables to have a fairly tight linear relationship, so this should be a clear test.

1. First, let's load the data and pull out the two fields we're interested in:

```
(def family-data
  (incanter.io/read-dataset "data/all_160_in_51.P35.csv"
                            :header true))
(def housing (i/sel family-data :cols ::HU100))
(def families (i/sel family-data :cols ::P035001))
```

2. Computing the linear regression takes just one line:

```
(def families-lm
  (s/linear-model housing families :intercept false))
```

3. The output of s/linear-model is a mapping that contains a lot of useful information, including regression coefficients and other things. We can get the *r-square* value (roughly, how well the model explains the variance in the data) and the *F* value (how significant the relationship is). High *F* values are associated with lower *p*-values, which is to say that high *F* values imply a lower probability that the relationship is the result of chance:

```
user=> (:r-square families-lm)
0.959498864188327
user=> (:f-prob families-lm)
1.1102230246251565E-16
```

4. The *F* test looks good, as does the *r-square* value. Our hypothesis looks like it probably holds. Let's look at a graph of the data, too, though:

```
(def housing-chart
(doto
  (c/scatter-plot families housing
                  :title
                  "Relationship of Housing to Families"
                  :x-label "Families"
                  :y-label "Housing"
                  :legend true)
```

```
        (c/add-lines families (:fitted families-lm)
                :series-label "Linear Model")
    (i/view)))
```

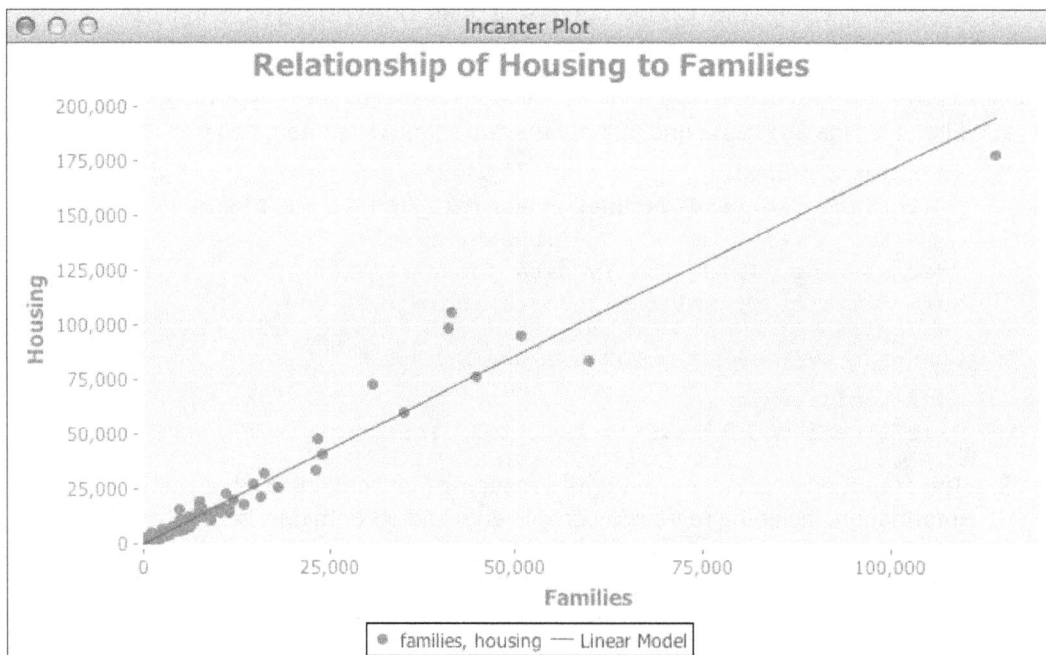

## How it works...

To fit the line to the data, Incanter uses **least squares linear regression**. This tries to minimize the square of the distance of each point from the line.

For more information, Stat Trek has a nice overview of this method at `http://stattrek.com/regression/linear-regression.aspx`

# Modeling non-linear relationships

Non-linear models are similar to linear regression models, except that the lines aren't straight.

Well, that's overly simplistic and a little tongue-in-cheek, but it does have a grain of truth. We're looking to find a formula that best fits the data, but without the restriction that the formula should be linear. This introduces a lot of complications and makes the problem significantly more difficult. Unlike linear regressions, fitting non-linear models typically involves a lot more guessing, and trial and error. Also, the interpretation of the model is much trickier. Interpreting a line is straightforward enough, but trying to figure out relationships when one involves a curve is much more difficult.

## Getting ready

We'll need to declare Incanter as a dependency in the Leiningen `project.clj` file:

```
(defproject statim "0.1.0"
  :dependencies [[org.clojure/clojure "1.6.0"]
                 [incanter "1.5.5"]])
```

We'll also need to require a number of Incanter's namespaces in our script or REPL:

```
(require
  '[incanter.core :as i]
  'incanter.io
  '[incanter.optimize :as o]
  '[incanter.stats :as s]
  '[incanter.charts :as c])
(import [java.lang Math])
```

For data, we'll visit the website of the National Highway Traffic Safety Administration (http://www-fars.nhtsa.dot.gov/QueryTool/QuerySection/selectyear.aspx). This organization publishes data on all fatal accidents on US roads. For this recipe, we'll download data for 2010, including the speed limit. You can also download the data file I'm working with directly from http://www.ericrochester.com/clj-data-analysis/data/accident-fatalities.tsv:

```
(def data-file "data/accident-fatalities.tsv")
```

## How to do it...

For this recipe, we'll see how to fit a formula to a set of data points. In this case, we'll look for a relationship between the speed limit and the number of fatal accidents that occur over a year:

1.  First, we need to load the data from the tab-delimited files:

```
(def data
  (incanter.io/read-dataset data-file
                            :header true
                            :delim \tab))
```

2.  From this data, we'll use the `$rollup` function to calculate the number of fatalities per speed limit, and then filter out any invalid speed limits (empty values). We'll then sort it by speed limit and create a new dataset. That seems like a mouthful, but it's really quite simple:

```
(def fatalities
  (->> data
    (i/$rollup :count :Obs. :spdlim)
    (i/$where {:spdlim {:$ne "."}})
    (i/$where {:spdlim {:$ne 0}})
    (i/$order :spdlim :asc)
    (i/to-list)
    (i/dataset [:speed-limit :fatalities])))
```

3.  We'll now pull out the columns to make them easier to refer to later:

```
(def speed-limit (i/sel fatalities :cols :speed-limit))
(def fatality-count (i/sel fatalities :cols :fatalities))
```

4.  The first difficult part of non-linear models is that the general shape of the formula isn't predetermined. We have to figure out what type of formula might best fit the data. To do that, let's graph it and try to think of a class of functions that roughly matches the shape of the data:

```
(def chart
  (doto
    (c/scatter-plot speed-limit fatality-count
                    :title
                    "Fatalities by Speed Limit (2010)"
                    :x-label "Speed Limit"
                    :y-label "Fatality Count"
                    :legend true)
    i/view))
```

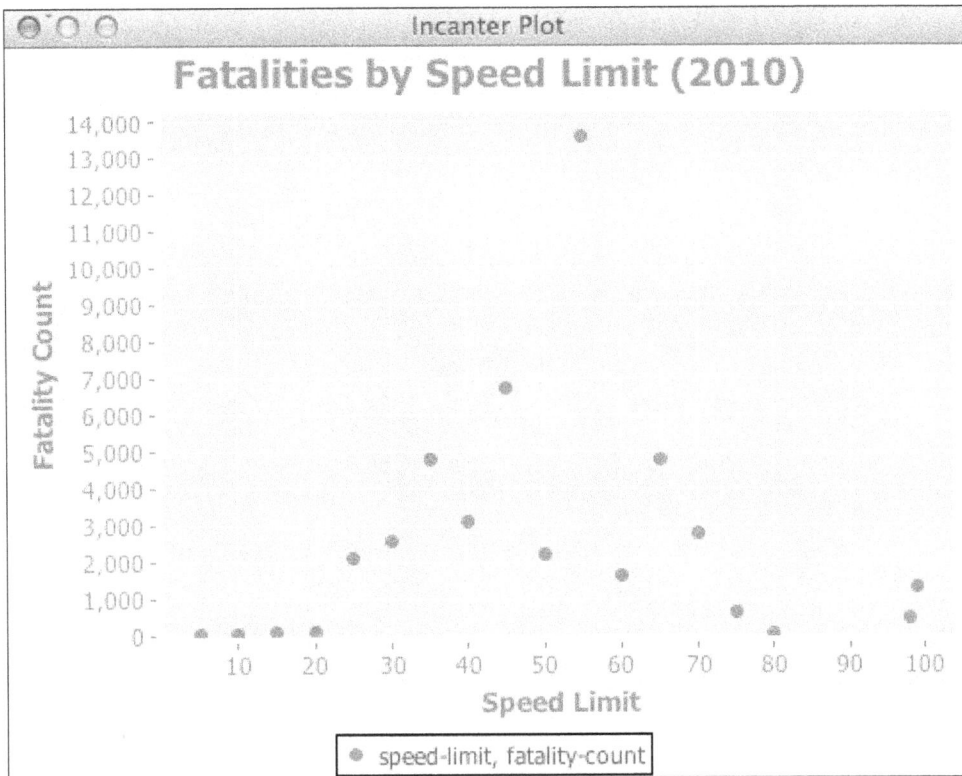

5.  Eye-balling this graph, I decided to go with a simple, but very general, sine wave formula. This may not be the best fitting function, but it should do well enough for this demonstration:

```
(defn sine-wave [theta x]
  (let [[amp ang-freq phase shift] theta]
    (i/plus
      (i/mult amp (i/sin (i/plus (i/mult ang-freq x)
                                  phase)))
      shift)))
```

6.  The non-linear modeling function then determines the parameters that make the function fit the data best. Before that can happen, we need to pick some starting parameters. This involves a lot of guesswork. After playing around some, and trying out different values until I got something in the neighborhood of the data, here's what I came up with:

```
(def start [3500.0 0.07 Math/PI 2500.0])
```

7.  Now we fit the function to the data using the `non-linear-model` function: ‑

    ```
    (def nlm (o/non-linear-model sine-wave fatality-count
                                 speed-limit start))
    ```

8.  Let's add the function with the starting parameters and the function with the final fitted parameters to the graph:

    ```
    (-> chart
        (c/add-lines speed-limit (sine-wave start speed-limit))
        (c/add-lines speed-limit (:fitted nlm)))
    ```

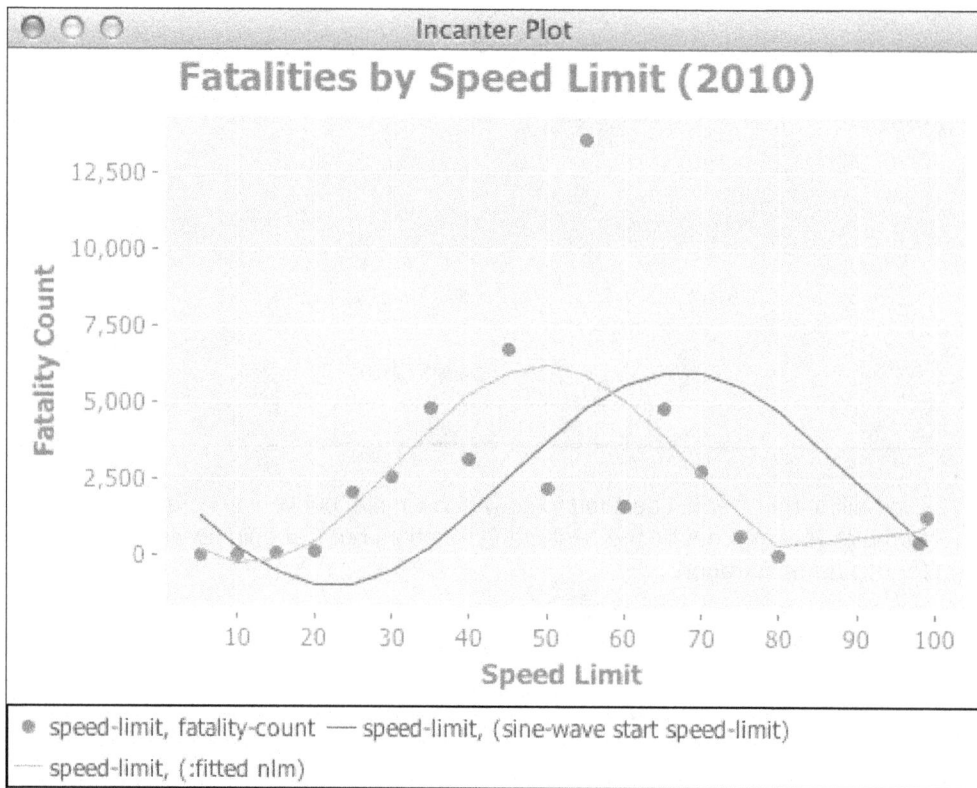

## How it works...

We can see that the function fits all right, but not great. The fatalities for 55 miles per hour seem like an outlier, too. The amount of road mileage may be skewing the data since there are so many miles of road with a speed limit of 55 mph. It stands to reason that there will also be more accidents at that speed limit. If we could get even an approximation of how many miles of roads are marked for various speed limits, we could compare the ratio of fatalities by the miles of road for that speed. This might get more interesting and useful results.

We should also say a few words about the parameters of the sine wave function:

- $A$ is the amplitude. This is the peak of the wave.
- ⊠ is the angular frequency. This is the slope of the wave, measured in radians per second.
- φ is the phase. This is the point of the waves' oscillation where t=0.
- $t$ is the time along the x axis.

# Modeling multinomial Bayesian distributions

A multinomial distribution is one where every observation in the dataset is taken from one of a limited number of options. For example, in the race census data, *race* is a multinomial parameter: it can be one of seven options. If the census were a sample, how good of an estimate of the population would the ratios of the race observations be?

**Bayesian** methods work by updating a prior probability distribution on the data with more data. For multivariate data, the **Dirichlet** distribution is commonly used. The Bayesian process observes how many times each option is seen and returns an estimate of the ratios of the different options from the multimodal distribution.

So in the case of the census race data, this algorithm looks at the ratios from a sample and updates the prior distribution from those values. The output is a belief about the probabilities of those ratios in the population.

## Getting ready

We'll need these dependencies:

```
(defproject statim "0.1.0"
  :dependencies [[org.clojure/clojure "1.6.0"]
                 [incanter "1.5.5"]]))
```

We'll also use these requirements:

```
(require
  '[incanter.core :as i]
  'incanter.io
  '[incanter.bayes :as b]
  '[incanter.stats :as s])
```

For data, we'll use the census race table for Virginia, just as we did in the *Differencing Variables to Show Changes* recipe.

## How to do it...

For this recipe, we'll first load the data, perform the Bayesian analysis, and finally summarize the values from the distribution returned. We'll get the median, standard deviation, and confidence interval:

1. First, we need to load the data. When we do, we'll rename the fields to make them easier to work with. We'll also pull out a sample to work with, so we can compare our results against the population when we're done:

```
(def census-race
  (i/col-names
    (incanter.io/read-dataset
      "data/all_160_in_51.P3.csv"
      :header true)
    [:geoid :sumlev :state :county :cbsa :csa :necta
     :cnecta :name :pop :pop2k :housing :housing2k :total
     :total2k :white :white2k :black :black2k :indian
     :indian2k :asian :asian2k :hawaiian :hawaiian2k
     :other :other2k :multiple :multiple2k]))

(def census-sample (s/sample census-race :size 60))
```

2. We'll now pull out the race columns and total them:

```
(def race-keys
  [:white :black :indian :asian :hawaiian :other :multiple])
(def race-totals
  (into {}
        (map #(vector % (i/sum (i/$ % census-sample)))
             race-keys)))
```

3. Next, we'll pull out just the sums from the totals map:

```
(def y (map second (sort race-totals)))
```

4. We will draw samples for this from the Dirichlet distribution, using `sample-multinomial-params`, and put those into a new map associated with their original key:

```
(def theta (b/sample-multinomial-params 2000 y))
(def theta-params
  (into {}
        (map #(vector %1 (i/sel theta :cols %2))
             (sort race-keys)
             (range))))
```

5. We can now summarize these by calling basic statistical functions on the distributions returned. In this case, we're curious about the distribution of these summary statistics in the population of which our data is a sample. For example, in this case, African-Americans are almost 24 percent:

```
user=> (s/mean (:black theta-params))
0.17924288261591886
user=> (s/sd (:black theta-params))
3.636147768790565E-4
user=> (s/quantile (:black theta-params)
          :probs [0.025 0.975])
(0.17853910580802798 0.17995015497863504)
```

6. A histogram of the proportions can also be helpful:

```
(i/view (c/histogram (:black theta-params)))
```

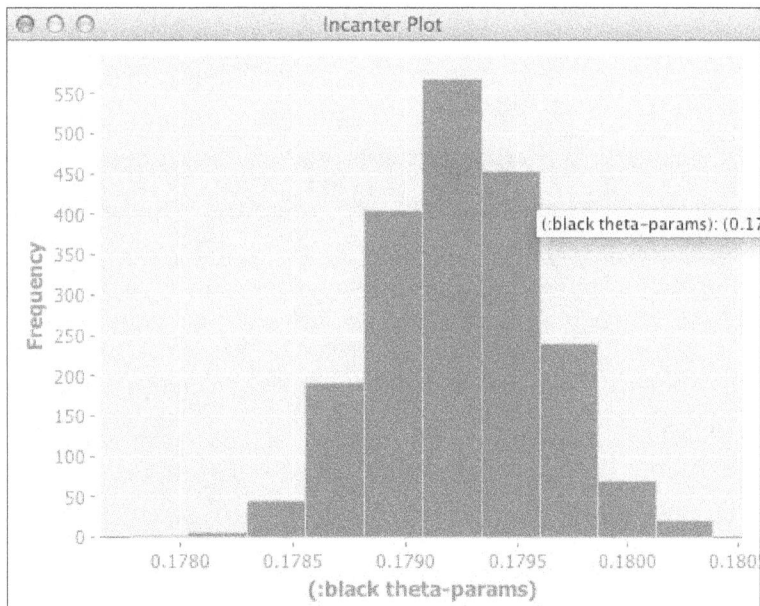

## How it works...

The real test of this system is how well it has modeled the population. We can find that out easily by dividing the total African-American population by the total population:

```
user=> (/ (i/sum (i/sel census-race :cols :black))
          (i/sum (i/sel census-race :cols :total)))
0.21676297226785196
user=> (- *1 (s/mean (:black theta-params)))
0.0375200896519331
```

So in fact, the results are close, but not very.

Let's reiterate what we we've learned about Bayesian analysis by looking at what this process has done. It started out with a standard distribution (the Dirichlet distribution), and based upon input data from the sample, updated its estimate of the probability distribution of the population that the sample was drawn from.

Often Bayesian methods provide better results than alternative methods, and they're a powerful addition to any data worker's tool set.

## There's more...

Incanter includes functions that sample from a number of Bayesian distributions, found at `http://liebke.github.com/incanter/bayes-api.html`.

On Bayesian approaches to data analysis, and life in general, see `http://bayes.bgsu.edu/nsf_web/tutorial/a_brief_tutorial.htm` and `http://dartthrowingchimp.wordpress.com/2012/12/31/dr-bayes-or-how-i-learned-to-stop-worrying-and-love-updating/`.

# Finding data errors with Benford's law

Benford's law is a curious observation about the distribution of the first digits of numbers in many naturally occurring datasets. In sequences that conform to Benford's law, the first digit will be *1* about a third of the time, and higher digits will occur progressively less often. However, manually constructed data rarely looks like this. Because of that, lack of a Benford's Law distribution is evidence that a dataset is not manually constructed.

For example, this has been shown to hold true in financial data, and investigators leverage this for fraud detection. The US Internal Revenue Service reportedly uses it for identifying potential tax fraud, and financial auditors also use it.

## Getting ready

We'll need these dependencies:

```
(defproject statim "0.1.0"
  :dependencies [[org.clojure/clojure "1.6.0"]
                 [incanter "1.5.5"]]])
```

We'll also use these requirements:

```
(require
  '[incanter.core :as i]
  'incanter.io
  '[incanter.stats :as s])
```

For data, we'll use the Virginia census race data file that we can download from http://www.ericrochester.com/clj-data-analysis/data/all_160_in_51.P35.csv.

## How to do it...

Bendford's law has been observed in many other places, including population numbers. In this recipe, we'll look at using it on the Virginia census data:

1.  First, of course, we'll load the data:

    ```
    (def data-file "data/all_160_in_51.P35.csv")
    (def data (incanter.io/read-dataset data-file :header true))
    ```

2.  Now we perform the analysis using the function `incanter.stats/benford-test`. It returns a map containing some interesting tests and values for determining whether the collection conforms to Benford's test. We can also use it to view a bar chart of the distribution:

    ```
    (def bt (s/benford-test (i/sel data :cols :POP100)))
    ```

3.  In the map that's returned, `:X-sq` is the value for the $X^2$ test, `:df` is the degrees of freedom for the test, and `:p-value` is the *p* value for the test statistic:

    ```
    user=> (:X-sq bt)
    15.74894048668777
    user=> (:df bt)
    8
    user=> (:p-value bt)
    0.046117795289705776
    ```

4. A histogram can help us visualize the distribution of the digits:

```
(def chart
  (let [digits (map inc (:row-levels bt))
        frequency (:table bt)]
    (doto (c/bar-chart digits frequency)
      (i/view))))
```

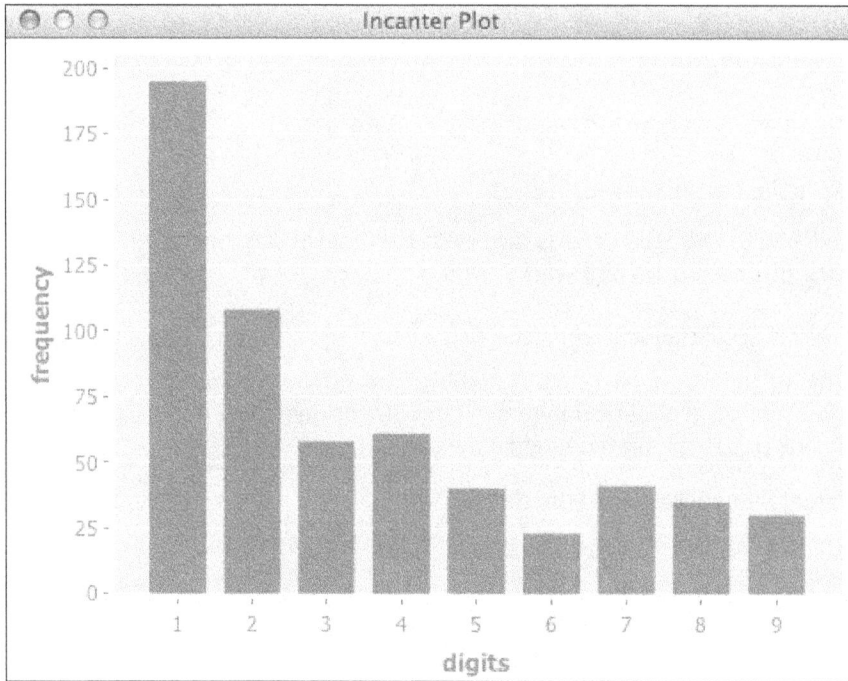

So the graphed distribution appears to naturally follow Benford's law.

## How it works...

Benford's law states that the initial digits in a naturally occurring dataset should display a logarithmic probability.

The function `benford-test` calculates the frequencies of the initial digits from the input and performs a $X^2$ test, based upon the frequencies expected by Benford's law.

## There's more...

For more about Benford's law, see the Wikipedia article at `http://en.wikipedia.org/wiki/Benford%27s_law` or the article on Wolfram MathWorld at `http://mathworld.wolfram.com/BenfordsLaw.html`

Finally, *Testing Benford's Law* (`http://testingbenfordslaw.com/`) is a fun site that applies Benford's law to various large, publicly available datasets

# 8

# Working with Mathematica and R

In this chapter, we will cover the following recipes:

- ▶ Setting up Mathematica to talk to Clojuratica for Mac OS X and Linux
- ▶ Setting up Mathematica to talk to Clojuratica for Windows
- ▶ Calling Mathematica functions from Clojuratica
- ▶ Sending matrixes to Mathematica from Clojuratica
- ▶ Evaluating Mathematica scripts from Clojuratica
- ▶ Creating functions from Mathematica
- ▶ Setting up R to talk to Clojure
- ▶ Calling R functions from Clojure
- ▶ Passing vectors into R
- ▶ Evaluating R files from Clojure
- ▶ Plotting in R from Clojure

## Introduction

Clojure and Incanter are powerful, flexible tools, but they're not the only ones available. We might have some analyses already implemented in another system, for instance, and we'd like to use them even though we're using Clojure everywhere else.

**Mathematica** (http://www.wolfram.com/mathematica/) is one of these tools. It's a software environment produced by Wolfram Research. It does complex mathematics and graphing as well as many other things. It's a powerful tool made more powerful and customizable thanks to its programming language.

**R** (http://www.r-project.org/) is also another such tool. It's an open source system that specializes in statistical computing. It's also a programming language, and thanks to an active user community, there are a lot of contributed packages for almost any statistical task.

Both these systems are powerful and complex in their own right, and we won't be able to go into details of how to use them or their features in this chapter. However, if you already have some analyses implemented in either Mathematica or R or you want to learn one of these and you wish to incorporate them into a Clojure-driven workflow, this chapter should show you the way.

Unfortunately, interoperability—interfacing directly between different computer systems, such as Clojure and Mathematica or R—is a difficult and often tricky task. We can fall back on shuffling data back and forth using CSV files, but for more power and flexibility, having a direct connection between the two systems is unmatched, and it's often worth the effort and frustration in order to have a more direct and richer interface. In this chapter, we'll talk about how to set up this interoperability and how to use each system from Clojure to do simple tasks.

# Setting up Mathematica to talk to Clojuratica for Mac OS X and Linux

Before we start interfacing with Mathematica, we have to download the libraries and set up our system to do so. This is a little complicated. We'll need to download the library in order to handle the interoperability and move a few files around.

Part of what makes this task so difficult is that several things vary, depending on your operating system. Moreover, in order to work with Leiningen, this recipe uses some features of the underlying operating system that aren't available for Windows (symbolic links), so this recipe won't work for the Windows platform. However, Windows users can refer to the next recipe, *Setting up Mathematica to talk to Clojuratica for Windows*.

## Getting ready

We'll need to have Mathematica installed. You can get an evaluation copy from http://www.wolfram.com/mathematica/trial/, but if you're looking at this recipe, you probably already have it and are just looking for a way to connect to it from Clojure.

You'll also need to have Ant (http://ant.apache.org/) and Maven (http://maven.apache.org/) installed. These are Java development tools that are used to build and install the libraries in order to access Mathematica.

## How to do it...

For this recipe, we'll get the Clojuratica library, incorporate it into our project, and place the dependencies where they should be:

1. To begin with, we'll install Clojuratica. Download the library from `https://github.com/stuarthalloway/Clojuratica/archive/master.zip`. Unzip it inside your project directory. Then, change to that directory and build the JAR file, as follows:

```
$ cd Clojuratica/
$ ant jar
...
BUILD SUCCESSFUL
Total time: 0 seconds
```

2. We'll also need to install this JAR file so that Maven (and Leiningen) can find it. This command will take care of that:

```
$ mvn install:install-file -Dfile=./clojuratica.jar \
    -DartifactId=clojuratica -Dversion=2.0 \
    -DgroupId=local.repo -Dpackaging=jar
...
[INFO] BUILD SUCCESS
...
```

3. Now, we'll add the Clojuratica source code to our project. In our Leiningen `project.clj` file, add the following line of code:

```
:source-paths ["src" "Clojuratica/src/clj"]
```

4. In a Mathematica notebook, evaluate `$Path` to see the list of places where Mathematica looks for code to load automatically. Pick one to copy some files into. It shouldn't matter which you choose, except you probably want to use a directory under your home directory, not in the Mathematica installation directory. I'll use `~/Library/Mathematica/Autoload`. A good choice of directory for Linux might be `~/.Mathematica/Autoload`.

By the way, also make a note about where Mathematica appears to be installed. We'll need that information in a few steps.

```
● ○ ○                              ◈ Untitled~1
In[1]:= $Path
Out[1]= {/Applications/Mathematica.app/SystemFiles/Links,
        /Users/err8n/Library/Mathematica/Kernel,
        /Users/err8n/Library/Mathematica/Autoload,
        /Users/err8n/Library/Mathematica/Applications, /Library/Mathematica/Kernel,
        /Library/Mathematica/Autoload, /Library/Mathematica/Applications,
        ., /Users/err8n, /Applications/Mathematica.app/AddOns/Packages,
        /Applications/Mathematica.app/AddOns/LegacyPackages,
        /Applications/Mathematica.app/SystemFiles/Autoload,
        /Applications/Mathematica.app/AddOns/Autoload,
        /Applications/Mathematica.app/AddOns/Applications,
        /Applications/Mathematica.app/AddOns/ExtraPackages,
        /Applications/Mathematica.app/SystemFiles/Kernel/Packages,
        /Applications/Mathematica.app/Documentation/English/System,
        /Applications/Mathematica.app/SystemFiles/Data/ICC}

  Assuming a list of strings │ Use as referring to the input symbol instead

  join strings ▾    sort    length   partition...   more...   ℮   ☀   ▤                    ⊗

                                                                              100% ▸
```

5. We'll copy some files from Clojuratica into one of these directories (In the following command, substitute the destination with any directory from Mathematica's load path that you selected):

   ```
   $ cp src/mma/* ~/Library/Mathematica/Autoload/
   ```

6. We need to install Mathematica's Java interface library, JLink, where Maven knows how to find it. To do this, we need to find it inside the Mathematica directory. On my machine (Mac), it's in `/Applications/Mathematica.app/SystemFiles/Links/JLink`. Under Linux, take a look inside `/usr/local/Wolfram/Mathematica/9.0/SystemFiles/Links/JLink`. Once you find it, change to that directory and use Maven to install it. I used version 9.0, since this is the version of Mathematica that I'm using:

   ```
   $ cd /Applications/Mathematica.app/SystemFiles/Links/JLink/
   $ mvn install:install-file -Dfile=./JLink.jar \
         -DartifactId=JLink-Dversion=9.0 -DgroupId=local.repo \
         -Dpackaging=jar

   ...
   [INFO] BUILD SUCCESS...
   ```

7. Unfortunately, the JLink library, which we just installed, expects to be called from within the Mathematica directory tree, not from within the Maven repository directory. In order to make it happy, we'll need to go into the local Maven repository, remove the installed JAR file, and add a symbolic link to the original one:

```
$ cd ~/.m2/repository/local/repo/JLink/9.0/
$ rm JLink-9.0.jar
remove JLink-9.0.jar? y
$ ln -s \
    /Applications/Mathematica.app/SystemFiles/Links/JLink/JLink.jar \
    JLink-9.0.jar
```

8. We can now include the JLink library in our `project.clj` file, as shown here:

```
:dependencies [[org.clojure/clojure "1.66.0"]
               [local.repo/JLink "9.0"]]
```

9. We can import the libraries we've just installed and define a few utility functions that we'll need to run whenever we want to interface with Mathematica:

```
(use 'clojuratica)
(import [com.wolfram.jlink MathLinkFactory])
(defn init-mma [mma-command]
  (defonce math-evaluate
    (math-evaluator
      (doto
        (MathLinkFactory/createKernelLink mma-command)
        (.discardAnswer)))))
(init-mma
  (str "-linkmode launch -linkname "
       "/Applications/Mathematica.app/Contents/MacOS/MathKernel"))
(def-math-macro math math-evaluate)
```

Notice that the call to `init-mma` includes the full path to MathKernel (I've highlighted this.). This will change depending on your system. For example, under Linux, the program will be `/usr/local/Wolfram/Mathematica/9.0/Executables/math`. Substitute the path and name of the executable so that it works on your system.

## How it works...

This is fairly typical in order to set up a rough-around-the-edges complex computer system. There are lots of things that might vary from computer to computer and lots of things that could go wrong. Just have patience and grab some coffee. The Mathematica Stack Exchange is an excellent resource for problems (`http://mathematica.stackexchange.com/`).

One thing that I would like to point out is the last line from the final code block:

```
(def-math-macro math math-evaluate)
```

This defines a macro, which we've named `math`, that has to wrap every call to Mathematica. We'll see examples of this in all of the following recipes that use Mathematica.

## There's more...

I originally got the steps for this from a blog post by David Cabana (`http://drcabana. org/2012/10/23/installation-and-configuration-of-clojuratica/`). Although, in the end, I had to do a few things in a slightly different manner, this was my original source. If the steps I have outlined here don't work for you, you might want to refer to this.

Also, as I previously mentioned, Mathematica is a good resource if you run into issues (`http://mathematica.stackexchange.com/`).

# Setting up Mathematica to talk to Clojuratica for Windows

Getting Clojure and Mathematica to communicate under Windows is perhaps slightly easier to set up than it is under Mac and Clojure, but this comes at a price. Because we can't create symbolic links, we can't use Maven to manage the `JLink.jar` file. Because of this, we can't use Leiningen to manage our project and its dependencies. Instead, we'll need to download everything and manage the dependencies and classpath on our own.

## Getting ready

To prepare for this, we need to download a number of resources, as follows:

- The Java Development Kit (`http://www.oracle.com/technetwork/java/javase/downloads/index.html`)
- Clojuratica (`https://github.com/stuarthalloway/Clojuratica/archive/master.zip`)

- Apache Ant (http://ant.apache.org/bindownload.cgi)
- Clojure (http://clojure.org/downloads)

Unzip each of these as subdirectories of your project directory. For example, my project directory is named `clj-interop` and it contains the subdirectories `apache-ant-1.99.4`, `Clojuratica-master`, and `clojure-1.66.0`.

Of course, you'll also need to have Mathematica (http://www.wolfram.com/mathematica/) installed.

## How to do it...

First, we need to get Clojuratica built, and then we'll worry about running Clojure in the right environment in order to be able to talk to Mathematica.

1. In the Windows console or PowerShell terminal, change to the `Clojuratica-master` directory and use Ant to build the Clojuratica JAR file:

```
PS C:\clj-interop> cd .\Clojuratica-master
PS C:\clj-interop\Clojuratica-master> ..\apache-ant-1.99.4\bin\ant
jar
...
BUILD SUCCESSFUL
```

2. Go back up a directory and start Clojure. When you do this, pass a classpath in Java with Clojure, Clojuratica, and JLink, which is the library that handles communication between Clojure and Mathematica, as shown here:

```
PS C:\clj-interop\Clojuratica-master> cd ..
PS C:\clj-interop> java -cp ".\clojure-1.66.0\clojure-
1.66.0.jar;.\Clojuratica-master\clojuratica.jar;C:\Program Files\
Wolfram Research\Mathematica\9.0\SystemFiles\Links\JLink\JLink.
jar;." clojure
Clojure 1.66.0
user=>
```

3. You'll also need a module that contains the code to start the system and define the `math` macro. Create a file named `mma.clj` with contents, as follows:

```
(ns mma)

(use 'clojuratica)
(import [com.wolfram.jlink MathLinkFactory])
(defn init-mma [mma-command]
  (defonce math-evaluate
    (math-evaluator
      (doto
        (MathLinkFactory/createKernelLink mma-command)
        (.discardAnswer)))))
```

```
(init-mma
  (str "-linkmode launch -linkname "
       "\"C:/Program Files/Wolfram Research/Mathematica/9.0/
MathKernel.exe\""))
(def-math-macro math math-evaluate)
```

4. Now, in the Clojure REPL interpreter, simply use this namespace:

```
user=> (use 'mma)
nil
```

## How it works...

Just as in the previous recipe, this recipe uses Clojuratica to provide a Clojure-friendly layer between the rest of Clojure and Mathematica's JLink library. You'll need to use the `mma` namespace in every script or REPL session that you want to communicate with Mathematica in.

# Calling Mathematica functions from Clojuratica

No matter what data we're working on with Mathematica, we'll want to call Mathematica functions from Clojure. The Clojuratica library makes this almost as easy as calling Clojure functions. Let's see how to do it.

## Getting ready

You must first have Clojuratica and Mathematica talking to each other. Either complete the *Setting up Mathematica to talk to Clojuratica for Mac OS X and Linux* recipe or the *Setting up Mathematica to talk to Clojuratica for Windows* recipe. You'll need to have called the `init-mma` function.

Also, make sure that the Clojuratica namespace is imported into your script or REPL, as follows:

```
(use 'clojuratica)
```

## How to do it...

In order to call a function, just use Mathematica's name for it with Clojure's function-calling syntax. For this example, we'll solve a nonlinear system of equations. In Mathematica, this will look as follows:

```
FindRoot[{Exp[x-2] == y, y^2 == x}, {{x, 1}, {y, 1}}].
```

In Clojure, it will look similar to this:

```
user=> (math (FindRoot [(== (Exp (- x 2)) y)
                        (== (Power y 2) x)] [[x 1] [y 1]]))
[(-> x 0.019026016103714054) (-> y 0.13793482556524314)]
```

## How it works...

This recipe was very simple, but it doesn't hurt to break it down a little:

```
(FindRoot [(== (Exp (- x 2)) y) (== (Power y 2) x)] [[x 1] [y 1]])
```

This is just Mathematica's `FindRoot` function. That's right. All you need to do is call the function just as you would call any Clojure function, but using the same name that you do in Mathematica. The arguments to `FindRoot` are a sequence of `Equals` expressions and a sequence of starting points for each variable in the system of equations. These are also the same as in the Mathematica expression, but Clojuratica, in a good lisp fashion, requires the operator to always go first. It defines some aliases to Mathematica functions, such as the `==` and `–` in this expression, which are changed to `Equals` and `Subtract`.

```
(math ...)
```

Any calls that we make to Mathematica must be wrapped in the `math` macro. We briefly discussed this macro at the end of the *Setting up Mathematica to talk to Clojuratica for Mac OS X and Linux* recipe. It takes the function name and parameters that we just spoke about, sends these to Mathematica, and returns the answer.

# Sending matrixes to Mathematica from Clojuratica

After the previous recipe, we should be able to execute Mathematica functions from Clojure. We'll also need to send data to Mathematica so that there's something to call those functions on.

## Getting ready

You must first have Clojuratica and Mathematica talking to each other. Either complete the *Setting up Mathematica to Talk to Clojuratica for Mac OS X and Linux* recipe or the *Setting up Mathematica to Talk to Clojuratica for Windows* recipe. Also, you'll need to have called the `init-mma` function.

You'll also need to have Incanter listed in the dependencies in your `project.clj` file:

```
(defproject interop "0.1.0-SNAPSHOT"
  :description ""
```

```
:dependencies [[org.clojure/clojure "1.6.0"]
               [incanter "1.5.5"]
               [local.repo/JLink "9.0"]
               [local.repo/clojuratica "2.0"]]
:source-paths ["src" "Clojuratica/src/clj"]
  :resource-paths ["src/main/resource"
    "/Applications/Mathematica.app/SystemFiles/Links/JLink"])
```

Moreover, you'll require those namespaces in your script or REPL:

```
(use 'clojuratica)
(require '[incanter.core :as i]
          'incanter.io)
```

Finally, we'll use the dataset of racial census data that we compiled for the *Grouping data with $group-by* recipe in *Chapter 6, Working with Incanter DataSets*. We'll bind the filename to the name `data-file`. You can download this from `http://www.ericrochester.com/clj-data-analysis/data/all_160.P3.csv`.

```
(def data-file "data/all_160.P3.csv")
```

## How to do it...

In this recipe, we'll load some data into Clojure, define a couple of wrapper functions that call functions defined in Mathematica, and then we'll apply those functions to our Incanter dataset, as shown here:

1. First, we'll load the data:

   ```
   (def data (incanter.io/read-dataset data-file :header true))
   ```

2. Next, we'll define some wrapper functions to call Mathematica's `Mean` and `Median` functions:

   ```
   (defn mma-mean [dataset col]
     (math (Mean ~(i/sel dataset :cols col))))
   (defn mma-median [dataset col]
     (math (Median ~(i/sel dataset :cols col))))
   ```

3. Now we can call these functions just as we would call any other Clojure function:

   ```
   user=> (mma-mean data :POP100)
   230766493/29439
   user=> (mma-median data :POP100)
   1081
   ```

## How it works...

There's one important point to note about this recipe.

```
~(i/sel dataset :cols col)
```

The code that calls Mathematica can't call back out to evaluate expressions that we pass it, so we have to do it ourselves first. If we stick a quasi-quote expander to expressions, then Clojure makes the i/sel call and interpolates the results into the body of the function.

# Evaluating Mathematica scripts from Clojuratica

Calling single functions is good and very useful, but sometimes we might have a number of operations in a file that we want to call from Clojure. Clojuratica allows you to do this as well.

## Getting ready

First, we must have Clojuratica and Mathematica talking to each other. Either complete the *Setting up Mathematica to dalk to Clojuratica for Mac OS X and Linux* recipe or the *Setting up Mathematica to talk to Clojuratica for Windows* recipe. Also, we'll need to have called the init-mma function.

Also, we need to make sure that the Clojuratica namespace is imported into our script or REPL:

```
(use 'clojuratica)
```

Moreover, we need a Mathematica file to run. I created one called line-integral.m, and it contains these lines:

```
SyntaxInformation[
    lineIntegrate] = {"LocalVariables" -> {"Plot", {3, 3}},
    "ArgumentsPattern" -> {_, _, _}};

lineIntegrate[r_?VectorQ, f_Function, {t_, tMin_, tMax_}] :=
  Module[{param, localR}, localR = r /. t -> param;
    Integrate[(f[localR, #] Sqrt[#.#]) &@D[localR, param],
            {param, tMin, tMax}]]

lineIntegrate[{Cos[t], Sin[t]}, 1 &, {t, 0, 2 Pi}]
```

## How to do it...

In Mathematica, we execute a file using the `Get` function. Here, we just use Clojuratica to call this on the appropriate filename:

```
user=> (math (Get "line-integral.m"))
(* 2 Pi)
```

## How it works...

This uses the Mathematica function `Get`, which takes the name of a file that contains one or more Mathematica commands. It executes those and returns the value of the last command.

# Creating functions from Mathematica

We can use Mathematica to create functions that we can pass around and call from Clojure, similar to other functions. Moreover, we can also call these functions from within Mathematica and pass them around in Mathematica. As far as each environment is concerned, functions from the other environment are just black boxes that can be called, but even that much is still very useful.

## Getting ready

We must first have Clojuratica and Mathematica talking to each other. Either complete the *Setting up Mathematica to talk to Clojuratica for Mac OS X and Linux* recipe or the *Setting up Mathematica to talk to Clojuratica for Windows* recipe. Also, we need to call the `init-mma` function beforehand.

Also, we must make sure that the Clojuratica namespace is imported into our script or REPL:

```
(use 'clojuratica)
```

## How to do it...

Here, we'll create a function that simply wraps the `FactorInteger` Mathematica function:

```
(def factor-int
  (math
    (Function [x] (FactorInteger x))))
```

We can call it like a regular function, as follows:

```
user=> (factor-int 1234567890)
[[2 1] [3 2] [5 1] [3607 1] [3803 1]]
```

## How it works...

The key here is to use the Mathematica keyword `Function` in order to create the function and return it. We assigned this to `factor-int`, and from that point onwards, we can treat the value as a regular function value.

# Setting up R to talk to Clojure

Another major statistical processing environment is R. It's an open source programming language and environment designed for statistical analysis. It's widely used and has an active community as well as a huge and growing body of useful add-on packages.

While there's no Clojure-specific interoperability library, there is one for Java, and we can use that to pass calls to R and to get results back. In this recipe, we'll set this system up.

## Getting ready

We'll need to have R installed. We can download it from `http://www.r-project.org/` by following the link to **CRAN**, picking a mirror, and downloading the correct version of R for our platform.

You'll also need to have Maven (`http://maven.apache.org/`) installed in order to build and install the libraries to access R.

## How to do it...

There are two parts to setting up this system. We'll get the R-side working, and then we'll see what Clojure needs to have in place.

### Setting up R

To set up the system, we first have to configure R to talk to Clojure:

1. Once R is installed, we'll download the interoperability package, `Rserve`. In my case, I went to `http://www.rforge.net/Rserve/files/` and downloaded `Rserver_1.88-1.tar.gz`, but you might have a more recent version available.

2. You'll need to extract the files from the tarball that you've downloaded. On Windows, **7-Zip** (`http://www.7-zip.org/`) can help:

```
$ tar xfzv Rserve_1.88-1.tar.gz
x Rserve/
x Rserve/configure.win
x Rserve/cleanup
...
```

3. Change into the `src/client/java` subdirectory of the `Rserve` directory:

```
$ cd Rserve/src/client/java/
```

4. Run `make` to create the JAR files:

```
$ make
```

5. Use Maven to install the two JAR files in that directory into your local Maven repository, as shown here:

```
$ mvn install:install-file -Dfile=./REngine.jar \
  -DartifactId=REngine -Dversion=1.88.1 -DgroupId=local.repo \
  -Dpackaging=jar
...
$ mvn install:install-file -Dfile=./Rserve.jar \
  -DartifactId=Rserve -Dversion=1.88.1 -DgroupId=local.repo \
  -Dpackaging=jar
...
```

6. Start R and install the package, as follows:

```
> install.packages("Rserve")
--- Please select a CRAN mirror for use in this session ---
```

At this point, a dialog window will pop up with a list of mirrors. Select one near you, and R will download the package and install it.

7. While still in R, load and start the Rserver. The code for this chapter has a shell script, `start-rserve.sh`, that starts the Rserver. You can also download the script from `https://gist.github.com/erochest/4974005`.

```
$ ./start-rserve.sh
R version 2.15.2 (2012-10-26) -- "Trick or Treat"
...
Rserv started in daemon mode.
```

## Setting up Clojure

Now we need to turn our attention to Clojure.

1. First, we must declare the two JAR files that we just installed as dependencies in our Leiningen `project.clj` file:

```
(defproject interop "0.1.0-SNAPSHOT"
  :description ""
  :dependencies [[org.clojure/clojure "1.6.0"]
                 [incanter "1.5.5"]
                 [local.repo/REngine "1.8.1"]
                 [local.repo/Rserve "1.8.1"]])
```

2. Then we'll import a couple of namespaces from them into our script or REPL:

```
(import '[org.rosuda.REngine REngine]
        '[org.rosuda.REngine.Rserve RConnection])
```

3. Finally, we create a connection to the R server. This will be a dynamic variable, so we can swap it out easily later. If the Rserve isn't running, this step will fail, so make sure that you have the Rserver running before you execute this (see step 6 from the previous section), and if this succeeds, you have R and Clojure successfully communicating:

```
(def ^:dynamic *r-cxn* (RConnection.))
```

## How it works...

The Rserve package runs a server in the background where the Java library communicates with. From Clojure, we can now feed data to the Rserver and get results. We'll see examples of this in the following recipes.

Because Rserve has to be running, step 6 from the previous section (load and start the Rserver) has to be performed in every session you want to call R from Clojure.

# Calling R functions from Clojure

R, and the many incredibly useful packages that have been developed for it, provides a rich environment to do statistical computing. To access any of this, however, we'll need to be able to call functions from Clojure. We do this by constructing R expressions as strings, sending them to the R server, and getting the results back. The Rserve Java library helps us convert the results to Java objects that we can access.

## Getting ready

We must first complete the recipe, *Setting up R to talk to Clojure*, and have Rserve running. We must also have the Clojure-specific parts of that recipe done and the connection to Rserve made.

## How to do it...

Once we have a connection to Rserver, we can call functions by passing the complete call—function and arguments—to the server as a string and evaluating it. Then, we have to pull the results back out, as follows:

```
user=> (map #(.asDouble %)
            (.. *r-cxn* (eval "qr(c(1,2,3,4,5,6,7))") asList))
(-11.832159566199232 1.0 1.0845154254728517 1.0)
```

## How it works...

To call an R function, we make a series of method calls on the RConnection object that we created in *Setting up R to talk to Clojure*. The first call, eval, takes the code to evaluate as a string and passes it to R.

Next, we have to convert the output to a Clojure data structure. We first call asList on the result, which converts it to a type that implements java.lag.Iterable. This can be passed to map, which is used to convert the list's members to doubles.

## There's more...

The example in this recipe called the R function qr. This calculates the QR decomposition of a matrix. For more information on this function, see http://www.math.montana.edu/Rweb/Rhelp/qr.html.

# Passing vectors into R

In order to do very complex or meaningful analysis, we'll need to be able to pass vector or matrix data into R to operate on and analyze.

Let's see how to do this.

## Getting ready

We must first complete the recipe, *Setting up R to talk to Clojure*, and have Rserve running. We must also have the Clojure-specific parts of that recipe done and the connection to Rserve made.

We'll also need access to the clojure.string namespace:

```
(require '[clojure.string :as str])
```

## How to do it...

To make passing values into R easier, we'll first define a protocol and then we'll use it to pass a matrix to R:

1. In order to handle the conversion of all the data types into a string that R can read, we'll define a protocol, ToR. Any data types that we want to marshal into R must implement this, as follows:

```
(defprotocol ToR
  (->r [x] "Convert an item to R."))
```

2.  Now we'll implement this protocol for sequences, vectors, and numeric types:

```
(extend-protocol ToR
  clojure.lang.ISeq
  (->r [coll] (str "c(" (str/join \, (map ->r coll)) ")"))
  clojure.lang.PersistentVector
  (->r [coll] (->r (seq coll)))
  java.lang.Integer
  (->r [i] (str i))
  java.lang.Long
  (->r [l] (str l))
  java.lang.Float
  (->r [f] (str f))
  java.lang.Double
  (->r [d] (str d)))
```

3.  We create a wrapper function to call R's `mean` function:

```
(defn r-mean
  ([coll] (r-mean coll *r-cxn*))
  ([coll r-cxn]
    (.. r-cxn
      (eval (str "mean(" (->r coll) ")"))
      asDouble)))
```

4.  With these in place, we can call them just as we would call any other function:

```
user=> (r-mean [1.0 2.0 3.0])
2.0
user=> (r-mean (map (fn [_] (rand)) (range 5)))
0.3966653617356786
```

## How it works...

For most data types, marshaling to R simply means converting it to a string. However, for sequences and vectors, it's a little more complicated. Clojure has to convert all the sequence's items to R strings, join the items with a comma, and wrap it in a call to R's `c` constructor.

This is a perfect place to use protocols. Defining methods in order to marshal more data types to R is simple. For example, we can define a naïve method to work with strings as shown here:

```
(extend-protocol ToR
  java.lang.String
  (->r [s] (str \' s \')))
```

Of course, this method isn't without its problems. If a string has a quote within it, for instance, it must be escaped. Also, having to marshal data types back and forth in this manner can be computationally expensive, especially for large or complex data types.

# Evaluating R files from Clojure

We might not always want to feed R code from Clojure directly into R. Many times, we might have files containing R expressions and we would want to evaluate the whole file.

We can do this quite easily too. Let's see how.

## Getting ready

We must first complete the recipe, *Setting up R to talk to Clojure*, and have Rserve running. We must also have the Clojure-specific parts of that recipe done and the connection to Rserve made.

Moreover, we'll need access to the `java.io.File` class:

```
(import '[java.io File])
```

## How to do it...

We'll first define a function to make evaluating a file in R easier, and then we'll find a file and execute it:

1.  The function to evaluate a file of R code takes a filename and (optionally) a connection to the R server. It feeds the file to R using R's `source` function, and it returns whatever R does:

    ```
    (defn r-source
      ([filename] (r-source filename *r-cxn*))
      ([filename r-cxn]
        (.eval r-cxn (str "source(\""
                          (.getAbsolutePath (File. filename))
                          "\")"))))
    ```

2.  For example, suppose we have a file named `chrsqr-example.R` that creates a random data table and performs a $X^2$ test on it:

    ```
    dat <- data.frame(q1=sample(c("A","B","C"),
        size=1000,replace=TRUE),
      sex=sample(c("M","F"),
        size=1000,replace=TRUE))
    dtab <- with(dat,table(q1,sex))

    (Xsq <- chisq.test(dtab))
    ```

3. The results that come back from are a little complicated, but with some trial and error, we can tease the answers back out, as follows:

```
user=> (def x-sqr (.asList (r-source "chisqr-example.R")))
#'user/x-sqr
;; X-square
user=> (.. x-sqr (at 0) asList (at "statistic") asDouble)
0.2166086470268894
;; degrees of freedon
user=> (.. x-sqr (at 0) asList (at "parameter") asInteger)
2
;; p-value
user=> (.. x-sqr (at 0) asList (at "p.value") asDouble)
0.897354468808211
```

## How it works...

The most difficult part of this is to deal with the return value. After calling `r-source`, we convert the output to an R list. We pull the *statistic* item from that and convert it to a double. That's the $X^2$ value. The *parameter* item is the degrees of freedom. Also, the *p.value* item is the p-value for the test.

Generally, when I'm picking out the results from their Java data structures, the REPL and documentation are the biggest help. For example, the value `x-sqr`, when printed on the REPL, displays this:

```
user=> x-sqr
[#<REXPGenericVector org.rosuda.REngine.REXPGenericVector@4e2f1185+[9]
named> #<REXPLogical org.rosuda.REngine.REXPLogical@43be5d17[1]>]
```

This tells me that the list's first item is a generic R vector and the second item is an R logical structure. Diving further into the first item shows the names of the members it contains:

```
user=> (.. x-sqr (at 0) asList names)
["statistic" "parameter" "p.value" "method" "data.name" "observed"
"expected" "residuals" "stdres"]
```

This helps me pick out the values I'm looking for, and by using some test data and referring to the documentation for the data types, I can easily write the code that is required to dig down to the results.

## There's more...

The documentation for R's Java data types is available at `http://rforge.net/org/docs/index.html?org/rosuda/REngine/package-tree.html`.

# Plotting in R from Clojure

One of R's strengths is its plotting ability. In this recipe, we'll see how to take some data and plot it on a graph. We won't really exercise R's graphic abilities, but this should be enough to get you started.

## Getting ready

We must first complete the recipe, *Setting up R to talk to Clojure*, and have Rserve running. We must also have the Clojure-specific parts of that recipe done and the connection to Rserve made.

We'll need the ToR protocol and the implementations that we defined in the *Passing vectors into R* recipe.

Also, we'll need access to the `java.io.File` class:

```
(import '[java.io File])
```

## How to do it...

This recipe will look a lot like a number of other R-related recipes. We'll create a function that assembles the string with the R expression and then we'll see it in action.

1. First, we'll define a function to initialize a PNG file for output, plot some data, and save the file, all from R:

```
(defn r-plot
  ([data filename] (r-plot data filename *r-cxn*))
  ([data filename r-cxn]
   (.. r-cxn
     (eval (str "png(filename=\""
                (.getAbsolutePath (File. filename))
                "\", height=300, width=250, bg=\"white\")\n"
                "plot(" (->r data) ")\n"
                "dev.off()\n")))))
```

2. Now, let's test it out at the start of the Fibonacci sequence:

```
user=> (r-plot [1.0 1.0 2.0 3.0 5.0 8.0 11.0] "fib.png")
#<REXPInteger org.rosuda.REngine.REXPInteger@7342054+[1]>
```

If we open up the `fib.png` file and take a look at it, we can see the results of the simple graphing call that we made, as shown here:

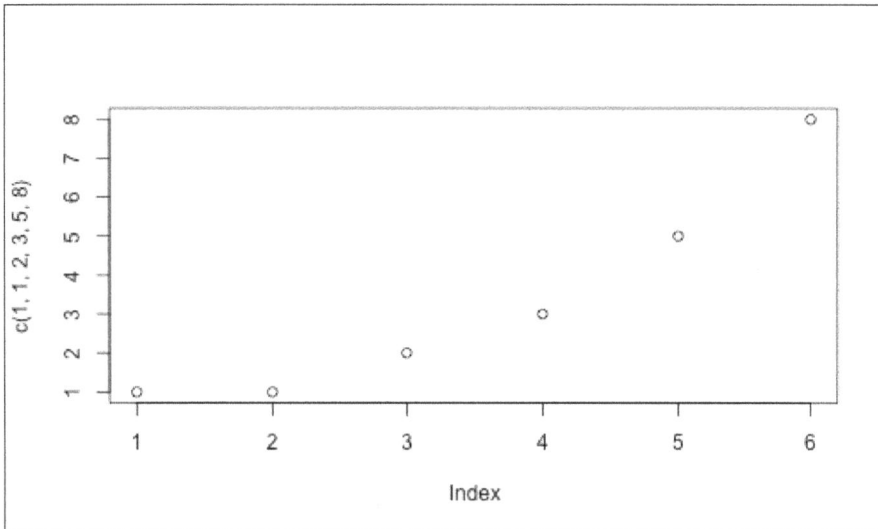

## How it works...

The body of this function is in the string that gets passed to R to evaluate. It's composed of three function calls. First, it initializes the PNG output with the `png` function:

```
"png(filename=\""
(.getAbsolutePath (File. filename))
"\", height=300, width=500, bg=\"white\")\n"
```

Then, we actually plot the data:

```
"plot(" (->r data) ")\n"
```

Finally, save the plot to the file:

```
"dev.off()\n"
```

## There's more...

A scatterplot is a very basic plot, which Incanter can do as well. However, R's graphing features are more sophisticated than what Incanter can currently do. To get a taste of what R's capable of, browse through the R gallery at http://gallery.r-enthusiasts.com/.

# 9

# Clustering, Classifying, and Working with Weka

In this chapter, we will cover the following recipes:

- ▶ Loading CSV and ARFF files into Weka
- ▶ Filtering, renaming, and deleting columns in Weka datasets
- ▶ Discovering groups of data using K-Means clustering
- ▶ Finding hierarchical clusters in Weka
- ▶ Clustering with SOMs in Incanter
- ▶ Classifying data with decision trees
- ▶ Classifying data with the Naive Bayesian classifier
- ▶ Classifying data with support vector machines
- ▶ Finding associations in data with the Apriori algorithm

## Introduction

Looking for patterns in our dataset is a large part of data analysis. Of course, a dataset of any complexity is too much for the human mind to see patterns in, so we rely on computers, statistics, and machine learning to augment our insights.

In this chapter, we'll take a look at a number of methods used to cluster and classify data. Depending on the nature of the data and the question(s) we're trying to answer, different algorithms will be more or less useful. For instance, while K-Means clustering is great for clustering numeric datasets, it's poorly suited for working with nominal data.

Most of the recipes in this chapter will use the Weka machine learning and data mining library (`http://www.cs.waikato.ac.nz/ml/weka/`). This is a full-featured library, which is used to analyze data using many different procedures and algorithms. It includes a more complete set of these algorithms than Incanter, which we've been using a lot so far. We'll start by seeing how to load CSV files into Weka and work with Weka datasets. However, for most of the chapter, we'll examine how to use this powerful library to perform different analyses. Weka's interface to the classes implementing these algorithms is very consistent. For the first recipe, in which we use one of these algorithms, *Discovering groups of data using K-Means clustering*, we'll define a macro that will facilitate creating wrapper functions for Weka algorithms. This is a great example shows using macros, and of how easy it is to create a wrapper over an external Java library to make it more natural to use from Clojure.

# Loading CSV and ARFF files into Weka

Weka is most comfortable when using its own file format: the **Attribute-Relation File Format** (**ARFF**). This format includes the types of data in the columns and other information that allow it to be loaded incrementally, and both of these can be important features. Because of this, Weka can load data more reliably. However, Weka can still import CSV files, and when it does, it attempts to guess the type of data in the columns.

In this recipe, we'll see what's necessary to load data from a CSV file and an ARFF file.

## Getting ready

First, we'll need to add Weka to the dependencies in our Leiningen `project.clj` file:

```
(defproject d-mining "0.1.0-SNAPSHOT"
  :dependencies [[org.clojure/clojure "1.6.0"]
                 [nz.ac.waikato.cms.weka/weka-dev "3.7.11"]]])
```

Then we'll import the right classes into our script or REPL:

```
(import [weka.core.converters ArffLoader CSVLoader]
        [java.io File])
```

Finally, we'll need to have a CSV file to import. In this recipe, I'll use the dataset of Chinese land use data that we compiled for the *Scaling variables to simplify variable relationships* recipe in *Chapter 7, Statistical Data Analysis with Incanter*. It's in the file named `data/chnchn-land.csv`. You can also download this file from `http://www.ericrochester.com/clj-data-analysis/data/chn-land.csv`.

## How to do it...

For this recipe, we'll write several utility functions and then use them to load the data:

1. First, we'll need a utility function to convert options into an array of strings:

```
(defn ->options
 [& opts]
  (into-array String
              (map str (flatten (remove nil? opts)))))
```

2. Next, we'll create a function that takes a filename and an optional `:header` keyword argument and returns the Weka dataset of instances:

```
(defn load-csv [filename & {:keys [header]
                             :or {header true}}]
  (let [options (->options (when-not header "-H"))
        loader (doto (CSVLoader.)
                 (.setOptions options)
                 (.setSource (File. filename)))]
    (.getDataSet loader)))
```

3. Finally, we can use this to load CSV files:

```
(def data (load-csv "data/chn-land.csv"))
```

4. Alternatively, if we have a file without a header row, we can do this:

```
(def data (load-csv "data/chn-land.csv"
                    :header false))
```

5. We can use a similar function to load ARFF files:

```
(defn load-arff [filename]
  (.getDataSet
    (doto (ArffLoader.)
      (.setFile (File. filename)))))
```

There are ARFF files of standard datasets already created and available to download from `http://weka.wikispaces.com/Datasets`. We'll use some of these in later recipes.

## How it works...

Weka can be used in a number of ways. Although we're using it as a library here, it is also possible to use it as a GUI or a command-line application. In fact, in a lot of ways, to use the interface as a library is the same as using it as a command-line application (just without calling it from the shell). Whether used from a GUI or programmatically, at some point, we're setting options using a command-line-style string array.

The `->options` function takes care of converting and cleaning up a list of these options, and `into-array` converts the sequence into a string array.

For all of the later recipes that use Weka, this function will be a template. Each time it's used, we'll essentially create an object, set the options as a string array, and perform the operation. In the *Discovering groups of data using K-Means clustering* recipe, we'll reify the process with the `defanalysis` macro.

The ARFF format, for which we created a function in Step 5, is a Weka-specific datafile format. CSV files don't include information about the types of data stored in the columns. Weka tries to be smart and figure out what they are, but it isn't always successful. However, ARFF files do contain information about the columns' datatypes, and this makes them Weka's preferred file format.

## There's more...

The columns may need filtering or renaming, especially if the CSV file doesn't have a header row. We'll see how to do that in the next recipe, *Filtering, renaming, and deleting columns in Weka datasets*.

## See also...

For more about Weka, see its website at `http://www.cs.waikato.ac.nz/ml/weka/`

# Filtering, renaming, and deleting columns in Weka datasets

Generally, data won't be quite in the form we'll need for our analyses. We spent a lot of time transforming data in Clojure in *Chapter 2, Cleaning and Validating Data*. Weka contains several methods for renaming columns and filtering the ones that will make it into the dataset.

Most datasets have one or more columns that will throw off clustering—row identifiers or name fields, for instance—so we must filter the columns in the datasets before we perform any analysis. We'll see lot of examples of this in the recipes to come.

## Getting ready

We'll use the dependencies, imports, and datafiles that we did in the *Loading CSV and ARFF files into Weka recipe*. We'll also use the dataset that we loaded in that recipe. We'll need to access a different set of Weka classes, as well as the `clojure.string` library:

```
(import [weka.filters Filter]
        [weka.filters.unsupervised.attribute Remove])
(require '[clojure.string :as str])
```

## How to do it...

In this recipe, we'll first rename the columns from the dataset. Then we'll look at two different ways to remove columns, one destructively and one not.

### Renaming columns

We'll create a function to rename the attributes with a sequence of keywords, and then we'll see this function in action:

1. First, we'll define a function that takes a dataset and a sequence of field names, and then renames the columns in the dataset to match those passed in:

```
(defn set-fields [instances field-seq]
  (doseq [n (range (.numAttributes instances))]
    (.renameAttribute instances
                      (.attribute instances n)
                      (name (nth field-seq n)))))
```

2. Now, let's look at the dataset's current column names:

```
user=> (map #(.. data (attribute %) name)
            (range (.numAttributes data)))
("Country-Code" "Year" "AG.SRF.TOTL.K2" "AG.LND.AGRI.ZS" "AG.LND.
AGRI.K2")
```

3. These are the names that World Bank gives these fields, but we can change the field names to something more obvious:

```
(set-fields data
            [:country-code :year
             :total-land :agri-percent :agri-total])
```

### Removing columns

This dataset also contains a number of columns that we won't use, for example, the field *agri-percent*. Since it won't ever be used, we'll destructively remove it from the dataset:

1. Weka allows us to delete attributes by index, but we want to specify them by name. We'll write a function that takes an attribute name and returns the index:

```
(defn attr-n [instances attr-name]
  (->> instances
    (.numAttributes)
    range
    (map #(vector % (.. instances (attribute %)
                        name)))
    (filter #(= (second %) (name attr-name)))
    ffirst))
```

2.  We can use that function to call `reduce` on the instances and remove the attributes as we go:

```
(defn delete-attrs [instances attr-names]
  (reduce (fn [is n]
            (.deleteAttributeAt is (attr-n is n)) is)
          instances
          attr-names))
```

3.  Finally, we can use the following to delete the attributes I mentioned earlier:

```
(delete-attrs data [:agri-percent])
```

## Hiding columns

There are a few attributes that we'll hide. Instead of destructively deleting attributes from one set of instances, filtering them creates a new dataset without the hidden attributes. It can be useful to have one dataset for clustering and another with the complete information for the dataset (for example, a name or ID attribute). For this example, I'll take out the country code:

1.  Weka does this by applying a `filter` class to a dataset to create a new dataset. We'll use the `Remove` filter in this function. This also uses the `attr-n` function, which was used earlier in this recipe:

```
(defn filter-attributes [dataset remove-attrs]
  (let [attrs (map inc
                   (map (partial attr-n dataset)
                        remove-attrs))
        options (->options
                  "-R"
                  (str/join \, (map str attrs)))
        rm (doto (Remove.)
              (.setOptions options)
              (.setInputFormat dataset))]
    (Filter/useFilter dataset rm)))
```

2.  We can call this function with the attribute names that we want to filter out:

```
(def data-numbers
     (filter-attributes data [:country-code]))
```

And we can see the results.

```
user=> (map #(.. data-numbers (attribute %) name)
            (range (.numAttributes data-numbers)))
("year" "total-land" "agri-total")
```

## How it works...

Weka's attributes are an integral part of its data model. Moreover, the later algorithms that we'll see can be sensitive to which columns are in the dataset. In order to work with only the attributes that are important, we can hide them or delete them altogether using the functions in this recipe.

# Discovering groups of data using K-Means clustering

One of the most popular and well-known clustering methods is **K-Means clustering**. It's conceptually simple. It's also easy to implement and is computationally cheap. We can get decent results quickly for many different datasets.

On the downside, it sometimes gets stuck in local optima and misses a better solution.

Generally, K-Means clustering performs best when groups in the data are spatially distinct and are grouped into separate circles. If the clusters are all mixed, this won't be able to distinguish them. This means that if the natural groups in the data overlap, the clusters that K-Means generates will not properly distinguish the natural groups in the data.

## Getting ready

For this recipe, we'll need the same dependencies in our `project.clj` file that we used in the *Loading CSV and ARFF files into Weka* recipe.

However, we'll need a slightly different set of imports in our script or REPL:

```
(import [weka.core EuclideanDistance]
        [weka.clusterers SimpleKMeans])
```

For data, we'll use the Iris dataset, which is often used for learning about and testing clustering algorithms. You can download this dataset from the Weka wiki at `http://weka.wikispaces.com/Datasets` or from `http://www.ericrochester.com/clj-data-analysis/UCI/iris.arff`. We will load it using `load-arff`, which was covered in *Loading CSV and ARFF files into Weka*.

## How to do it...

For this recipe, we'll first define a function and macro that will greatly facilitate writing wrapper functions around Weka classes and processes. Then we'll use that macro for the first time to wrap the `weka.clusters.SimpleKMeans` class:

1. First, we'll define a function to generate a random seed from the current time. By default, Weka always uses *1* as the random seed. This function will allow us to use the current time by specifying `nil` as the seed:

```
(defn random-seed [seed]
  (if (nil? seed)
    (.intValue (.getTime (java.util.Date.)))
    seed))
```

2. Most of the Weka analyses follows the same pattern. We'll take keyword parameters and turn them into a command-line-style string array. We'll create a Weka object and pass it the options array. This is the kind of boilerplate that the Lisp and Lisp macros are particularly good at abstracting away.

   The most complicated part of this will involve parsing a sequence of vectors into the wrapper function's parameter list and the options array. Each vector will list the option, a variable name for it, and a default value. Optionally, they may also contain a keyword indicating how the value is converted to an option and under what circumstances it's included. The highlighted comments in the code show some examples of these near the place where they're passed. Here's the function to parse an options vector into the code to pass to `->options`:

```
(defn analysis-parameter [parameter]
  (condp = (count parameter)
    ;; [option-str variable-name default-value]
    ;; ["-N" k 2]
    3 '[~(first parameter) ~(second parameter)]

    ;; [option-str variable-name default-value flag]
    ;; ["-V" verbose false :flag-true]
    4 (condp = (last parameter)
        :flag-true '[(when ~(second parameter)
                       ~(first parameter))]
        :flag-false '[(when-not ~(second parameter)
                        ~(first parameter))]
        :not-nil '[(when-not
                     (nil? ~(second parameter))
                     [~(first parameter)
```

```
                        ~(second parameter))]))]
        :seq (let [name (second parameter)]
                (apply concat
                    (map-indexed
                        (fn [i flag]
                          '[~flag (nth ~name ~i)])
                        (first parameter))))


      '[~(first parameter)
        (~(last parameter) ~(second parameter))])

;; [option-str variable-name default-value flag
;;  option]
;; ["-B" distance-of :node-length :flag-equal
;;  :branch-length]
5 (condp = (nth parameter 3)
    :flag-equal '[(when (= ~(second parameter)
                          ~(last parameter))
                    ~(first parameter))]

    :predicate '[(when ~(last parameter)
                   [~(first parameter)
                    ~(second parameter)])])))))
```

3. Now we can create a macro that takes a name for the wrapper function, a class and a method for it, and a sequence of parameter vectors. It then defines the analysis as a function:

```
(defmacro defanalysis
  [a-name a-class a-method parameters]
  '(defn ~a-name
    [dataset# &
      ;; The variable-names and default-values are
      ;; used here to build the function's
      ;; parameter list.
      {:keys ~(mapv second parameters)
       :or ~(into {}
                  (map #(vector (second %) (nth % 2))
                       parameters))}]
      ;; The options, flags, and predicats are used to
      ;; construct the options list.
      (let [options# (->options
                        ~@(mapcat analysis-parameter
                                  parameters))]
```

```
;; The algorithm's class and invocation
;; function are used here to actually
;; perform the processing.
(doto (new ~a-class)
  (.setOptions options#)
  (. ~a-method dataset#)))))
```

4.  Now we can define a wrapper for K-Means clustering (as well as the other algorithms we'll introduce later in the chapter) very quickly. This also makes clear how the macro has helped us. It's allowed us to **DRY**-up (**Don't Repeat Yourself**) the options list. Now we can clearly see what options an algorithm takes and how it uses them:

```
(defanalysis
  k-means SimpleKMeans buildClusterer
  [["-N" k 2]
   ["-I" max-iterations 100]
   ["-V" verbose false :flag-true]
   ["-S" seed 1 random-seed]
   ["-A" distance EuclideanDistance .getName]])
```

5.  We can now call this wrapper function and get the results. We'll first load the dataset and then filter it into a new dataset that only includes the columns related to the petal size. Our clustering will be based upon those attributes:

```
user=> (def iris (load-arff "data/UCI/iris.arff"))
user=> (def iris-petal
           (filter-attributes iris
                   [:sepallength :sepalwidth :class]))
user=> (def km (k-means iris-petal :k 3))
user=> km
#<SimpleKMeans
kMeans
======

Number of iterations: 8
Within cluster sum of squared errors: 1.7050986081225123
...
```

## How it works...

There are several interesting things to talk about in this recipe.

# Clustering with K-Means

As far as clustering algorithms (or as far as any algorithms) are concerned, K-Means is simple. To group the input data into $K$ clusters, we initially pick $K$ random points in the data's domain space. Now follow the steps listed here:

1.  Assign each of the data points to the nearest cluster
2.  Move the cluster's position to the centroid (or mean position) of the data assigned to that cluster
3.  Repeat

We keep following these steps until either we've performed a maximum number of iterations or until the clusters are stable, that is, when the set of data points assigned to each cluster doesn't change. We saw this in the example in this recipe. The maximum number of iterations was set to 100, but the clusters stabilized after eight iterations.

K-Means clustering does have a number of quirks to be aware of. First, it must be used with numeric variables. After all, what would the distance be between two species in the Iris dataset? What's the distance between Virginica and Setosa?

Another factor is that it won't work well if the natural classifications within the data (for example, the species in the Iris dataset) aren't in separate circles. If the data points for each class tend to run into each other, then K-Means won't be able to reliably distinguish between the classifications.

## Analyzing the results

The following graph shows petal dimensions of the items in the Iris dataset and distinguishes each point by species (shape) and classification (color). Generally, the results are good, but I've highlighted half a dozen points that the algorithm put into the wrong category (some green crosses or yellow diamonds):

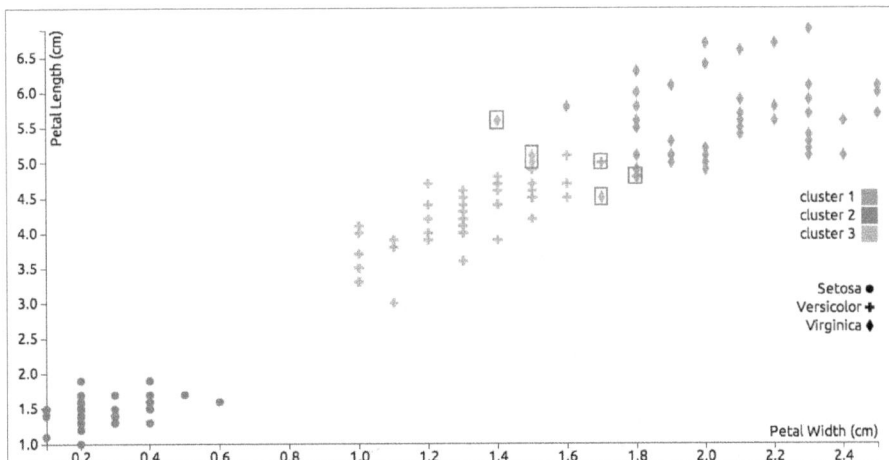

This chart helps us visually verify the results, but the most important part of the algorithm's output is probably the **within-cluster sum of squared errors (WCSS)**. This should be as low as possible for a given number of clusters. In the example, this value is approximately 1.71, which is fine.

## Building macros

Another interesting aspect of this recipe is the use of a macro to create a wrapper function for the cluster analysis. Because Clojure, like other lisps, is written in its own data structures, it's common to write programs to manipulate programs. In fact, this is so common that Clojure provides a stage of compilation dedicated to letting the user manipulate the input program. These meta-programs are called macros. The Clojure compiler reads forms, uses macros to manipulate them, and finally compiles the output of the macros. Macros are a powerful tool that allows users to define their own control structures and other forms far beyond what programmers of other languages have available to them.

We can easily see how the macro is turned into a function using `macroexpand-1`, like this:

```
(macroexpand-1 '(defanalysis
                  k-means SimpleKMeans buildClusterer
                  [["-N" k 2]
                   ["-I" iterations 100]
                   ["-V" verbose false :flag-true]
                   ["-S" seed 1 random-seed]
                   ["-A" distance EuclideanDistance .getName]]))
```

I cleaned up this output to make it look more like something we'd type. The function that the macro creates is listed here:

```
(defn k-means
  [dataset__1216__auto__ &
   {:or {k 2,
         max-iterations 100,
         verbose false,
         seed 1,
         distance EuclideanDistance},
    :keys [k max-iterations verbose seed distance]}]
  (let [options__1217__auto__
        (->options "-N" k
                   "-I" max-iterations
                   (when verbose "-V")
                   "-S" (random-seed seed)
                   "-A" (.getName distance))]
    (doto (new SimpleKMeans)
      (.setOptions options__1217__auto__)
      (.buildClusterer dataset__1216__auto__))))
```

**See also...**

- For information about K-Means clustering, Wikipedia provides a good introduction at `http://en.wikipedia.org/wiki/K-means_clustering`

- For information about Weka's `SimpleKMeans` class, including an explanation of its options, see `http://weka.sourceforge.net/doc.dev/weka/clusterers/SimpleKMeans.html`

- For more about macros in Clojure, see `http://clojure.org/macros`. Also, I've written a longer tutorial on macros, which is available at `http://writingcoding.blogspot.com/2008/07/stemming-part-8-macros.html`

# Finding hierarchical clusters in Weka

Another common way to cluster data is the hierarchical way. This involves either splitting the dataset down to pairs (divisive or top-down) or building the clusters up by pairing the data or clusters that are closest to each other (agglomerative or bottom-up).

Weka has a class `HierarchicalClusterer` to perform agglomerative hierarchical clustering. We'll use the `defanalysis` macro that we created in the *Discovering groups of data using K-Means clustering* recipe to create a wrapper function for this analysis as well.

## Getting ready

We'll use the same `project.clj` dependencies that we did in the *Loading CSV and ARFF files into Weka* recipe, and this set of imports:

```
(import [weka.core EuclideanDistance]
        [weka.clusterers HierarchicalClusterer])
(require '[clojure.string :as str])
```

Because hierarchical clustering can be memory intensive, we'll use the Iris dataset, which is fairly small. The easiest way to get this dataset is to download it from `http://www.ericrochester.com/clj-data-analysis/data/UCI/iris.arff`. You can also download it, and other datasets, in a JAR file from `http://weka.wikispaces.com/Datasets`. I loaded it using the `load-arff` function from the *Loading CSV and ARFF files into Weka* recipe:

```
(def iris (load-arff "data/UCI/iris.arff"))
```

We'll also use the `defanalysis` macro that we defined in the *Discovering groups of data using K-Means clustering* recipe.

## How to do it...

Now we see some return on having defined the `defanalysis` macro. We can create a wrapper function for Weka's `HierarchicalClusterer` in just a few lines:

1. We define the wrapper function like this:

```
(defanalysis
  hierarchical HierarchicalClusterer buildClusterer
  [["-A" distance EuclideanDistance .getName]
   ["-L" link-type :centroid
    #(str/upper-case (str/replace (name %) \- \_))]
   ["-N" k nil :not-nil]
   ["-D" verbose false :flag-true]
   ["-B" distance-of :node-length :flag-equal
    :branch-length]
   ["-P" print-newick false :flag-true]])
```

2. Using this, we can filter the petal dimensions fields and perform the analysis:

```
(def iris-petal
  (filter-attributes
    iris
    [:sepallength :sepalwidth :class]))
```

3. Now we can use this data to train a new classifier:

```
(def hc
  (hierarchical iris-petal :k 3 :print-newick true))
```

4. To see which cluster an instance falls in, we use `clusterInstance`, and we can check the same index in the full dataset to see all of the attributes for that instance:

```
user=> (.clusterInstance hc (.get iris-petal 2))
0
user=> (.get iris 2)
#<DenseInstance 4.7,3.2,1.3,0.2,Iris-setosa>
```

## How it works...

Hierarchical clustering usually works in a bottom-up manner. Its process is fairly simple:

1. Identify the two data points or clusters that are closest to each other

2. Group them into a new cluster positioned at the centroid of the pair

3. In the population, replace the pair with the new group

4. Repeat until we're left with only the number of clusters we expect (the "-N" option mentioned previously)

If we look at a graph of the results, we can see that the results are very similar to what K-Means clustering produced. Actually, there's only one data point that was classified differently, which I've highlighted. In this case, hierarchical clustering grouped that data point incorrectly, possibly pairing it with one of the points to its right:

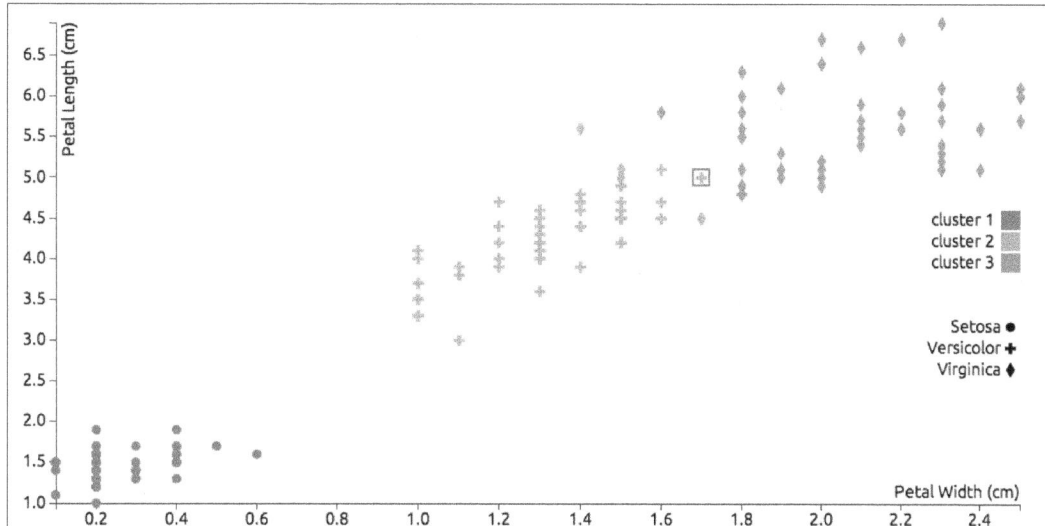

Like K-Means clustering, hierarchical clustering is based on a distance measurement, so it will also have trouble correctly classifying data points along the margins between two groups with close, non-distinct data points.

## There's more...

▶ The documentation for the `HierarchicalClusterer` at `http://weka.sourceforge.net/doc.dev/weka/clusterers/HierarchicalClusterer.html` has more information about the options available for this algorithm

▶ Wikipedia has a good introduction to hierarchical clustering at `http://en.wikipedia.org/wiki/Hierarchical_clustering`

▶ David Blei has a set of slides that provides another excellent summary of this algorithm, at `http://www.cs.princeton.edu/courses/archive/spr08/cos424/slides/clustering-2.pdf`

▶ The book, *Introduction to Information Retrieval*, also has a more in-depth look at hierarchical clustering. You can find it online at `http://nlp.stanford.edu/IR-book/html/htmledition/hierarchical-clustering-1.html`

# Clustering with SOMs in Incanter

**Self-organizing maps** (**SOMs**) are a type of neural network that cluster and categorize the data without supervision. An SOM starts from a random set of groupings and competitively updates the values in the network to eventually match those in the distribution of the training data. In this way, it learns the clusters in the data by looking at the attributes of the data.

Incanter has an easy-to-use implementation of SOMs. We'll use it here to look for clusters in the Iris dataset.

## Getting ready

First, we'll need to have these dependencies in our `project.clj` file:

```
(defproject d-mining "0.1.0-SNAPSHOT"
  :dependencies [[org.clojure/clojure "1.6.0"]
                 [incanter "1.5.5"]])
```

We'll also need to have these libraries loaded into our script or REPL:

```
(require '[incanter.core :as i]
         '[incanter.som :as som]
         'incanter.datasets)
```

We'll use the Iris dataset for this recipe:

```
(def iris (incanter.datasets/get-dataset :iris))
```

## How to do it...

Incanter includes the SOM algorithm in its core library. We'll use it from there:

1. To cluster this dataset, we'll use the `incanter.som/som-batch-train` function on a matrix of our data. This time, we'll use all measurement attributes, so the SOM will map the four-dimensional attribute vectors onto two dimensions:

```
(def iris-clusters
  (som/som-batch-train
    (i/to-matrix
      (i/sel iris
             :cols [:Sepal.Length :Sepal.Width
                    :Petal.Length :Petal.Width])))))
```

2. Now we can get the indexes of the data rows that are in each cluster by looking at the `:sets` key of `iris-clusters`. Then we can pull the species from each cluster's rows to look at the frequency of each species in each cluster:

```
user=> (doseq [[pos rws] (:sets iris-clusters)]
          (println pos \:
                     (frequencies
                        (i/sel iris :cols :Species
                                     :rows rws))))
[4 1] : {virginica 23}
[8 1] : {virginica 27, versicolor 50}
[9 0] : {setosa 50}
```

So we can see that `setosa` and `versicolor` are each put into their own clusters, and half of the virginica are in their own cluster and half are with the versicolors.

## How it works...

SOMs use a neural network to map data points onto a grid. As the neural network is trained, the data points converge into cells in the grid, based on the similarities between the items.

We can get the size of the output map using the `:dims` key:

```
user=> (:dims iris-clusters)
[10.0 2.0]
```

We can use this information, combined with the cell frequencies, to graph the clustering of data in the SOM:

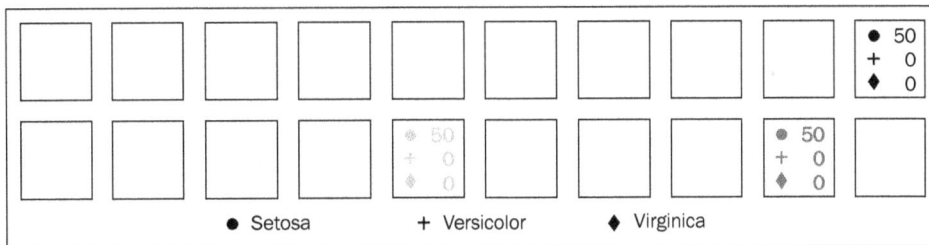

One of the downsides of SOMs is that the network's weights are largely opaque. We can see the groupings, but figuring out why the algorithm grouped them the way it did is difficult to define.

▸ The Incanter documentation at `http://clojuredocs.org/incanter/incanter.som/som-batch-train` has more information about the `som/som-batch-train` function and its parameters

▸ Tom Germano has a more in-depth discussion of SOMs at `http://davis.wpi.edu/~matt/courses/soms/`

# Classifying data with decision trees

One way to classify documents is to follow a hierarchical tree of rules, finally placing an instance into a bucket. This is essentially what decision trees do. Although they can work with any type of data, they are especially helpful in classifying nominal variables (discrete categories of data such as the `species` attribute of the Iris dataset), where statistics designed for working with numerical data—such as K-Means clustering—doesn't work as well.

Decision trees have another handy feature. Unlike many types of data mining where the analysis is somewhat of a black box, decision trees are very intelligible. We can easily examine them and readily tell how and why they classify our data the way they do.

In this recipe, we'll look at a dataset of mushrooms and create a decision tree to tell us whether a mushroom instance is edible or poisonous.

## Getting ready

First, we'll need to use the dependencies that we specified in the `project.clj` file in the *Loading CSV and ARFF files into Weka* recipe.

We'll also need these imports in our script or REPL:

```
(import [weka.classifiers.trees J48])
(require '[clojure.java.io :as io])
```

For data, we'll use one of the UCI datasets that Weka provides. You can download this set from `http://www.cs.waikato.ac.nz/ml/weka/datasets.html`, or more directly from `http://www.ericrochester.com/clj-data-analysis/data/UCI/mushroom.arff`. We can load the datafile using the `load-arff` function from the *Loading CSV and ARFF files into Weka* recipe.

We'll also use the `defanalysis` macro from the *Discovering groups of data using K-Means clustering in Weka* recipe.

As a bonus, if you have Graphviz installed (`http://www.graphviz.org/`), you can use it to generate a graph of the decision tree. Wikipedia lists other programs that can display DOT or GV files, at `http://en.wikipedia.org/wiki/DOT_language#Layout_programs`.

## How to do it...

We'll build a wrapper for the `J48` class. This is Weka's implementation of the C4.5 algorithm for building decision trees:

1. First, we create the wrapper function for this algorithm:

```
(defanalysis
  j48 J48 buildClassifier
  [["-U" pruned true :flag-false]
   ["-C" confidence 0.25]
   ["-M" min-instances 2]
   ["-R" reduced-error false :flag-true]
   ["-N" folds 3 :predicate reduced-error]
   ["-B" binary-only false :flag-true]
   ["-S" subtree-raising true :flag-false]
   ["-L" clean true :flag-false]
   ["-A" smoothing true :flag-true]
   ["-J" mdl-correction true :flag-false]
   ["-Q" seed 1 random-seed]])
```

2. We can use this function to create a decision tree of the mushroom data, but before that, we have to load the file and tell it which field contains the classification for each one. In this case, it's the last field that tells whether the mushroom is poisonous or edible:

```
(def shrooms
  (doto (load-arff "data/UCI/mushroom.arff")
    (.setClassIndex 22)))
(def d-tree (j48 shrooms :pruned true))
```

3. The decision tree outputs Graphviz dot data, so we can write the data to a file and generate an image from that:

```
(with-open [w (io/writer "decision-tree.gv")]
  (.write w (.graph d-tree)))
```

4. Now, from the command line, process `decision-tree.gv` with dot. If you're using another program to process the Graphviz file, substitute that here:

```
$ dot -O -Tpng decision-tree.gv
```

## How it works...

The following graph is created by Graphviz:

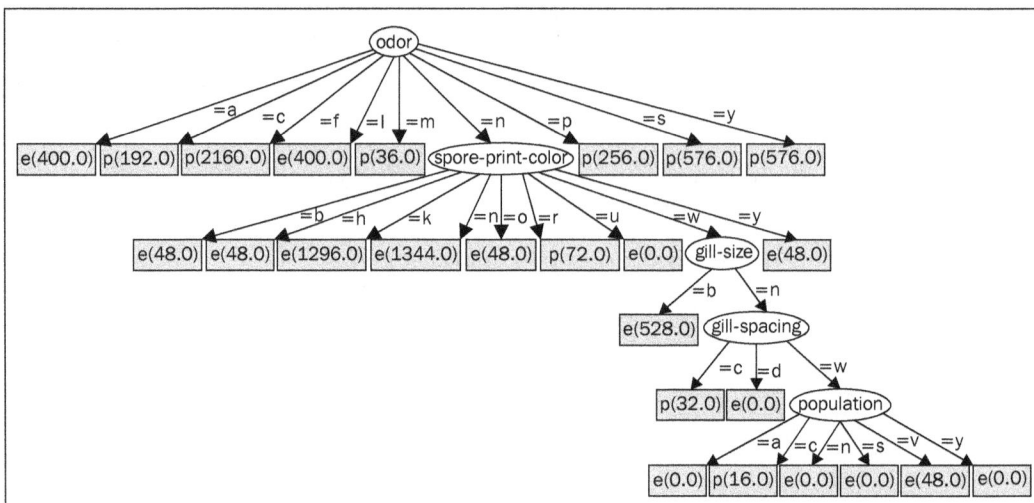

The decision tree starts from the root looking at the odor attribute. Instances that have a value of *a* (almond) go to the leftmost node, which is marked *e* (edible). Instances that have a value of *c* (creosote) go to the next node, which is marked *p* (poisonous).

However, instances with an odor value of *n* (none) go to the oval child. It looks at the spore-print-color attribute. If that value is *b* (buff), then the instance is edible. Other sequences of attributes and values end in different categories of mushrooms.

## There's more...

- Giorgio Ingargiola, of Temple University, has a tutorial page for a class that breaks down the C4.5 algorithm and the ID3 algorithm it's based on, at http://www.cis.temple.edu/~giorgio/cis587/readings/id3-c45.html
- The overview page for the mushroom dataset at http://archive.ics.uci.edu/ml/datasets/Mushroom has information about the attributes used

# Classifying data with the Naive Bayesian classifier

Bayesian classification is a way of updating your estimate of the probability that an item is in a given category, depending on what you already know about that item, category, and the world at large. In the case of a Naive Bayesian system, we assume that all features of the items are independent. For example, elevation and average snowfall are *not* independent (higher elevations tend to have more snow), but elevation and median income should be independent. This algorithm has been useful in a number of interesting areas, for example, spam detection in emails, automatic language detection, and document classification. In this recipe, we'll apply it to the mushroom dataset that we looked at in the *Classifying data with decision trees* recipe.

## Getting ready

First, we'll need to use the dependencies that we specified in the `project.clj` file in the *Loading CSV and ARFF files into Weka* recipe. We'll also use the `defanalysis` macro from the *Discovering groups of data using K-Means clustering* recipe, and we'll need this import in our script or REPL:

```
(import [weka.classifiers.bayes NaiveBayes]
        [weka.core Instances])
```

For data, we'll use the mushroom dataset that we did in the *Classifying data with decision trees* recipe. You can download it from http://www.ericrochester.com/clj-data-analysis/data/UCI/mushroom.arff. We'll also need to ensure that the class attribute is marked, just as we did in that recipe:

```
(def shrooms (doto (load-arff "data/UCI/mushroom.arff")
               (.setClassIndex 22)))
```

## How to do it...

In order to test the classifier, we'll take a sample of the data and train the classifier on that. We'll then see how well it classifies the entire dataset:

1. The following function takes a dataset of instances and a sample size, and it returns a sample of the dataset:

```
(defn sample-instances [instances size]
  (let [inst-count (.numInstances instances)]
    (if (<= inst-count size)
      instances
```

```
(let [indexes
        (loop [sample #{}]
          (if (= (count sample) size)
            (sort sample)
            (recur
              (conj sample
                    (rand-int inst-count)))))
      sample (Instances. instances size)]
  (doall
    (map #(.add sample (.get instances %))
         indexes))
  sample)))))
```

2. We also need to create the wrapper function for the Bayesian analyzer:

```
(defanalysis
  naive-bayes NaiveBayes buildClassifier
  [["-K" kernel-density false :flag-true]
   ["-D" discretization false :flag-true]])
```

3. Now we can create a sample of the mushroom data and apply the analyzer to it:

```
(def shroom-sample (sample-instances shrooms 2000))
(def bayes (naive-bayes shroom-sample))
```

4. We can pull an instance from the original dataset and use the Bayesian model to classify it. In this dataset, edible (*e*) is 0 and poisonous (*p*) is 1, so the model has correctly classified this data:

```
user=> (.get shrooms 2)
#<DenseInstance b,s,w,t,l,f,c,b,n,e,c,s,s,w,w,p,w,o,p,n,n,m,e>
user=> (.classifyInstance bayes (.get shrooms 2))
0.0
```

## How it works...

Bayesian models work by initially assuming that there's usually a fifty-fifty chance that a mushroom is edible or poisonous. For each item in the training set, it uses the values of each mushroom's attributes to nudge this fifty-fifty chance in the direction of the classification for that mushroom. So if a mushroom has a bell-shaped cap, smells of anise, and is edible, the model will assume that if it sees another mushroom with a bell-shaped cap that smells of anise, it's slightly more likely to be edible than poisonous.

By classifying each instance in the mushroom dataset, we can evaluate how well the model has done. The following code snippet will do this:

```
user=> (frequencies
          (map #(vector (.classValue (.get shrooms %))
                          (.classifyInstance bayes (.get shrooms %)))
              (range (.numInstances shrooms)))))
{[1.0 0.0] 383, [0.0 0.0] 4173, [1.0 1.0] 3533, [0.0 1.0] 35}
```

Thus, it classified approximately 95 percent of the data correctly (4173 plus 3533). It thought that 383 poisonous mushrooms were edible and 35 edible mushrooms were poisonous. This isn't a bad result, although we might wish that it erred on the side of caution!

## There's more...

▸ Weka's documentation for the `NaiveBayes` class at `http://weka.sourceforge.net/doc.dev/weka/classifiers/bayes/NaiveBayes.html` has information about the options available

▸ Alexandru Nedelcu has a good introduction to Bayesian modeling and classifiers at `https://www.bionicspirit.com/blog/2012/02/09/howto-build-naive-bayes-classifier.html`

# Classifying data with support vector machines

**Support vector machines** (**SVMs**) try to divide two groups of data along a plane. An SVM finds the plane that is the farthest from both groups. If a plane comes much closer to group B, it will prefer a plane that is approximately an equal distance from both. SVMs have a number of nice properties. While other clustering or classification algorithms work well with defined clusters of data, SVMs may work fine with data that isn't in well-defined and delineated groupings. They are also not affected by the local minima. Algorithms such as K-Means or SOMs—which begin from a random starting point—can get caught in solutions that aren't bad for the area around the solution, but aren't the best for the entire space. This isn't a problem for SVMs.

## Getting ready

First, we'll need these dependencies in our `project.clj` file:

```
(defproject d-mining "0.1.0-SNAPSHOT"
  :dependencies [[org.clojure/clojure "1.6.0"]
                 [nz.ac.waikato.cms.weka/weka-dev "3.7.11"]
                 [nz.ac.waikato.cms.weka/LibSVM "1.0.6"]])
```

In the script or REPL, we'll import the SVM library:

```
(import [weka.classifiers.functions LibSVM])
```

We'll also use the ionosphere dataset from the Weka datasets. (You can download this from http://www.ericrochester.com/clj-data-analysis/data/UCI/ionosphere.arff.) This data is taken from a phased-array antenna system in Goose Bay, Labrador. For each observation, the first 34 attributes are from 17 pulse numbers (a pulse for each observation) for the system, with two attributes per pulse number. The thirty-fifth attribute indicates whether the reading is good or bad. Good readings show evidence of some kind of structure in the ionosphere. Bad readings do not; their signals pass through the ionosphere. We'll load this and set the last column, the "good" or "bad" column as the class index:

```
(def ion (doto (load-arff "data/UCI/ionosphere.arff")
           (.setClassIndex 34)))
```

Finally, we'll use the `defanalysis` macro from the *Discovering groups of data with K-Means clustering* recipe and the `sample-instances` function from the *Classifying data with Naive Bayesian classifiers* recipe.

## How to do it...

For this recipe, we'll define some utility functions and the analysis algorithm wrapper. Then we'll put it through its paces:

1.  A number of the options for the SVM analysis have to be converted from Clojure-friendly values. For example, we want to pass `true` to one option and a mnemonic keyword to another, but Weka wants both of these as integers. So to make the parameter values more natural to Clojure, we'll use several functions that convert the Clojure parameters to the integer strings that Weka wants:

    ```
    (defn bool->int [b] (if b 1 0))
    (def svm-types
      {:c-svc 0, :nu-svc 1, :one-class-svm 2,
       :epsilon-svr 3, :nu-svr 4})
    (def svm-fns
      {:linear 0, :polynomial 1, :radial-basis 2,
       :sigmoid 3})
    ```

2.  We'll use these to define the wrapper function for the `LibSVM` class, which is a standalone library that works with Weka:

    ```
    (defanalysis
      svm LibSVM buildClassifier
      [["-S" svm-type :c-svc svm-types]
       ["-K" kernel-fn :radial-basis svm-fns]
    ```

```
    ["-D" degree 3]
    ["-G" gamma nil :not-nil]
    ["-R" coef0 0]
    ["-C" c 1]
    ["-N" nu 0.5]
    ["-Z" normalize false bool->int]
    ["-P" epsilon 0.1]
    ["-M" cache-size 40]
    ["-E" tolerance 0.001]
    ["-H" shrinking true bool->int]
    ["-W" weights nil :not-nil]])
```

3.  Before we use this, let's also write a function to calculate the classification accuracy by re-classifying each instance and tracking whether the SVM identified the class values correctly or not. We'll use this to see how well the trained SVM is:

```
(defn eval-instance
  ([] {:correct 0, :incorrect 0})
  ([_] {:correct 0, :incorrect 0})
  ([classifier sums instance]
   (if (= (.classValue instance)
          (.classifyInstance classifier instance))
     (assoc sums
            :correct (inc (sums :correct)))
     (assoc sums
            :incorrect (inc (sums :incorrect))))))
```

4.  Now, let's get a sample of 35 of the observations (about 10 percent of the total) and train the SVM on them:

```
(def ion-sample (sample-instances ion 35))
(def ion-svm (svm ion-sample))
```

5.  It'll output some information about the optimizations, and then it will be ready to use. We'll use `eval-instance` to see how it did:

```
user=> (reduce (partial eval-instance ion-svm)
               (eval-instance) ion)
{:incorrect 81, :correct 270}
```

This gives us a total correct of 77 percent.

## There's more...

▸ The Weka website's documentation has a good page on the `LibSVM` class at
  `http://weka.wikispaces.com/LibSVM`

▸ R. Berwick has written *An Idiot's guide to Support vector machines (SVMs)*, which is
  an excellent introduction to the history and theoretical background of SVMs. You can
  find it at `http://www.cs.ucf.edu/courses/cap6412/fall2009/papers/`
  `Berwick2003.pdf`

▸ More information on the ionosphere dataset is available at `http://archive.ics.`
  `uci.edu/ml/datasets/Ionosphere`

# Finding associations in data with the Apriori algorithm

One of the main goals of data mining and clustering is to learn the implicit relationships
in the data. The Apriori algorithm helps to do this by teasing out such relationships into an
explicit set of association rules. A common example of this type of analysis is what is done by
groceries stores. They analyze receipts to see which items are commonly bought together, and
then they can modify the store layout and marketing to suggest the second item once you've
decided to buy the first item.

In this recipe, we'll use this algorithm to extract the relationships from the mushroom dataset
that we've already seen several times in this chapter.

## Getting ready

First, we'll use the same dependencies that we did in the *Loading CSV and ARFF files
into Weka* recipe.

We'll use only one import in our script or REPL:

```
(import [weka.associations Apriori])
```

We'll also use the mushroom dataset that we introduced in the *Classifying data with decision
trees* recipe. We'll set the class attribute to the column indicating whether the mushroom is
edible or poisonous:

```
(def shrooms (doto (load-arff "data/UCI/mushroom.arff")
                   (.setClassIndex 22)))
```

Finally, we'll use the `defanalysis` macro from the *Discovering groups of data using K-Means
clustering* recipe.

## How to do it...

We'll train an instance of the `Apriori` class, extract the classification rules, and use them to classify the instances:

1. First, we need a function that converts keywords into integers for one of the options to the `Apriori` class:

```
(def rank-metrics
  {:confidence 0 :lift 1 :leverage 2 :conviction 3})
```

2. Now we'll use that in our definition of a wrapper function for the `Apriori` class:

```
(defanalysis
  apriori Apriori buildAssociations
  [["-N" rules 10]
   ["-T" rank-metric :confidence rank-metrics]
   ["-C" min-metric 0.9]
   ["-D" min-support-delta 0.05]
   [["-M" "-U"] min-support-bounds [0.1 1.0] :seq]
   ["-S" significance nil :not-nil]
   ["-I" output-itemsets false :flag-true]
   ["-R" remove-missing-value-columns
    false :flag-true]
   ["-V" progress false :flag-true]
   ["-A" mine-class-rules false :flag-true]
   ["-c" class-index nil :not-nil]])
```

3. With this in place, we can use it the way we have used the other wrapper functions:

```
(def a (apriori shrooms))
```

4. Then we can print the association rules:

```
user=> (doseq [r (.. a getAssociationRules getRules)]
         (println
           (format "%s => %s %s = %.4f"
                   (mapv str (.getPremise r))
                   (mapv str (.getConsequence r))
                   (.getPrimaryMetricName r)
                   (.getPrimaryMetricValue r))))
["veil-color=w"] => ["veil-type=p"] Confidence = 1.0000
["gill-attachment=f"] => ["veil-type=p"] Confidence = 1.0000
...
```

## How it works...

The Apriori algorithm looks for items that are often associated together within a transaction. This can be used for things such as analyzing shopping patterns. In this case, we're viewing the constellation of attributes related to each mushroom as a transaction, and we're using the Apriori algorithm to see which traits are associated with which other traits.

The algorithm attempts to find the premises that imply a set of consequences. For instance, white veil colors (the premise) imply a partial veil type with a confidence of 1.0, so whenever the premise is found, the consequence is also found. A white veil color also implies a free gill attachment, but the confidence is 99 percent, so we know that these two aren't associated all of the time.

The abbreviated data dump of the preceding traits isn't particularly legible, so here's the same information as a table:

| Premise | Consequence | Confidence |
| --- | --- | --- |
| veil-color=w | veil-type=p | 1.0000 |
| gill-attachment=f | veil-type=p | 1.0000 |
| gill-attachment=f, veil-color=w | veil-type=p | 1.0000 |
| gill-attachment=f | veil-color=w | 0.9990 |
| gill-attachment=f, veil-type=p | veil-color=w | 0.9990 |
| gill-attachment=f | veil-type=p, veil-color=w | 0.9990 |
| veil-color=w | gill-attachment=f | 0.9977 |
| veil-type=p, veil-color=w | gill-attachment=f | 0.9977 |
| veil-color=w | gill-attachment=f, veil-type=p | 0.9977 |
| veil-type=p | veil-color=w | 0.9754 |

From this, we can see that a white veil is associated with a partial veil type, a free gill attachment is associated with a partial white veil, and so on. If we want more information, we can request more rules using the `rules` parameter.

## There's more...

The Weka documentation at `http://weka.sourceforge.net/doc.dev/weka/associations/Apriori.html` has more information about the `Apriori` class and its options

For more about the algorithm itself, see Wikipedia's page on the Apriori algorithm at `http://en.wikipedia.org/wiki/Apriori_algorithm`

# 10
# Working with Unstructured and Textual Data

In this chapter, we will cover the following recipes:

- ▶ Tokenizing text
- ▶ Finding sentences
- ▶ Focusing on content words with stoplists
- ▶ Getting document frequencies
- ▶ Scaling document frequencies by document size
- ▶ Scaling document frequencies with TF-IDF
- ▶ Finding people, places, and things with Named Entity Recognition
- ▶ Mapping documents to a sparse vector space representation
- ▶ Performing topic modeling with MALLET
- ▶ Performing naïve Bayesian classification with MALLET

# Introduction

We've been talking about all of the data that's out there in the world. However, structured or semistructured data—the kind you'd find in spreadsheets or in tables on web pages—is vastly overshadowed by the unstructured data that's being produced. This includes news articles, blog posts, tweets, Hacker News discussions, StackOverflow questions and responses, and any other natural text that seems like it is being generated by the petabytes daily.

This unstructured content contains information. It has rich, subtle, and nuanced data, but getting it is difficult. In this chapter, we'll explore some ways to get some of the information out of unstructured data. It won't be fully nuanced and it will be very rough, but it's a start. We've already looked at how to acquire textual data. In *Chapter 1, Importing Data for Analysis*, we looked at this in the *Scraping textual data from web pages* recipe. Still, the Web is going to be your best source for data.

# Tokenizing text

Before we can do any real analysis of a text or a corpus of texts, we have to identify the words in the text. This process is called **tokenization**. The output of this process is a list of words, and possibly includes punctuation in a text. This is different from tokenizing formal languages such as programming languages: it is meant to work with natural languages and its results are less structured.

It's easy to write your own tokenizer, but there are a lot of edge and corner cases to take into consideration and account for. It's also easy to include a **natural language processing** (**NLP**) library that includes one or more tokenizers. In this recipe, we'll use the OpenNLP (`http://opennlp.apache.org/`) and its Clojure wrapper (`https://clojars.org/clojure-opennlp`).

## Getting ready

We'll need to include the `clojure-opennlp` in our `project.clj` file:

```
(defproject com.ericrochester/text-data "0.1.0-SNAPSHOT"
  :dependencies [[org.clojure/clojure "1.6.0"]
                 [clojure-opennlp "0.3.2"]])
```

We will also need to require it into the current namespace, as follows:

```
(require '[opennlp.nlp :as nlp])
```

Finally, we'll download a model for a statistical tokenizer. I downloaded all of the files from `http://opennlp.sourceforge.net/models-1.5/`. I then saved them into `models/`.

## How to do it...

In order to tokenize a document, we'll need to first create the tokenizer. We can do this by loading the model:

```
(def tokenize (nlp/make-tokenizer "models/en-token.bin"))
```

Then, we use it by passing a string to this `tokenizer` object:

```
user=> (tokenize "This is a string.")
["This" "is" "a" "string" "."]
user=> (tokenize "This isn't a string.")
["This" "is" "n't" "a" "string" "."]
```

## How it works...

In OpenNLP, tokenizers are statistically trained to identify tokens in a language, based on the language used in the text. The `en-token.bin` file contains the information for a trained tokenizer for English. In the second example of the previous section, we can see that it correctly pulls the contracted *not* from the base word, *is*.

Once we load this data back into a tokenizer, we can use it again to pull the tokens out.

The main catch is that the language used to generate the model data has to match the language in the input string that we're attempting to tokenize.

# Finding sentences

Words (tokens) aren't the only structures that we're interested in, however. Another interesting and useful grammatical structure is the sentence. In this recipe, we'll use a process similar to the one we used in the previous recipe, *Tokenizing text*, in order to create a function that will pull sentences from a string in the same way that tokenize pulled tokens from a string in the last recipe.

## Getting ready

We'll need to include `clojure-opennlp` in our `project.clj` file:

```
(defproject com.ericrochester/text-data "0.1.0-SNAPSHOT"
  :dependencies [[org.clojure/clojure "1.6.0"]
                 [clojure-opennlp "0.3.2"]])
```

We will also need to require it into the current namespace:

```
(require '[opennlp.nlp :as nlp])
```

Finally, we'll download a model for a statistical sentence splitter. I downloaded `en-sent.bin` from `http://opennlp.sourceforge.net/models-1.5/`. I then saved it into `models/en-sent.bin`.

## How to do it...

As in the *Tokenizing text* recipe, we will start by loading the sentence identification model data, as shown here:

```
(def get-sentences
  (nlp/make-sentence-detector "models/en-sent.bin"))
```

Now, we use that data to split a text into a series of sentences, as follows:

```
user=> (get-sentences "I never saw a Purple Cow.
          I never hope to see one.
          But I can tell you, anyhow.
          I'd rather see than be one.")
["I never saw a Purple Cow."
 "I never hope to see one."
 "But I can tell you, anyhow."
 "I'd rather see than be one."]
```

## How it works...

The data model in `models/en-sent.bin` contains the information that OpenNLP needs to recreate a previously-trained sentence identification algorithm. Once we have reinstantiated this algorithm, we can use it to identify the sentences in a text, as we did by calling `get-sentences`.

# Focusing on content words with stoplists

**Stoplists** or **stopwords** are a list of words that should not be included in further analysis. Usually, this is because they're so common that they don't add much information to the analysis.

These lists are usually dominated by what are known as **function words**—words that have a grammatical purpose in the sentence, but which themselves do not carry any meaning. For example, *the* indicates that the noun that follows is singular, but it does not have a meaning by itself. Others prepositions, such as *after*, have a meaning, but they are so common that they tend to get in the way.

On the other hand, *chair* has a meaning beyond what it's doing in the sentence, and in fact, it's role in the sentence will vary (subject, direct object, and so on).

You don't always want to use stopwords since they throw away information. However, since function words are more frequent than content words, sometimes focusing on the content words can add clarity to your analysis and its output. Also, they can speed up the processing.

## Getting ready

This recipe will build on the work that we've done so far in this chapter. As such, it will use the same `project.clj` file that we used in the *Tokenizing text* and *Finding sentences* recipes:

```
(defproject com.ericrochester/text-data "0.1.0-SNAPSHOT"
  :dependencies [[org.clojure/clojure "1.6.0"]
                 [clojure-opennlp "0.3.2"]])
```

However, we'll use a slightly different set of requirements for this recipe:

```
(require '[opennlp.nlp :as nlp]
         '[clojure.java.io :as io])
```

We'll also need to have a list of stopwords. You can easily create your own list, but for the purpose of this recipe, we'll use the English stopword list included with the Natural Language Toolkit (http://www.nltk.org/). You can download this from http://nltk.github.com/nltk_data/packages/corpora/stopwords.zip. Unzip it into your project directory and make sure that the `stopwords/english` file exists.

We'll also use the `tokenize` and `get-sentences` functions that we created in the previous two recipes.

## How to do it...

We'll need to create a function in order to process and normalize the tokens. Also, we'll need a utility function to load the stopword list. Once these are in place, we'll see how to use the stopwords. To do this, perform the following steps:

1. The words in the stopword list have been lowercased. We can also do this with the tokens that we create. We'll use the `normalize` function to handle the lowercasing of each token:

```
(defn normalize [token-seq]
  (map #(.toLowerCase %) token-seq))
```

2. The stoplist will actually be represented by a Clojure set. This will make filtering a lot easier. The `load-stopwords` function will read in the file, break it into lines, and fold them into a set, as follows:

```
(defn load-stopwords [filename]
  (with-open [r (io/reader filename)]
    (set (doall (line-seq r)))))
(def is-stopword (load-stopwords "stopwords/english"))
```

3. Finally, we can load the tokens. This will break the input into sentences. Then, it will tokenize each sentence, normalize its tokens, and remove its stopwords, as follows:

```
(def tokens
  (map #(remove is-stopword (normalize (tokenize %)))
       (get-sentences
         "I never saw a Purple Cow.
         I never hope to see one.
         But I can tell you, anyhow.
         I'd rather see than be one.")))
```

Now, you can see that the tokens returned are more focused on the content and are missing all of the function words:

```
user=> (pprint tokens)
(("never" "saw" "purple" "cow" ".")
 ("never" "hope" "see" "one" ".")
 ("tell" "," "anyhow" ".")
 ("'d" "rather" "see" "one" "."))
```

# Getting document frequencies

One common and useful metric to work with text corpora is to get the counts of the tokens in the documents. This can be done quite easily by leveraging standard Clojure functions.

Let's see how.

## Getting ready

We'll continue building on the previous recipes in this chapter. Because of that, we'll use the same `project.clj` file:

```
(defproject com.ericrochester/text-data "0.1.0-SNAPSHOT"
  :dependencies [[org.clojure/clojure "1.6.0"]
                 [clojure-opennlp "0.3.2"]])
```

We'll also use `tokenize`, `get-sentences`, `normalize`, `load-stopwords`, and `is-stopword` from the earlier recipes.

We'll also use the value of the tokens that we saw in the *Focusing on content words with stoplists* recipe. Here it is again:

```
(def tokens
  (map #(remove is-stopword (normalize (tokenize %)))
       (get-sentences
         "I never saw a Purple Cow.
         I never hope to see one.
         But I can tell you, anyhow.
         I'd rather see than be one.")))
```

## How to do it...

Of course, the standard function to count items in a sequence is `frequencies`. We can use this to get the token counts for each sentence, but then we'll also want to fold those into a frequency table using `merge-with`:

```
(def token-freqs
  (apply merge-with + (map frequencies tokens)))
```

We can print or query this table to get the count for any token or piece of punctuation, as follows:

```
user=> (pprint token-freqs)
{"see" 2,
 "purple" 1,
 "tell" 1,
 "cow" 1,
 "anyhow" 1,
 "hope" 1,
 "never" 2,
 "saw" 1,
 "'d" 1,
 "." 4,
 "one" 2,
 "," 1,
 "rather" 1}
```

# Scaling document frequencies by document size

While raw token frequencies can be useful, they often have one major problem: comparing frequencies with different documents is complicated if the document sizes are not the same. If the word *customer* appears 23 times in a 500-word document and it appears 40 times in a 1,000-word document, which one do you think is more focused on that word? It's difficult to say.

To work around this, it's common to scale the tokens frequencies for each document by the size of the document. That's what we'll do in this recipe.

## Getting ready

We'll continue building on the previous recipes in this chapter. Because of that, we'll use the same `project.clj` file:

```
(defproject com.ericrochester/text-data "0.1.0-SNAPSHOT"
  :dependencies [[org.clojure/clojure "1.6.0"]
                 [clojure-opennlp "0.3.2"]])
```

We'll use the token frequencies that we figured from the *Getting document frequencies* recipe. We'll keep them bound to the name `token-freqs`.

## How to do it...

The function used to perform this scaling is fairly simple. It calculates the total number of tokens by adding the values from the frequency hashmap and then it walks over the hashmap again, scaling each frequency, as shown here:

```
(defn scale-by-total [freqs]
  (let [total (reduce + 0 (vals freqs))]
    (->> freqs
         (map #(vector (first %) (/ (second %) total)))
         (into {}))))
```

We can now use this on `token-freqs` from the last recipe:

```
user=> (pprint (scale-by-total token-freqs))
{"see" 2/19,
 "purple" 1/19,
 "tell" 1/19,
```

```
"cow" 1/19,
"anyhow" 1/19,
"hope" 1/19,
"never" 2/19,
"saw" 1/19,
"'d" 1/19,
"." 4/19,
"one" 2/19,
"," 1/19,
"rather" 1/19}
```

Now, we can easily compare these values to the frequencies generated from other documents.

## How it works...

This works by changing all of the raw frequencies into ratios based on each document's size.

These numbers are comparable. In our example, from the introduction to this recipe, 0.046 (23/500) is obviously slightly more than 0.040 (40/1000). However, both of these numbers are ridiculously high. Words that typically occur this much in English are words such as *the*.

Document-scaled frequencies do have problems with shorter texts. For example, take this tweet by the Twitter user @LegoAcademics:

> *"Dr Brown's random number algorithm is based on the baffling floor sequences chosen by the Uni library elevator".*

In this tweet, let's see what the scaled frequency of *random* is:

```
(-> (str "Dr Brown's random number algorithm is based "
         "on the baffling floor seqeuences chosen by "
         "the Uni library elevator.")
    tokenize
    normalize
    frequencies
    scale-by-total
    (get "random")
    float)
```

This gives us 0.05. Again, this is ridiculously high. Most other tweets won't include the term *random* at all. Because of this, you still can only compare tweets.

# Scaling document frequencies with TF-IDF

In the last few recipes, we've seen how to generate term frequencies and scale them by the size of the document so that the frequencies from two different documents can be compared.

Term frequencies also have another problem. They don't tell you how important a term is, relative to all of the documents in the corpus.

To address this, we will use **term frequency-inverse document frequency (TF-IDF)**. This metric scales the term's frequency in a document by the term's frequency in the entire corpus.

In this recipe, we'll assemble the parts needed to implement TF-IDF.

## Getting ready

We'll continue building on the previous recipes in this chapter. Because of that, we'll use the same `project.clj` file:

```
(defproject com.ericrochester/text-data "0.1.0-SNAPSHOT"
  :dependencies [[org.clojure/clojure "1.6.0"]
                 [clojure-opennlp "0.3.2"]])
```

We'll also use two functions that we've created earlier in this chapter. From the *Tokenizing text* recipe, we'll use `tokenize`. From the *Focusing on content words with stoplists* recipe, we'll use `normalize`.

Aside from the imports required for these two functions, we'll also want to have this available in our source code or REPL:

```
(require '[clojure.set :as set])
```

For this recipe, we'll also need more data than we've been using. For this, we'll use a corpus of **State of the Union (SOTU)** addresses from United States presidents over time. These are yearly addresses that presidents make where they talk about the events of the past year and outline their priorities over the next twelve months. You can download these from `http://www.ericrochester.com/clj-data-analysis/data/sotu.tar.gz`. I've unpacked the data from this file into the `sotu` directory.

## How to do it...

The following image shows the group of functions that we'll be coding in this recipe:

$$tf(t,d) = 0.5 + \frac{0.5 \times f(t,d)}{\max\{f(w,d) : w \in \text{d}\}}$$

$$idf(t,D) = \log \frac{N}{|\{d \in D : t \in d\}|}$$

$$tfidf(t,d,D) = tf(t,d) \times idf(t,D)$$

So, in English, the function for _tf_ represents the frequency of the term _t_ in the document _d_, scaled by the maximum term frequency in _d_. In other words, unless you're using a stoplist, this will almost always be the frequency of the term _the_.

The function for _idf_ is the log of the number of documents (_N_) divided by the number of documents that contain the term _t_.

These equations break the problem down well. We can write a function for each one of these. We'll also create a number of other functions to help us along. Let's get started:

1.  For the first function, we'll implement the `tf` component of the equation. This is a transparent translation of the _tf_ function from earlier. It takes a term's frequency and the maximum term frequency from the same document, as follows:

    ```
    (defn tf [term-freq max-freq]
      (+ 0.5 (/ (* 0.5 term-freq) max-freq)))
    ```

2.  Now, we'll do the most basic implementation of `idf`. Like the `tf` function used earlier, it's a close match to the _idf_ equation:

    ```
    (defn idf [corpus term]
      (Math/log
        (/ (count corpus)
           (inc (count
                  (filter #(contains? % term) corpus)))))))
    ```

3. Now, we'll take a short detour in order to optimize prematurely. In this case, the IDF values will be the same for each term across the corpus, but if we're not careful, we'll code this so that we're computing these terms for each document. For example, the IDF value for *the* will be the same, no matter how many times *the* actually occurs in the current document. We can precompute these and cache them. However, before we can do that, we'll need to obtain the set of all the terms in the corpus. The get-corpus-terms function does this, as shown here:

```
(defn get-corpus-terms [corpus]
  (->> corpus
       (map #(set (keys %)))
       (reduce set/union #{})))
```

4. The get-idf-cache function takes a corpus, extracts its term set, and returns a hashmap associating the terms with their IDF values, as follows:

```
(defn get-idf-cache [corpus]
  (reduce #(assoc %1 %2 (idf corpus %2)) {}
          (get-corpus-terms corpus)))
```

5. Now, the tf-idf function is our lowest-level function that combines tf and idf. It just takes the raw parameters, including the cached IDF value, and performs the necessary calculations:

```
(defn tf-idf [idf-value freq max-freq]
  (* (tf freq max-freq) idf-value))
```

6. The tf-idf-pair function sits immediately on top of tf-idf. It gets the IDF value from the cache, and for one of its parameters, it takes a term-raw frequency pair. It returns the pair with the frequency being the TF-IDF for that term:

```
(defn tf-idf-pair [idf-cache max-freq pair]
  (let [[term freq] pair]
    [term (tf-idf (idf-cache term) freq max-freq)]))
```

7. Finally, the tf-idf-freqs function controls the entire process. It takes an IDF cache and a frequency hashmap, and it scales the frequencies in the hashmap into their TF-IDF equivalents, as follows:

```
(defn tf-idf-freqs [idf-cache freqs]
  (let [max-freq (reduce max 0 (vals freqs))]
    (->> freqs
         (map #(tf-idf-pair idf-cache max-freq %))
         (into {}))))
```

Now, we have all of the pieces in place to use this.

1. For this example, we'll read all of the State of the Union addresses into a sequence of raw frequency hashmaps. This will be bound to the name `corpus`:

```
(def corpus
  (->> "sotu"
       (java.io.File.)
       (.list)
       (map #(str "sotu/" %))
       (map slurp)
       (map tokenize)
       (map normalize)
       (map frequencies)))
```

2. We'll use these frequencies to create the IDF cache and bind it to the name `cache`:

```
(def cache (get-idf-cache corpus))
```

3. Now, actually calling `tf-idf-freqs` on these frequencies is straightforward, as shown here:

```
(def freqs (map #(tf-idf-freqs cache %) corpus))
```

## How it works...

TF-IDF scales the raw token frequencies by the number of documents they occur in within the corpus. This identifies the distinguishing words for each document. After all, if the word occurs in almost every document, it won't be a distinguishing word for any document. However, if a word is only found in one document, it helps to distinguish that document.

For example, here are the 10 most distinguishing words from the first SOTU address:

```
user=> (doseq [[term idf-freq] (->> freqs
                                     first
                                     (sort-by second)
                                     reverse
                                     (take 10))]
         (println [term idf-freq ((first corpus) term)]))
[intimating 2.39029215473352 1]
[licentiousness 2.39029215473352 1]
[discern 2.185469574348983 1]
[inviolable 2.0401456408424132 1]
[specify 1.927423640693998 1]
```

```
[comprehending 1.8353230604578765 1]
[novelty 1.8353230604578765 1]
[well-digested 1.8353230604578765 1]
[cherishing 1.8353230604578765 1]
[cool 1.7574531294111173 1]
```

You can see that these words all occur once in this document, and in fact, *intimating* and *licentiousness* are only found in the first SOTU, and all 10 of these words are found in six or fewer addresses.

# Finding people, places, and things with Named Entity Recognition

One thing that's fairly easy to pull out of documents is named items. This includes things such as people's names, organizations, locations, and dates. These algorithms are called **Named Entity Recognition** (**NER**), and while they are not perfect, they're generally pretty good. Error rates under 0.1 are normal.

The OpenNLP library has classes to perform NER, and depending on what you train them with, they will identify people, locations, dates, or a number of other things. The clojure-opennlp library also exposes these classes in a good, Clojure-friendly way.

## Getting ready

We'll continue building on the previous recipes in this chapter. Because of this, we'll use the same `project.clj` file:

```
(defproject com.ericrochester/text-data "0.1.0-SNAPSHOT"
  :dependencies [[org.clojure/clojure "1.6.0"]
                 [clojure-opennlp "0.3.2"]])
```

From the *Tokenizing text* recipe, we'll use `tokenize`, and from the *Focusing on content words with stoplists* recipe, we'll use `normalize`.

Pretrained models can be downloaded from `http://opennlp.sourceforge.net/models-1.5/`. I downloaded `en-ner-person.bin`, `en-ner-organization.bin`, `en-ner-date.bin`, `en-ner-location.bin`, and `en-ner-money.bin`. Then, I saved these models in `models/`.

## How to do it...

To set things up, we have to load the models and bind them to function names. To load the models, we'll use the `opennlp.nlp/make-name-finder` function. We can use this to load each recognizer individually, as follows:

```
(def get-persons
  (nlp/make-name-finder "models/en-ner-person.bin"))
(def get-orgs
  (nlp/make-name-finder "models/en-ner-organization.bin"))
(def get-date
  (nlp/make-name-finder "models/en-ner-date.bin"))
(def get-location
  (nlp/make-name-finder "models/en-ner-location.bin"))
(def get-money
  (nlp/make-name-finder "models/en-ner-money.bin"))
```

Now, in order to test this out, let's load the latest SOTU address in our corpus. This is Barak Obama's 2013 State of the Union:

```
(def sotu (tokenize (slurp "sotu/2013-0.txt")))
```

We can call each of these functions on the tokenized text to see the results, as shown here:

```
user=> (get-persons sotu)
("John F. Kennedy" "Most Americans—Democrats" "Government" "John
McCain" "Joe Lieberman" "So" "Tonight I" "Joe Biden" "Joe" "Tonight"
"Al Qaida" "Russia" "And" "Michelle" "Hadiya Pendleton" "Gabby
Giffords" "Menchu Sanchez" "Desiline Victor" "Brian Murphy" "Brian")
user=> (get-orgs sotu)
("Congress" "Union" "Nation" "America" "Tax" "Apple" "Department
of Defense and Energy" "CEOs" "Siemens America—a" "New York Public
Schools" "City University of New York" "IBM" "American" "Higher
Education" "Federal" "Senate" "House" "CEO" "European Union" "It")
user=> (get-date sotu)
("this year" "18 months ago" "Last year" "Today" "last 15" "2007"
"today" "tomorrow" "20 years ago" "This" "last year" "This spring"
"next year" "2014" "next two decades" "next month" "a")
user=> (get-location sotu)
("Washington" "United States of America" "Earth" "Japan" "Mexico"
"America" "Youngstown" "Ohio" "China" "North Carolina" "Georgia"
"Oklahoma" "Germany" "Brooklyn" "Afghanistan" "Arabian Peninsula"
"Africa" "Libya" "Mali" "And" "North Korea" "Iran" "Russia" "Asia"
"Atlantic" "United States" "Rangoon" "Burma" "the Americas" "Europe"
"Middle East" "Egypt" "Israel" "Chicago" "Oak Creek" "New York City"
"Miami" "Wisconsin")
user=> (get-money sotu)
("$ 2.5 trillion" "$ 4 trillion" "$ 140 to" "$")
```

## How it works...

When you glance at the results, you can see that it appears to have performed well. We need to look into the document and see what it missed to be certain, of course.

The process to use this is similar to the tokenizer or sentence chunker: load the model from a file and then call the result as a function.

# Mapping documents to a sparse vector space representation

Many text algorithms deal with **vector space representations** of the documents. This means that the documents are normalized into vectors. Each individual token type is assigned one position across all the documents' vectors. For instance, *text* might have position 42, so index 42 in all the document vectors will have the frequency (or other value) of the word *text*.

However, most documents won't have anything for most words. This makes them **sparse vectors**, and we can use more efficient formats for them.

The Colt library (`http://acs.lbl.gov/ACSSoftware/colt/`) contains implementations of sparse vectors. For this recipe, we'll see how to read a collection of documents into these.

## Getting ready...

For this recipe, we'll need the following in our `project.clj` file:

```
(defproject com.ericrochester/text-data "0.1.0-SNAPSHOT"
  :dependencies [[org.clojure/clojure "1.6.0"]
                 [clojure-opennlp "0.3.2"]
                 [colt/colt "1.2.0"]])
```

For our script or REPL, we'll need these libraries:

```
(require '[clojure.set :as set]
         '[opennlp.nlp :as nlp])
(import [cern.colt.matrix DoubleFactory2D])
```

From the previous recipes, we'll use several functions. From the *Tokenizing text* recipe, we'll use `tokenize` and `normalize`, and from the *Scaling document frequencies with TF-IDF* recipe, we'll use `get-corpus-terms`.

For the data, we'll again use the State of the Union address that we first saw in the *Scaling document frequencies in TF-IDF* recipe. You can download these from `http://www.ericrochester.com/clj-data-analysis/data/sotu.tar.gz`. I've unpacked the data from this file into the `sotu` directory.

## How to do it...

In order to create vectors of all the documents, we'll first need to create a token index that maps tokens to the indexes in the vector. We'll then use that to create a sequence of Colt vectors. Finally, we can load the SOTU addresses and generate sparse feature vectors of all the documents, as follows:

1. Before we can create the feature vectors, we need to have a token index so that the vector indexes will be consistent across all of the documents. The `build-index` function takes care of this:

```
(defn build-index [corpus]
   (into {}
         (zipmap (tfidf/get-corpus-terms corpus)
                 (range))))
```

2. Now, we can use `build-index` to convert a sequence of token-frequency pairs into a feature vector. All of the tokens must be in the index:

```
(defn ->matrix [index pairs]
   (let [matrix (.make DoubleFactory2D/sparse
                    1 (count index) 0.0)
         inc-cell (fn [m p]
                     (let [[k v] p,
                           i (index k)]
                        (.set m 0 i v)
                        m))]
      (reduce inc-cell matrix pairs)))
```

With these in place, let's make use of them by loading the token frequencies in a corpus and then create the index from this:

```
(def corpus
   (->> "sotu"
        (java.io.File.)
        (.list)
        (map #(str "sotu/" %))
        (map slurp)
        (map tokenize)
        (map normalize)
        (map frequencies)))
(def index (build-index corpus))
```

With the index, we can finally move the information of the document frequencies into sparse vectors:

```
(def vecs (map #(->matrix index %) corpus))
```

# Performing topic modeling with MALLET

Previously in this chapter, we looked at a number of ways to programmatically see what's present in documents. We saw how to identify people, places, dates, and other things in documents. We saw how to break things up into sentences.

Another, more sophisticated way to discover what's in a document is to use **topic modeling**. Topic modeling attempts to identify a set of topics that are contained in the document collection. Each topic is a cluster of words that are used together throughout the corpus. These clusters are found in individual documents to varying degrees, and a document is composed of several topics to varying extents. We'll take a look at this in more detail in the explanation for this recipe.

To perform topic modeling, we'll use **MALLET** (`http://mallet.cs.umass.edu/`). This is a library and utility that implements topic modeling in addition to several other document classification algorithms.

## Getting ready

For this recipe, we'll need these lines in our `project.clj` file:

```
(defproject com.ericrochester/text-data "0.1.0-SNAPSHOT"
  :dependencies [[org.clojure/clojure "1.6.0"]
                 [cc.mallet/mallet "2.0.7"]]])
```

Our imports and requirements for this are pretty extensive too, as shown here:

```
(require '[clojure.java.io :as io])
(import [cc.mallet.util.*]
        [cc.mallet.types InstanceList]
        [cc.mallet.pipe
         Input2CharSequence TokenSequenceLowercase
         CharSequence2TokenSequence SerialPipes
         TokenSequenceRemoveStopwords
         TokenSequence2FeatureSequence]
        [cc.mallet.pipe.iterator FileListIterator]
        [cc.mallet.topics ParallelTopicModel]
        [java.io FileFilter])
```

Again, we'll use the State of the Union addresses that we've already seen several times in this chapter. You can download these from `http://www.ericrochester.com/clj-data-analysis/data/sotu.tar.gz`. I've unpacked the data from this file into the `sotu` directory.

## How to do it...

We'll need to work the documents through several phases to perform topic modeling, as follows:

1. Before we can process any documents, we'll need to create a processing pipeline. This defines how the documents should be read, tokenized, normalized, and so on:

```
(defn make-pipe-list []
  (InstanceList.
    (SerialPipes.
      [(Input2CharSequence. "UTF-8")
       (CharSequence2TokenSequence.
         #"\p{L}[\p{L}\p{P}]+\p{L}")
       (TokenSequenceLowercase.)
       (TokenSequenceRemoveStopwords. false false)
       (TokenSequence2FeatureSequence.)]))))
```

2. Now, we'll create a function that takes the processing pipeline and a directory of data files, and it will run the files through the pipeline. This returns an `InstanceList`, which is a collection of documents along with their metadata:

```
(defn add-directory-files [instance-list corpus-dir]
  (.addThruPipe
    instance-list
    (FileListIterator.
      (.listFiles (io/file corpus-dir))
      (reify FileFilter
        (accept [this pathname] true))
      #"/([^/]*).txt$"
      true)))
```

3. The last function takes the `InstanceList` and some other parameters and trains a topic model, which it returns:

```
(defn train-model
  ([instances] (train-model 100 4 50 instances))
  ([num-topics num-threads num-iterations instances]
   (doto (ParallelTopicModel. num-topics 1.0 0.01)
     (.addInstances instances)
     (.setNumThreads num-threads)
     (.setNumIterations num-iterations)
     (.estimate))))
```

Now, we can take these three functions and use them to train a topic model. While training, it will output some information about the process, and finally, it will list the top terms for each topic:

```
user=> (def pipe-list (make-pipe-list))
user=> (add-directory-files pipe-list "sotu/")
user=> (def tm (train-model 10 4 50 pipe-list))
...
INFO:
0       0.1       government federal year national congress war
1       0.1       world nation great power nations people
2       0.1       world security years programs congress program
3       0.1       law business men work people good
4       0.1       america people americans american work year
5       0.1       states government congress public people united
6       0.1       states public made commerce present session
7       0.1       government year department made service legislation
8       0.1       united states congress act government war
9       0.1       war peace nation great men people
```

## How it works...

It's difficult to succinctly and clearly explain how topic modeling works. Conceptually, it assigns words from the documents to buckets (topics). This is done in such a way that randomly drawing words from the buckets will most probably recreate the documents.

Interpreting the topics is always interesting. Generally, it involves taking a look at the top words for each topic and cross-referencing them with the documents that scored most highly for this topic.

For example, take the fourth topic, with the top words *law*, *business*, *men*, and *work*. The top-scoring document for this topic was the 1908 SOTU, with a distribution of 0.378. This was given by Theodore Roosevelt, and in his speech, he talked a lot about labor issues and legislation to rein in corrupt corporations. All of the words mentioned were used a lot, but understanding exactly what the topic is about isn't evident without actually taking a look at the document itself.

## See also...

There are a number of good papers and tutorials on topic modeling. There's a good tutorial written by Shawn Graham, Scott Weingart, and Ian Milligan at `http://programminghistorian.org/lessons/topic-modeling-and-mallet`

For a more rigorous explanation, check out Mark Steyvers's introduction *Probabilistic Topic Models*, which you can see at `http://psiexp.ss.uci.edu/research/papers/ SteyversGriffithsLSABookFormatted.pdf`

For some information on how to evaluate the topics that you get, see `http://homepages. inf.ed.ac.uk/imurray2/pub/09etm`

# Performing naïve Bayesian classification with MALLET

MALLET has gotten its reputation as a library for topic modeling. However, it also has a lot of other algorithms in it.

One popular algorithm that MALLET implements is naïve Bayesian classification. If you have documents that are already divided into categories, you can train a classifier to categorize new documents into those same categories. Often, this works surprisingly well.

One common use for this is in spam e-mail detection. We'll use this as our example here too.

## Getting ready

We'll need to have MALLET included in our `project.clj` file:

```
(defproject com.ericrochester/text-data "0.1.0-SNAPSHOT"
  :dependencies [[org.clojure/clojure "1.6.0"]
                 [cc.mallet/mallet "2.0.7"]])
```

Just as in the *Performing topic modeling with MALLET* recipe, the list of classes to be included is a little long, but most of them are for the processing pipeline, as shown here:

```
(require '[clojure.java.io :as io])
(import [cc.mallet.util.*]
        [cc.mallet.types InstanceList]
        [cc.mallet.pipe
         Input2CharSequence TokenSequenceLowercase
         CharSequence2TokenSequence SerialPipes
         SaveDataInSource Target2Label
         TokenSequence2FeatureSequence
         TokenSequenceRemoveStopwords
         FeatureSequence2AugmentableFeatureVector]
        [cc.mallet.pipe.iterator FileIterator]
        [cc.mallet.classify NaiveBayesTrainer])
```

For data, we can get preclassified emails from the SpamAssassin website. Take a look at `https://spamassassin.apache.org/publiccorpus/`. From this directory, I downloaded `20050311_spam_2.tar.bz2`, `20030228_easy_ham_2.tar.bz2`, and `20030228_hard_ham.tar.bz2`. I decompressed these into the `training` directory. This added three subdirectories: `training/easy_ham_2`, `training/hard_ham`, and `training/spam_2`.

I also downloaded two other archives: `20021010_hard_ham.tar.bz2` and `20021010_spam.tar.bz2`. I decompressed these into the `test-data` directory in order to create the `test-data/hard_ham` and `test-data/spam` directories.

## How to do it...

Now, we can define the functions to create the processing pipeline and a list of document instances, as well as to train the classifier and classify the documents:

1. We'll create the processing pipeline separately. A single instance of this has to be used to process all of the training, test, and actual data. Hang on to this:

```
(defn make-pipe-list []
  (SerialPipes.
    [(Target2Label.)
     (SaveDataInSource.)
     (Input2CharSequence. "UTF-8")
     (CharSequence2TokenSequence.
        #"\p{L}[\p{L}\p{P}]+\p{L}")
     (TokenSequenceLowercase.)
     (TokenSequenceRemoveStopwords.)
     (TokenSequence2FeatureSequence.)
     (FeatureSequence2AugmentableFeatureVector.
        false)]))
```

2. We can use that to create the instance list over the files in a directory. When we do, we'll use the documents' parent directory's name as its classification. This is what we'll be training the classifier on:

```
(defn add-input-directory [dir-name pipe]
  (doto (InstanceList. pipe)
    (.addThruPipe
      (FileIterator. (io/file dir-name)
                     #".*/([^/]*?)/\d+\..*$"))))
```

3. Finally, these two are relatively short and not strictly necessary, but it is good to have these two utility functions:

```
(defn train [instance-list]
  (.train (NaiveBayesTrainer.) instance-list))
(defn classify [bayes instance-list]
  (.classify bayes instance-list))
```

Now, we can use these functions to load the training documents from the `training` directory, train the classifier, and use it to classify the test files:

```
(def pipe (make-pipe-list))
(def instance-list (add-input-directory "training" pipe))
(def bayes (train instance-list))
```

Now we can use it to classify the test files.

```
(def test-list (add-input-directory "test-data" pipe))
(def classes (classify bayes test-list))
```

Moreover, finding the results just takes digging into the class structure:

```
user=> (.. (first (seq classes)) getLabeling getBestLabel
           toString)
"hard_ham"
```

We can use this to construct a matrix that shows how the classifier performs, as follows:

|  | Expected ham | Expected spam |
| --- | --- | --- |
| **Actually ham** | 246 | 99 |
| **Actually spam** | 4 | 402 |

From this confusion matrix, you can see that it does pretty well. Moreover, it errs on misclassifying spam as ham. This is good because this means that we'd only need to dig into our spam folder for four emails.

## How it works...

Naïve Bayesian classifiers work by starting with a reasonable guess about how likely a set of features are to be marked as spam. Often, this might be 50/50. Then, as it sees more and more documents and their classifications, it modifies this model, getting better results.

For example, it might notice that the word *free* is found in 100 ham emails but in 900 spam emails. This makes it a very strong indicator of spam, and the classifier will update its expectations accordingly. It then combines all of the relevant probabilities from the features it sees in a document in order to classify it one way or the other.

## There's more...

Alexandru Nedelcu has a good introduction to Bayesian modeling and classifiers at
`https://www.bionicspirit.com/blog/2012/02/09/howto-build-naive-bayes-classifier.html`

## See also...

We'll take a look at how to use the Weka machine learning library to train a naïve Bayesian classifier in order to sort edible and poisonous mushrooms in the *Classifying data with the Naïve Bayesian classifier* recipe in *Chapter 9, Clustering, Classifying, and Working with Weka*.

# 11

# Graphing in Incanter

In this chapter, we will cover the following recipes:

- ▶ Creating scatter plots with Incanter
- ▶ Graphing non-numeric data in bar charts
- ▶ Creating histograms with Incanter
- ▶ Creating function plots with Incanter
- ▶ Adding equations to Incanter charts
- ▶ Adding lines to scatter charts
- ▶ Customizing charts with JFreeChart
- ▶ Customizing chart colors and styles
- ▶ Saving Incanter graphs to PNG
- ▶ Using PCA to graph multi-dimensional data
- ▶ Creating dynamic charts with Incanter

## Introduction

Graphs serve a couple of important functions in data analysis. First, when exploring data, they can help us understand our data and the relationships in it.

But data analysis isn't all about wrangling data and crunching numbers. We must also communicate our findings and convey evidence for our arguments. Graphs serve an important role in succinctly communicating complex relationships. Although graphs can be unclear, confusing, or not too informative, well-made graphs can clarify concepts and relationships that are difficult to explain verbally.

Designing good, informative, and beautiful charts is difficult, and if you want to dive into that topic, and there's a lot of good information out there. Anything by Edward Tufte (http://www.edwardtufte.com/tufte/) is an excellent place to start, and his book, *The Visual Display of Quantitative Information*, is considered a classic in the field of data visualization design. To create charts and graphs, there are a number of options. There are a lot of solutions for graphing. In the next chapter, we'll look at some solutions involving ClojureScript (https://github.com/clojure/clojurescript) and d3 (http://d3js.org/). We also have R (http://www.r-project.org/), especially with its ggplot2 library (http://ggplot2.org/), and Mathematica (http://www.wolfram.com/mathematica/), which we worked with in *Chapter 8*, *Working with Mathematica and R*, both of which have strong graphing libraries.

In this chapter, we'll focus on Incanter charts. They are built on the JFreeChart library (http://www.jfree.org/jfreechart/), which provides a powerful set of functions to graph data. In this chapter, we'll use them to create a variety of types of graphs. We'll also look at how to save graphs as PNG images. We'll use **principal component analysis** (**PCA**) to project multidimensional data down to two dimensions so that they can be graphed easily. Finally, we'll create an interactive, dynamic graph.

# Creating scatter plots with Incanter

One of the most common types of charts is a scatter plot. This helps us visualize the relationship between two numeric variables.

## Getting ready

We'll need to list Incanter as a dependency in our Leiningen `project.clj` file:

```
(defproject reports "0.1.0-SNAPSHOT"
  :dependencies [[org.clojure/clojure "1.6.0"]
                 [incanter "1.5.5"]]])
```

We'll also require several of Incanter's namespaces into our script or REPL:

```
(require '[incanter.core :as i]
         '[incanter.charts :as c]
         'incanter.datasets)
```

Finally, we'll use the iris dataset, which we saw in several recipes in *Chapter 9*, *Clustering, Classifying, and Working with Weka*:

```
(def iris (incanter.datasets/get-dataset :iris))
```

## How to do it...

For this recipe, we'll create a chart plotting the dimensions of the iris' petals:

1. We'll create the chart, but hang on to the object created so that we can do things with the chart, such as displaying it, later:

```
(def iris-petal-scatter
  (c/scatter-plot
    (i/sel iris :cols :Petal.Width)
    (i/sel iris :cols :Petal.Length)
    :title "Irises: Petal Width by Petal Length"
    :x-label "Width (cm)"
    :y-label "Length (cm)"))
```

2. To actually display this chart, we pass it to the `incanter.core/view` function:

```
(i/view iris-petal-scatter)
```

The output of the preceding line resembles the following screenshot:

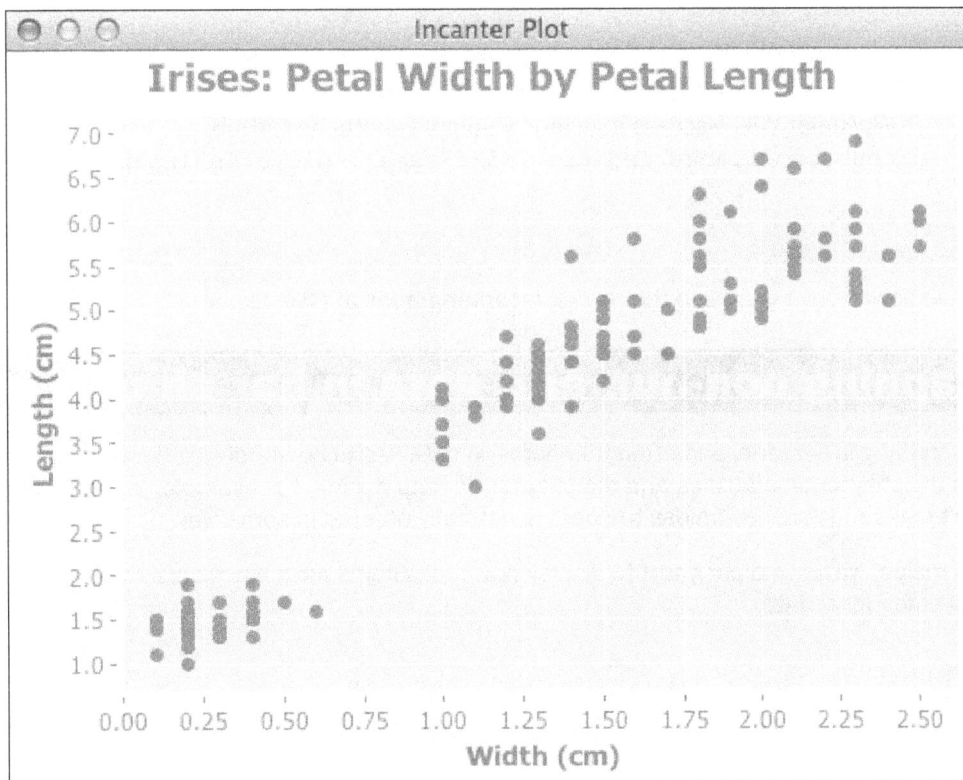

## How it works...

The `incanter.charts/scatter-plot` function takes two sequences, one of the points' *x* coordinates and one of their *y* coordinates.

By default, Incanter labels the x- and y-axes from the expressions we use in the call to `scatter-plot`. In this case, that would be `(i/sel race-data :cols :Petal.Width)` for the x-axis and `(i/sel race-data :cols :Petal.Length)` for the y-axis. That's not very readable, so we specify the axes' labels with the `:x-label` and `:y-label` parameters.

However, the `scatter-plot` function only creates the chart object. To view it, we have to pass it to the `incanter.core/view` function.

If we right-click on a displayed graph, several other options show up as well. From the context menu, we can zoom in and out, print the chart, and change the labels. The charts are also interactive. Clicking and dragging on the graph zooms the view into focus on the area we selected.

## There's more...

> ▶ The Incanter API documentation that lists the supported charts and the options for each is at `http://liebke.github.com/incanter/charts-api.html`.

> ▶ The Incanter Wiki also has a gallery of sample charts on GitHub, at `https://github.com/liebke/incanter/wiki/sample-plots-in-incanter`.

## See also

We'll see how to save graphs in the *Saving Incanter graphs to PNG* recipe.

# Graphing non-numeric data in bar charts

Not everything is numeric, and often non-numeric data has to be handled differently, as we saw in the chapter on statistics and the chapter on data mining. For example, a scatter plot doesn't make much sense unless the data is naturally ordered in some way.

In this recipe, we'll use a bar chart to display how many items have a possible value each for a field of categorical data.

## Getting ready

We'll use the same dependencies in our `project.clj` file as we did in *Creating scatter plots with Incanter*.

We'll also use this set of imports in our script or REPL:

```
(require '[incanter.core :as i]
         '[incanter.charts :as c]
         '[incanter.io :as iio])
```

For this chart, we'll use the mushroom dataset from the UCI machine learning archive. The web page with the information about this dataset is at `http://archive.ics.uci.edu/ml/datasets/Mushroom`, and we can download a copy of it with the header names directly from `http://www.ericrochester.com/clj-data-analysis/data/agaricus-lepiota.data`. I've downloaded it in a data directory, so I can load it with this expression:

```
(def shrooms
  (iio/read-dataset "data/agaricus-lepiota.data"
                    :header true))
```

## How to do it...

In order to graph this, we need to summarize the data in some way:

1. Here, we'll get the number of mushrooms with a cap shape and create a bar chart with that data:

```
(def shroom-cap-bar
  (i/with-data
    (->> shrooms
      (i/$group-by :cap-shape)
      (map (fn [[k v]] (assoc k :count (i/nrow v))))
      (sort-by :cap-shape)
      i/to-dataset)
    (c/bar-chart :cap-shape :count)))
```

2. Now we view it:

```
(i/view shroom-cap-bar)
```

In the output of the preceding line, we see something like the following screenshot:

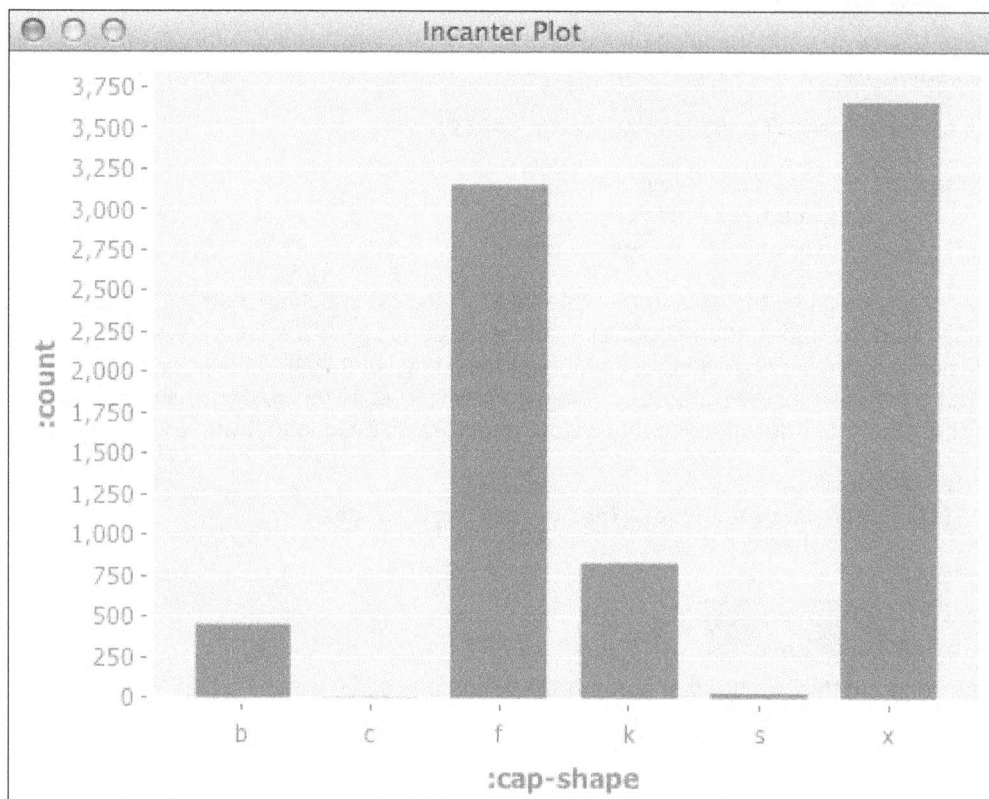

## How it works...

The most complicated part of this recipe is the transformation of the data to get the counts. Let's break that apart line-by-line:

1. We start with the dataset we loaded from the CSV file:

   ```
   (->> shrooms
   ```

2. We group that by the `:cap-shape` field. This produces a hash map going from a map like `{:cap-shape 0.0}` to a dataset:

   ```
   (i/$group-by :cap-shape)
   ```

3. We take each key-value pair in the group hash map and add the number of rows in the dataset to the key. The output of this operation is a sequence of maps, such as `{:cap-shape 0.0, :count 452}`:

   ```
   (map (fn [[k v]] (assoc k :count (i/nrow v))))
   ```

4. We sort that by the cap shape:

```
(sort-by :cap-shape)
```

5. Then we convert it to a new dataset:

```
i/to-dataset)
```

We implicitly pass the output of that expression to the `incanter.charts/bar-chart` using `incanter.core/with-data`, and we have our chart.

# Creating histograms with Incanter

Histograms are useful when we want to see the distribution of data. They are even effective with continuous data. In a histogram, the data is divided into a limited number of buckets, commonly 10, and the number of items in each bucket is counted. Histograms are especially useful for finding how much data are available for various percentiles. For instance, these charts can clearly show how much of your data was in the 90th percentile or lower.

## Getting ready

We'll use the same dependencies in our `project.clj` file as we did in *Creating scatter plots with Incanter*.

We'll use this set of imports in our script or REPL:

```
(require '[incanter.core :as i]
         '[incanter.charts :as c]
         'incanter.datasets)
```

For this recipe, we'll use the iris dataset that we used in *Creating scatter plots in Incanter*:

```
(def iris (incanter.datasets/get-dataset :iris))
```

## How to do it...

As we did in the previous recipes, we just create the graph and display it with `incanter.core/view`:

1. We create a histogram of the iris' petal length:

```
(def iris-petal-length-hist
  (c/histogram (i/sel iris :cols :Petal.Length)
               :title "Iris Petal Lengths"
               :x-label "cm"
               :nbins 20))
```

2. Now we view it:

```
(i/view iris-petal-length-hist)
```

The preceding line gives us a graph, as shown in the following screenshot:

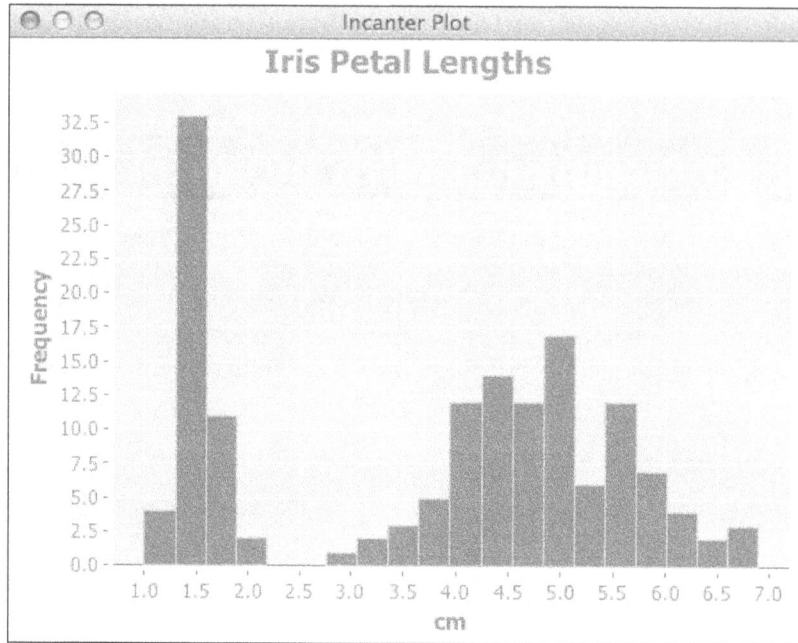

## How it works...

By looking at the graph created, the distribution of the data becomes clear. We can observe that the data does not fit a normal distribution, and in fact, the distribution has two well-separated clusters of values. If we compare this to the graph from *Creating scatter plots with Incanter*, we can see the cluster of smaller petals there also. Looking at the data, this seems to be the data for Iris Setosa. Versicolor and Virginica are grouped in the upper cluster.

By default, Incanter creates histograms with ten bins. When we made this graph, we wanted more detail and resolution, so we doubled the number of bins by adding the `:nbins 20` option when we created the graph.

# Creating function plots with Incanter

Sometimes we don't want to graph data, but plot the values of a function over a given domain instead. In this recipe, we'll see how to graph an inverse log function, although any other function would work just as well.

## Getting ready

We'll use the same dependencies in our `project.clj` file as we did in *Creating scatter plots with Incanter*.

We'll use this set of imports in our script or REPL:

```
(require '[incanter.core :as i]
         '[incanter.charts :as c])
```

## How to do it...

We just create and display a `function-plot` object:

```
(def f-plot
  (c/function-plot
    #(/ 1.0 (Math/log %)) 0.0 0.99
    :title "Inverse log function."
    :y-label "Inverse log"))
  i/view f-plot)
```

The graph is, as we would expect, like this:

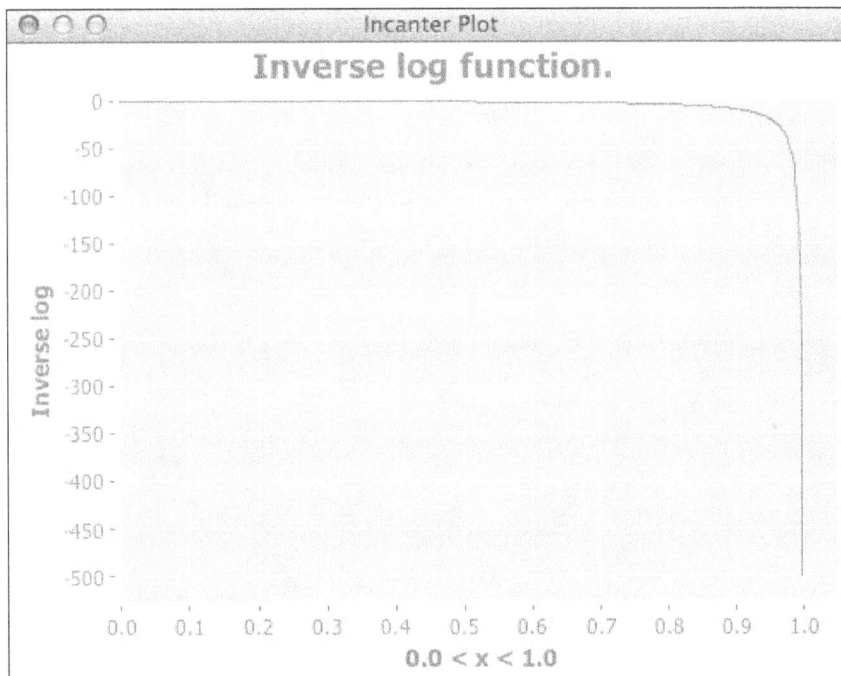

## How it works...

The `incanter.charts/function-plot` function takes the function to plot and the range of the domain (from 0.0 to 1.0 in this case). We've added some labels to make things clearer, but overall, this is a very straightforward function. Not having to worry about messy data simplifies a lot of things!

## See also

▸ *Adding lines to scatter charts.*

# Adding equations to Incanter charts

We've seen how to add a title to the charts and labels on the axes, but so far, they've all used only plain, unformatted text. Sometimes, we might want to use a formula instead.

Incanter lets you add a formula to a chart using LaTeX's mathematical notation. **LaTeX** (`http://www.latex-project.org/`) is a professional grade document typesetting system. We won't go into the details of its math notation—there are plenty of books and tutorials out there already. Instead, we'll just see how to use it with Incanter.

In this recipe, we'll take the chart from the last recipe, *Creating function plots with Incanter*, and add the function as a subtitle.

## Getting ready

We'll use the same dependencies in our `project.clj` file as we did in *Creating scatter plots with Incanter*.

We'll use this set of imports in our script or REPL:

```
(require '[incanter.core :as i]
         '[incanter.charts :as c]
         '[incanter.latex :as latex])
```

We'll also use the chart that we made in *Creating function plots with Incanter*. We'll still use the variable `f-plot` for it.

## How to do it...

The LaTeX string that we want to add is fairly simple, and it gives us a good taste of what the syntax for this notation is:

1. We bind the LaTeX string to `inv-log`:

   ```
   (def inv-log "f(x)=\\frac{1.0}{\\log x}")
   ```

2. We apply that to a chart using the `incanter.latex/add-latex-subtitle` function:

   ```
   (latex/add-latex-subtitle f-plot inv-log)
   ```

   The chart reflects the change immediately, as shown in the following screenshot:

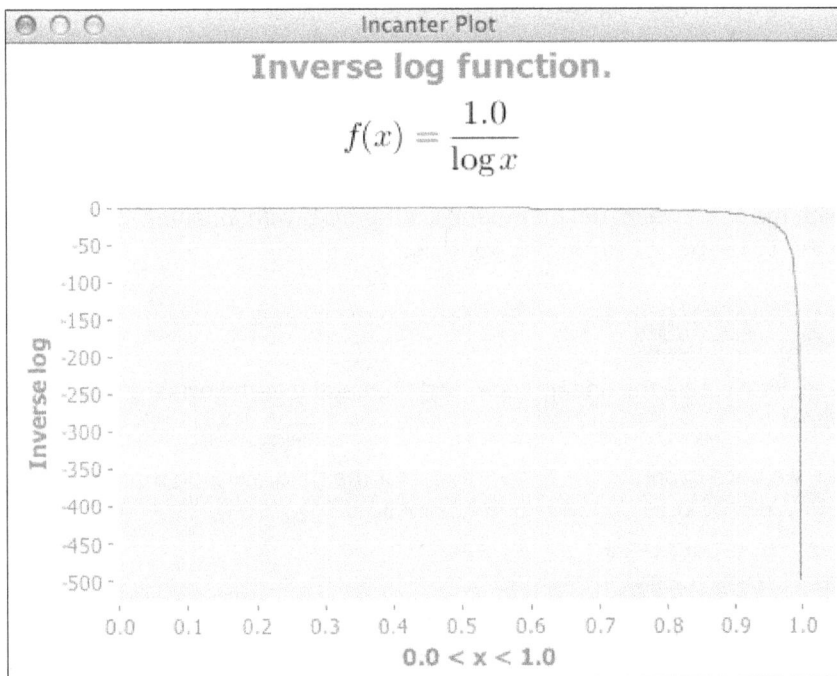

## There's more...

Full information about LaTeX and its math notation is beyond the scope of this recipe. The website for LaTeX is `http://www.latex-project.org/`. The LaTeX wikibook has a good chapter on typesetting mathematical equations, at `http://en.wikibooks.org/wiki/LaTeX/Mathematics`, and *The Not So Short Introduction to LaTeX 2ε* (`http://tobi.oetiker.ch/lshort/lshort.pdf`) is another good resource for learning LaTeX, including the math syntax.

# Adding lines to scatter charts

So far, all the recipes in this chapter have only created one type of chart. Incanter also lets us combine chart types. This allows us to add extra information and create a more useful, compelling chart. For instance, showing the interaction between the raw data and the output of a machine learning algorithm is a common use for overlaying lines onto scatter plots.

In this recipe, we'll take the chart from the *Creating scatter plots with Incanter* recipe and add a line from a linear regression.

## Getting ready

We'll use the same dependencies in our `project.clj` file as we did in *Creating scatter plots with Incanter*. We'll also use this set of imports in our script or REPL:

```
(require '[incanter.core :as i]
         '[incanter.charts :as c]
         '[incanter.io :as iio]
         '[incanter.stats :as s])
```

We'll start with the chart we made in *Creating scatter plots with Incanter*. We'll keep it assigned to the `iris-petal-scatter` variable.

## How to do it...

For this recipe, we'll create the linear model and then add it to the existing chart from the previous recipe:

1. First, we have to create the linear model for the data. We'll do that using the `incanter.stats/linear-model` function:

   ```
   (def iris-petal-lm
     (s/linear-model
       (i/sel iris :cols :Petal.Length)
       (i/sel iris :cols :Petal.Width)
       :intercept false))
   ```

2. Next, we take the `:fitted` data from the model and add it to the chart using `incanter.charts/add-lines`:

   ```
   (c/add-lines
     iris-petal-scatter
     (i/sel iris :cols :Petal.Width)
     (:fitted iris-petal-lm)
     :series-label "Linear Relationship")
   ```

Once we've added that, our chart resembles the following screenshot:

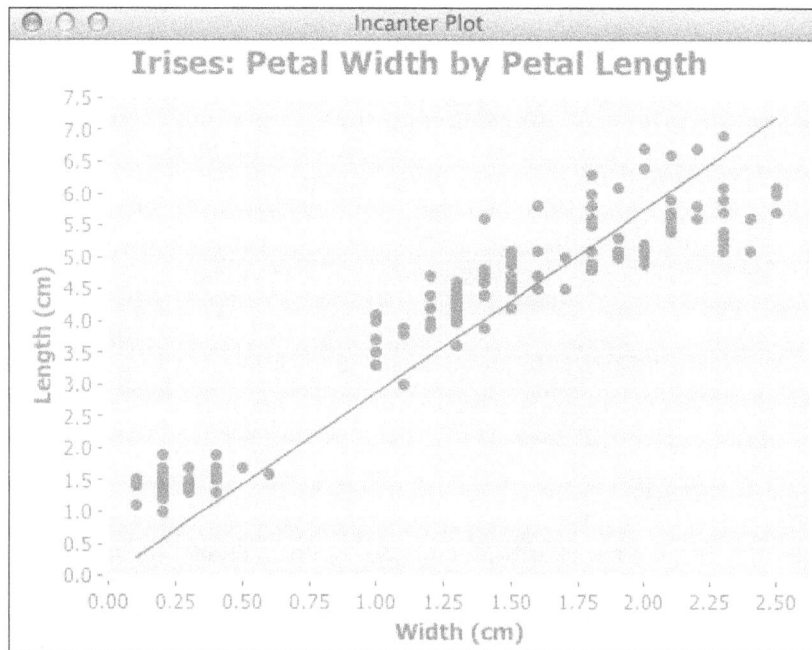

## How it works...

The fitted values for the linear regression are just a sequence of *y* values corresponding to the sequence of *x* values. When we add that line to the graph, Incanter pairs the *x* and *y* values together and draws a line on the graph linking each point. Since the points describe a straight line, we end up with the line found by the linear regression.

## See also

- ► The *Modeling linear relationships* recipe in *Chapter 7, Statistical Data Analysis with Incanter*.

# Customizing charts with JFreeChart

Incanter's chart API is easy to use and provides a powerful wrapper around JFreeChart (http://www.jfree.org/jfreechart/). However, it doesn't expose JFreeChart's full variety of chart types or all the options that JFreeChart provides. In order to access those, we have to dive from Incanter's API into the JFreeChart objects. Fortunately, that's quite easy to do. Let's see how.

## Getting ready

We'll use the same dependencies in our `project.clj` file as we did in *Creating scatter plots with Incanter*.

We'll use this set of imports in our script or REPL:

```
(require '[incanter.core :as i]
         '[incanter.charts :as c]
         'incanter.datasets)
(import org.jfree.chart.renderer.category.LayeredBarRenderer
        org.jfree.util.SortOrder)
```

We'll use the Iris dataset again. Here's how to load it in Incanter:

```
(def iris (incanter.datasets/get-dataset :iris))
```

## How to do it...

For this recipe, we'll create a bar chart with multiple columns, one for each measurement column in the Iris dataset:

1.  We'll first create the bar chart and add a category for each measurement:

    ```
    (def iris-dimensions
      (i/with-data
        iris
        (doto (c/bar-chart :Species :Petal.Width
                           :title "iris' dimensions"
                           :x-label "species"
                           :y-label "cm"
                           :series-label "petal width"
                           :legend true)
          (c/add-categories
            :Species :Sepal.Width
            :series-label "sepal width")
          (c/add-categories
            :Species :Petal.Length
            :series-label "petal length")
          (c/add-categories
            :Species :Sepal.Length
            :series-label "sepal length")))))
    ```

2. The `iris-dimensions` object is the `JFreeChart` object for this chart. We can call its methods to change how the chart is created. In this case, we'll change the renderer to layer the bars on top of each other, and we'll change the rendering order so that we can see each bar in the stack:

```
(doto (.getPlot iris-dimensions)
  (.setRenderer (doto (LayeredBarRenderer.)
                  (.setDrawBarOutline false)))
  (.setRowRenderingOrder SortOrder/DESCENDING))
```

3. Now, like the other charts, we display this chart using `incanter.core/view`:

```
(i/view iris-dimensions)
```

The results of the preceding line are something we can't get from Incanter's chart API alone. The resulting chart is as follows:

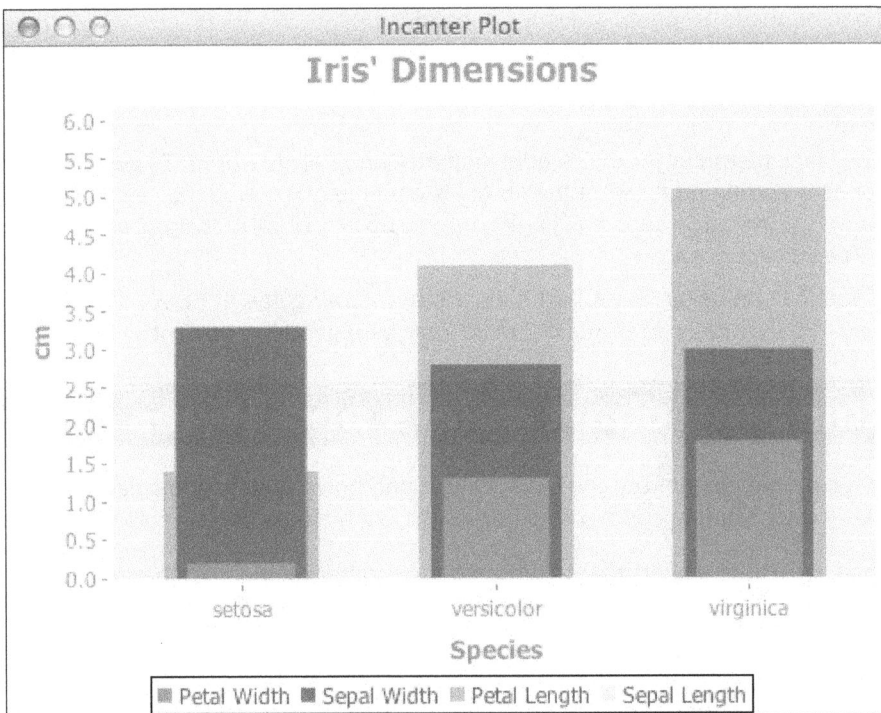

## How it works...

The object returned by the Incanter chart functions is the `JFreeChart` object. This is the builder class for all the charts. From this object, we can access the plot objects, which provide interfaces for different types of charts, and from the plot objects, we can access options such as axes, annotations, colors, and renderers, which handle the actual drawing of the chart.

That's what we do in this recipe. The relevant code snippet is as follows:

```
(doto (.getPlot iris-dimensions)
  (.setRenderer (doto (LayeredBarRenderer.)
                  (.setDrawBarOutline false)))
  (.setRowRenderingOrder SortOrder/DESCENDING))
```

In this code, we get the plot, set the renderer to an instance of `LayeredBarRenderer`, and then change the order of row rendering. If we don't do that, then the shorter rows get rendered behind the taller ones, which isn't useful.

## See also

▶ The class hierarchy for this is quite complex and fully featured. To get a good feel for its breadth and for what the library is capable of, browse the Java docs for it at `http://www.jfree.org/jfreechart/api/javadoc/org/jfree/chart/JFreeChart.html`.

▶ If you plan on using JFreeChart a lot, the developer guide at `http://www.jfree.org/jfreechart/devguide.html` may be a good investment.

# Customizing chart colors and styles

In the last recipe, we customized the type of chart and how the data is displayed and laid out. However, we'll often want to customize other things, such as the chart's color scheme or style.

In this recipe, we'll take a chart that we created for another recipe and change the way it looks. This will give an example of how to customize the color and other parts of how the chart displays.

## Getting ready

We'll use the same dependencies in our `project.clj` file as we did in *Creating scatter plots with Incanter,* and this set of imports in our script or REPL:

```
(require '[incanter.core :as i]
         '[incanter.charts :as c]
         '[incanter.io :as iio]
         '[incanter.stats :as s])
```

```
(import org.jfree.chart.renderer.category.LayeredBarRenderer
        org.jfree.util.SortOrder)
```

We'll start with the chart we made in *Adding lines to scatter charts*. We'll keep it assigned to the `iris-petal-scatter` variable.

## How to do it...

For this example, we'll take the Iris petal scatter plot, with the line added, and we'll change the color scheme for St. Patrick's Day (lots of green).

1. First, we'll pick the colors that we want in the color scheme:

   ```
   (def colors [(java.awt.Color. 0x00 0xb3 0x66)
                (java.awt.Color. 0x80 0xff 0xc9)])
   ```

2. Then we'll set the series color for each renderer on this chart:

   ```
   (doseq [[i c] (map vector (range) colors)]
     (.. iris-petal-scatter
         getPlot
         (getRenderer i)
         (setSeriesPaint 0 c)))
   ```

3. Finally, we'll just view it as we viewed the previous charts:

   ```
   (i/view iris-petal-scatter)
   ```

   This gives us the same chart as before, but with an updated color scheme. The updated chart looks like the following:

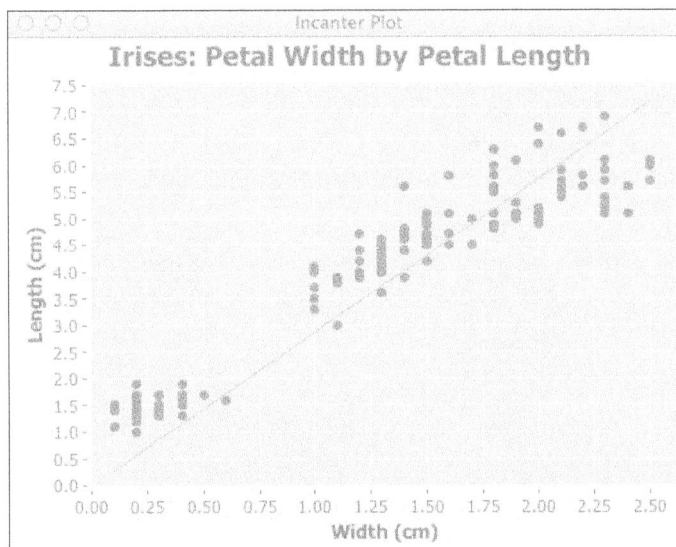

# Saving Incanter graphs to PNG

So far, we've been viewing the graphs we've created in a window on our computer. This is extremely handy, especially to quickly generate a graph and see what's in it. However, the chart would be more useful if we could save it. Then we could embed it in Word documents or web pages or print it so that we can hang it on the wall.

In this recipe, we'll save a graph of the iris data that we created in *Creating scatter plots with Incanter*.

## Getting ready

We'll use the same dependencies in our `project.clj` file as we did in *Creating scatter plots with Incanter*, and this set of imports in our script or REPL:

```
(require '[incanter.core :as i]
         '[incanter.charts :as c])
```

We'll also use the chart object that we created in *Creating scatter plots with Incanter*, and we'll keep using the `iris-petal-scatter` variable name for it.

## How to do it...

Since we already have the chart, saving it is simple. We just call `incanter.core/save` on it with the filename we want to save it to:

```
(i/save iris-petal-scatter "iris-petal-scatter.png")
```

## How it works...

Calling `incanter.core/save` on a chart saves it as a PNG file. We can also include options to the `save` function to set the output image's dimensions using the `:height` and `:width` parameters.

There's also another way to save images. If we right-click on a chart after displaying it with `incanter.core/view`, it gives us the option to save the chart from there.

# Using PCA to graph multi-dimensional data

So far, we've been limiting ourselves to two-dimensional data. After all, the human mind has a lot of trouble dealing with more than three dimensions, and even two-dimensional visualizations of three-dimensional space can be difficult to comprehend.

However, we can use PCA to help. It projects higher-dimensional data down to lower dimensions, but it does this in a way that preserves the most significant relationships in the data. It re-projects the data on a lower dimension in a way that captures the maximum amount of variance in the data. This makes the data easier to visualize in three- or two-dimensional space, and it also provides a way to select the most relevant features in a dataset.

In this recipe, we'll take the data from the US census by race that we've worked with in previous chapters, and create a two-dimensional scatter plot of it.

## Getting ready

We'll use the same dependencies in our `project.clj` file as we did in *Creating Scatter Plots with Incanter,* and this set of imports in our script or REPL:

```
(require '[incanter.core :as i]
         '[incanter.charts :as c]
         '[incanter.io :as iio]
         '[incanter.stats :as s])
```

We'll use the aggregated census race data for all states. You can download this from `http://www.ericrochester.com/clj-data-analysis/data/all_160.P3.csv`. We'll assign it to the `race-data` variable:

```
(def race-data (iio/read-dataset "data/all_160.P3.csv"
                                 :header true))
```

## How to do it...

We'll first summarize the data to make it more manageable and easier to visualize. Then we'll use PCA to project it on a two-dimensional space. We'll graph this view of the data:

1. First, we need to summarize the columns that we're interested in, getting the total population of each racial group by state:

```
(def fields [:P003002 :P003003 :P003004 :P003005
             :P003006 :P003007 :P003008])
```

```
(def race-by-state
  (reduce #(i/$join [:STATE :STATE] %1 %2)
          (map #(i/$rollup :sum % :STATE race-data)
               fields)))
```

2. Next, we'll take the summary and create a matrix from it. From that matrix, we'll extract the columns that we're interested in analyzing and graphing:

```
(def race-by-state-matrix (i/to-matrix race-by-state))
(def x (i/sel race-by-state-matrix :cols (range 1 8)))
```

3. Now we'll perform the principal component analysis:

```
(def pca (s/principal-components x))
```

4. From the output of the PCA, we'll get the components for the first two dimensions and multiply all the columns in the data matrix by each component:

```
(def components (:rotation pca))
(def pc1 (i/sel components :cols 0))
(def pc2 (i/sel components :cols 1))
(def x1 (i/mmult x pc1))
(def x2 (i/mmult x pc2))
```

5. We can plot x1 and x2. We'll use them to create a two-dimensional scatter plot:

```
(def pca-plot
  (c/scatter-plot
    x1 x2
    :x-label "PC1", :y-label "PC2"
    :title "Census Race Data by State"))
```

6. We can view that chart as we normally would:

```
(i/view pca-plot)
```

This provides us with a graph expressing the most salient features of the dataset in two dimensions:

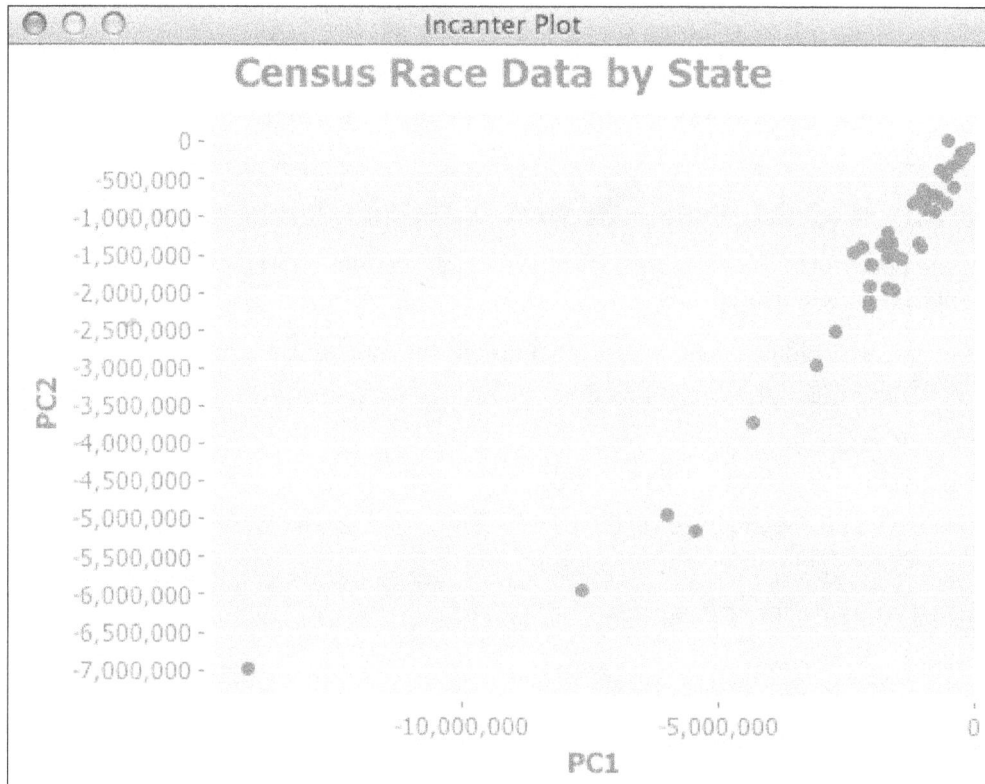

## How it works...

Conceptually, PCA projects the entire dataset on a lower-dimensional space and rotates to a view that captures the maximum variability it can see from that dimension.

In the preceding chart, we can see that most of the data clusters are around the origin. A few points trail off to the higher numbers of the graph.

## There's more...

▶ For an easy, visual explanation of PCA, see the *A layman's introduction to principle component analysis* video at `http://youtu.be/BfTMmoDFXyE`.

▶ For more details on PCA, see *A Tutorial on Principle Component Analysis* by Jonathon Shlens at `http://www.snl.salk.edu/~shlens/pca.pdf`.

# Creating dynamic charts with Incanter

Charts are powerful tools to explore data, and dynamic charts—charts that react to user input—are even more useful.

In this recipe, we'll create a simple chart that graphs the quadratic equation and lets us play with the parameters and see the results in real time.

## Getting ready

We'll use the same dependencies in our `project.clj` file as we did in *Creating scatter plots with Incanter*.

We'll use this set of imports in our script or REPL:

```
(require '[incanter.core :as i]
         '[incanter.charts :as c])
```

## How to do it...

It seems like creating a dynamic chart would be difficult, but it's not. We just define a `dynamic-xy-plot` with the variables and relationships that we want, and Incanter will do the rest:

```
(def d-plot
  (let [x (range -1 1 0.1)]
    (c/dynamic-xy-plot
      [a (range -1.0 1.0 0.1)
       b (range -1.0 1.0 0.1)
       c (range -1.0 1.0 0.1)]
      [x (i/plus (i/mult a x x) (i/mult b x) c)])))
(i/view d-plot)
```

This presents us with a slider for each dynamic variable. Here's the slider for *a*:

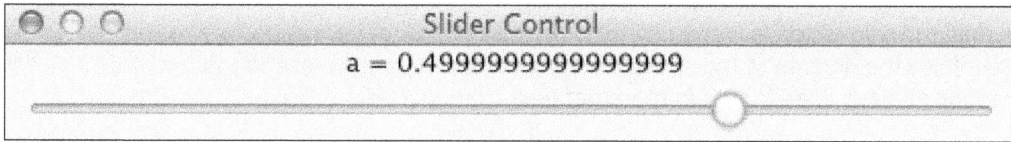

We can use these to control the values and the line in the graph. Here is what my screen looked like after I played with the code a little:

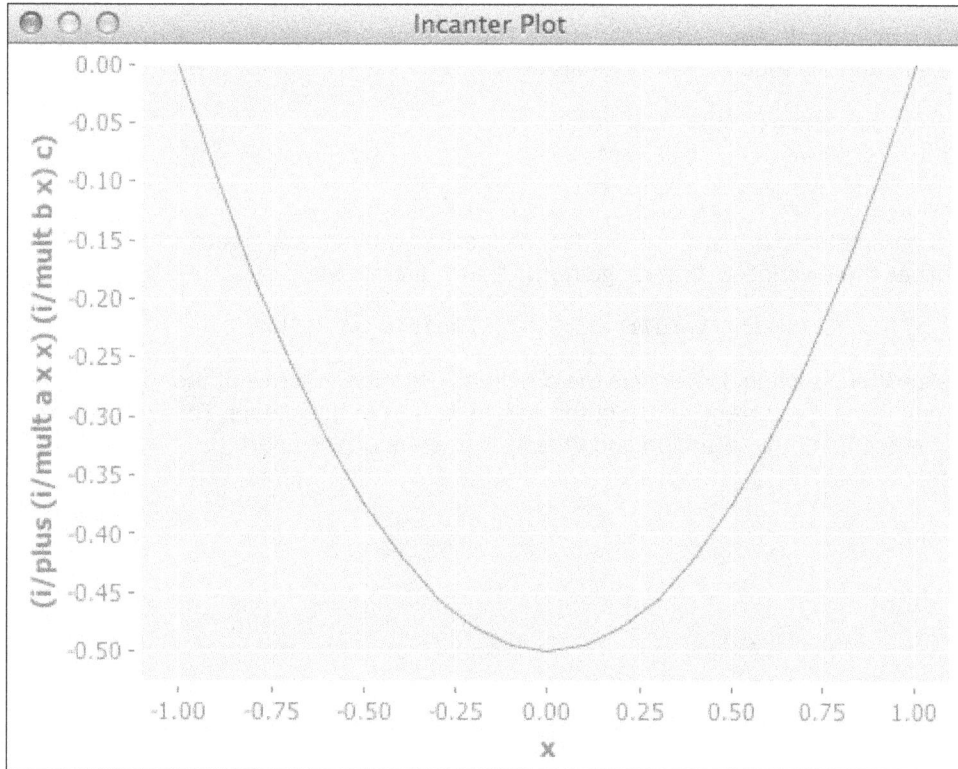

## How it works...

The magic in this recipe is in the call to `incanter.charts/dynamic-xy-plot`. This defines the domain of the chart, the range of the parameters, and the function. Let's look at a few lines from it in more detail:

```
(let [x (range -1 1 0.1)]
```

This defines the domain of the chart, that is, the extent of the x-axis:

```
(c/dynamic-xy-plot
```

This is the macro call that creates the chart. The parameters passed to this define the parameters and the function for the chart:

```
[a (range -1.0 1.0 0.1)
 b (range -1.0 1.0 0.1)
 c (range -1.0 1.0 0.1)]
```

The first parameter to `dynamic-xy-plot` defines the function parameters for the chart. This defines three variables that range from -1 to 1, incremented by 0.1:

```
[x (i/plus (i/mult a x x) (i/mult b x) c)]))
```

This defines the function. It specifies the quadratic equation in terms of the range of the x-axis, and using the current values of the parameters from the sliders. The dynamic plot shows the output of this equation and those parameters on the chart.

# 12
# Creating Charts for the Web

In this chapter, we will cover the following recipes:

- Serving data with Ring and Compojure
- Creating HTML with Hiccup
- Setting up to use ClojureScript
- Creating scatter plots with NVD3
- Creating bar charts with NVD3
- Creating histograms with NVD3
- Creating time series charts with D3
- Visualizing graphs with force-directed layouts
- Creating interactive visualizations with D3

## Introduction

In the previous chapter, we explored how to create graphs in order to publish in print or online by creating PNGs. Of course, the Internet can do a lot more than publish static images. Much of the power of the Internet lies in the fact that it's interactive. Adding rich data visualizations to the web's interactions makes a powerful environment in which you can explore and gain insights into the questions you're researching. In this chapter, we'll explore how to create a full web application using Clojure, including interactive graphs.

First, we'll set up a web application with **Ring** (`https://github.com/ring-clojure/ring`) and **Compojure** (`http://compojure.org`). Ring is an interface between web servers and web applications. Compojure is a small web framework that provides a convenient way to define and handle routes (the associations between URLs and functions to provide data for them).

Next, we'll see how to use **Hiccup** (`https://github.com/weavejester/hiccup`) in order to generate HTML from data structures.

We'll complete our web stack with **ClojureScript** (`https://github.com/clojure/clojurescript`). This is just Clojure, but instead of compiling to a JVM, it compiles to JavaScript. We can load its output into our web pages and use it to create stunning graphs.

The rest of the chapter will involve what we can create using this Clojure-dominated web stack. We'll use the **D3** (`http://d3js.org/`) and **NVD3** (`http://nvd3.org/`) JavaScript libraries to create visualizations from the data. In the end, we'll wind up with some good graphs and a productive environment to publish the results of our data analysis.

The stack from this chapter can be easily deployed to services such as **Heroku** (`http://www.heroku.com/`), which makes for a fast way to set up the server side of this system and to make our information available to the general public.

# Serving data with Ring and Compojure

While we can precompile ClojureScript and load the generated JavaScript files as static assets, we'll often want to combine the dynamic charts with dynamic pages. For instance, we might want to provide a search form to filter the data that's graphed.

In this recipe, we'll get started with a typical Clojure web stack. Even if we don't use ClojureScript, this system is useful for creating web applications. We'll use **Jetty** (`http://jetty.codehaus.org/jetty/`) to serve the requests, Ring (`https://github.com/ring-clojure/ring`) to connect the server to the different parts of our web application, and Compojure (`http://compojure.org`) to define the routes and handlers.

## Getting ready

We'll first need to include Jetty, Ring, and Compojure in our Leiningen `project.clj` file. We'll also want to use Ring as a development plugin for this project, so let's include it in the `project.clj` file under the `:plugins` key. The following is the full Leiningen project file:

```
(defproject web-viz "0.1.0-SNAPSHOT"
  :dependencies [[org.clojure/clojure "1.6.0"]
                 [ring/ring-core "1.3.1"]
```

```
                    [ring/ring-jetty-adapter "1.3.1"]
                    [compojure "1.2.0"]]
      :plugins [[lein-ring "0.8.3"]]
      :ring {:handler web-viz.web/app})
```

Also, we'll need data to serve. For this recipe, we'll serve the 2010 US census race data that we've been using throughout this book. I've converted it to JSON, though, so we can load it into D3 more easily. You can download this file from `http://www.ericrochester.com/clj-data-analysis/data/census-race.json`.

## How to do it...

Setting up a web application is relatively simple, but a number of steps are involved. We'll create the namespace and configuration, then we'll set up the application, and finally we'll add resources.

### Configuring and setting up the web application

The code for the web application will need to be run again and again, so we'll need to make sure that our code makes it into files. Let's create a namespace inside our Leiningen project for it. Right now, my Leiningen project is named `web-viz`, so I'll use it in this example, but you should replace it with whatever your project is named. To do this, perform the following steps:

1. Inside the project's `src` directory, let's create a file named `web.clj`. It's full path will be `src/web_viz/web.clj`. This will contain the web application and routes.

2. We'll use this namespace declaration at the top of `web.clj`. Note that you'll need to change the namespace to match your project:

```
(ns web-viz.web
  (:require [compojure.route :as route]
            [compojure.handler :as handler])
  (:use compojure.core
        ring.adapter.jetty
        [ring.middleware.content-type
         :only (wrap-content-type)]
        [ring.middleware.file
         :only (wrap-file)]
        [ring.middleware.file-info
         :only (wrap-file-info)]
        [ring.middleware.stacktrace
         :only (wrap-stacktrace)]
        [ring.util.response
         :only (redirect)] ))
```

3. Now that we have a namespace for it, we need to tell Ring where our web application is. We've actually already done this. If you look toward the bottom of the `project.clj` file, you'll find this line:

```
:ring {:handler web-viz.web/app}
```

## Serving data

For this recipe, we'll serve the JSON datafile statically. By default, Ring serves static files out of the `/resources` directory of our project. In this case, create the `/resources/data` directory and put the datafile that you downloaded from `http://www.ericrochester.com/clj-data-analysis/data/census-race.json` into it.

## Defining routes and handlers

Now, we can connect the IBM dataset to the Internet. To do this, perform the following steps:

1. In the `src/web_viz/web.clj` file, we'll define the routes using Compojure's `defroutes` macro, as shown here:

```
(defroutes
  site-routes
  (GET "/" [] (redirect "/data/census-race.json"))
  (route/resources "/")
  (route/not-found "Page not found"))
```

This creates a GET request that redirects to our datafile. It also defines routes to serve any static resources from the classpath—in this case, to serve the resources directory—and a 404 (resource missing) page.

2. We use these routes as the basis of our web app:

```
(def app
  (-> (handler/site site-routes)
      (wrap-file "resources")
      (wrap-file-info)
      (wrap-content-type)))
```

Along with serving the routes we defined, this function adds more functionality to our web app. We serve static files from the resources directory (`wrap-file`). We add content-type and other HTTP headers whenever we serve files (`wrap-file-info`). Also, we make sure to always include a content-type header, even if it's just an *application/octet-stream* (`wrap-content-type`).

## Running the server

Starting the server for development is a Leiningen task handled by the Ring plugin, as shown here:

```
$ lein ring server
2013-01-16 09:01:47.630:INFO:oejs.Server:jetty-7.6.1.v20120215
Started server on port 3000
2013-01-16 09:01:47.687:INFO:oejs.AbstractConnector:Started
SelectChannelConnector@0.0.0.0:3000
```

This starts the server on port 3000 and opens a web browser to the home page of the site at `http://localhost:3000/`. In this case, that just redirects you to the census data, so your browser should resemble the following screenshot, unless your browser attempts to download JSON and save it to your drive (Although, your text editor should still be able to open it):

## How it works...

The first part of this system, and the foundation of it, is Ring (`https://github.com/ring-clojure/ring`). Ring is an abstraction over HTTP. This makes it easier to write web applications that will work in a variety of settings and that run under a variety of servers. You can write the web application to work with the Ring specification, and you can connect Ring to the web server using an adapter.

There are a number of central concepts in Ring, which are described as follows:

- ▶ **Handlers**: These are the core of a web application. Handlers are Clojure functions that take a map with information about the request and return a map with the response. Each web application has one handler function.

- ▶ **Middleware**: This transforms incoming requests or outgoing responses. Generally, middleware wraps an existing handler to provide extra functionality. For instance, authentication can be handled through middleware. The project Friend (`https://github.com/cemerick/friend`) does this. Middleware can also handle requests for static resources, cookies, and many other things.

- ▶ **Adapters**: These connect Ring to web servers. Ring has an adapter for the Jetty web server (`http://jetty.codehaus.org/jetty/`) and this is what we use in this recipe.

Ring's a good option to connect a web application to a web server, but it's a little too close to the metal. You wouldn't want to write your web application to talk to Ring directly. Compojure (`https://github.com/weavejester/compojure/wiki`) steps into the gap. It provides a simple DSL to define routes and response functions and composes them into a single Ring application handler function. It allows you to define the type of HTTP request that each route function can accept (`GET`, `POST`, and so on) and what parameters each expect.

Here's how the preceding example breaks down into the components we just discussed:

- ▶ `site-routes`: This is composed of Compojure routes, which act as the Ring handler
- ▶ `app`: This is composed of the Ring handler function with some middleware

In our `project.clj` file, we define connect Ring to our handler function with this line:

```
:ring {:handler web-viz.web/app}
```

## There's more...

- ▶ The Ring wiki at `https://github.com/ring-clojure/ring/wiki` has a lot of useful information to get started and work with Ring.

- ▶ The Ring's API documentation at `http://ring-clojure.github.com/ring/` is also very helpful.

- ▶ However, if you want to get more complete information, you should take a look at the Ring specification, available at `https://github.com/ring-clojure/ring/blob/master/SPEC`. It's really quite readable.

- ▶ The Compojure wiki at `https://github.com/weavejester/compojure/wiki` has information on the many aspects of using Compojure.

- ▶ The Compojure API documentation at `http://weavejester.github.com/compojure/` is helpful too.

# Creating HTML with Hiccup

In the last recipe, we set up a server and returned some data. However, most people want to view HTML, not JSON. In this recipe, we'll take a look at Hiccup (`https://github.com/weavejester/hiccup`). This is a library that allows you to build web pages from Clojure expressions and data structures. It takes vectors, maps, keywords, and strings—or functions that return these—and turns them into HTML. This is a good solution for generating HTML from within Clojure web applications.

This recipe will build on the *Serving data with Ring and Compojure* recipe. I'll point out where you need to change or add things from that recipe, highlighting them as necessary. By the end of this recipe, we'll be serving a simple index page along with the census dataset.

## Getting ready

First, we'll use the same dependencies in our `project.clj` file as we did in the last recipe, plus one more. Here's the full list:

```
:dependencies [[org.clojure/clojure "1.6.0"]
               [ring/ring-core "1.3.1"]
               [ring/ring-jetty-adapter "1.3.1"]
               [compojure "1.2.0"]
               [hiccup "1.0.5"]]
```

We'll also add Hiccup to the namespace declaration, as shown here:

```
(ns web-viz.web
  (:require [compojure.route :as route]
            [compojure.handler :as handler])
  (:use compojure.core
        ring.adapter.jetty
        [ring.middleware.content-type :only (wrap-content-type)]
        [ring.middleware.file :only (wrap-file)]
        [ring.middleware.file-info :only (wrap-file-info)]
        [ring.middleware.stacktrace :only (wrap-stacktrace)]
        [ring.util.response :only (redirect)]
        [hiccup core element page]
        [hiccup.middleware :only (wrap-base-url)]]))
```

## How to do it...

In Hiccup, HTML is represented as vectors with keyword tag names and attribute maps.

1. We'll define a function that builds a simple web page with a link to the data set:

```
(defn index-page []
  (html5
    [:head
     [:title "Web Charts"]]
    [:body
     [:h1 {:id "web-charts"} "Web Charts"]
     [:ol
      [:li [:a {:href "/data/census-race.json"}
            "2010 Census Race Data"]]]]))
```

2. Now, instead of redirecting the root URL, we'll have it serve the function, as shown here:

```
(defroutes
  site-routes
  (GET "/" [] (index-page))
  (route/resources "/")
  (route/not-found "Page not found"))
```

3. Now, when we run the server and visit the home page at `http://localhost:3000/`, we'll get something different, as shown in the following screenshot:

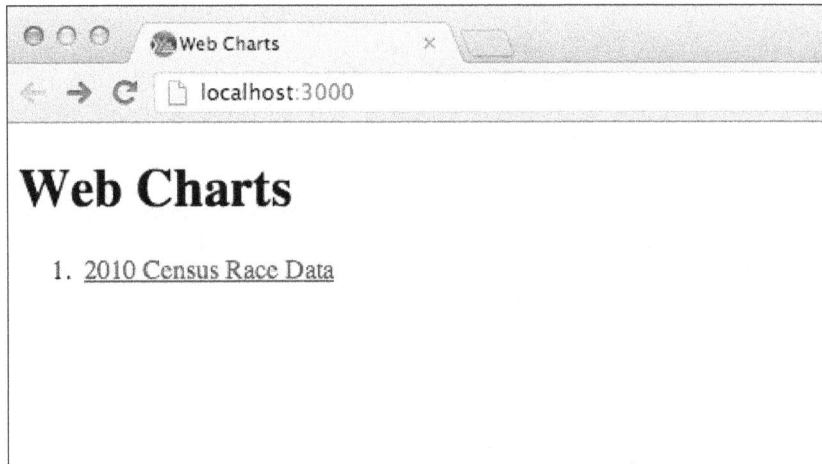

## How it works...

The Hiccup DSL is quite simple, and we can see examples of almost all of its syntax in this recipe, as shown here:

1.  We have an HTML tag with some text content, as shown here:

    ```
    [:title "Web Charts"]
    ```

2.  We have nested elements:

    ```
    [:head
      [:title "Web Charts"]]
    ```

3.  We can include attributes as a hashmap after the tag-name keyword:

    ```
    [:h1 {:id "web-charts"} "Web Charts"]
    ```

4.  Irrespective of the structure, we eventually pass it to one of the rendering functions. In this case, we're displaying it as HTML5, so we use this builder function:

    ```
    (html5
    ```

Hiccup also has a number of functions that can be used to insert links to CSS files and script elements. We'll see examples of these in the *Creating scatter plots with NVD3* recipe.

## There's more...

► The Hiccup site and wiki at `https://github.com/weavejester/hiccup` are a good starting point to use Hiccup

► In order to actually write HTML pages using Hiccup, the page on its syntax at `https://github.com/weavejester/hiccup/wiki/Syntax` will be particularly useful

# Setting up to use ClojureScript

The only thing that's missing is JavaScript. We can also generate this with ClojureScript (`https://github.com/clojure/clojurescript`). This is an implementation of Clojure that compiles to JavaScript.

Why will we want to write JavaScript in Clojure? First, it simplifies your project when both the client and the server are written in the same language. It also allows you to share code between the two sides of your application, which can cut down the complexity of your code as well as the lines of code.

For the rest of this chapter, we'll be creating charts and graphs using ClojureScript. These recipes will show you how to install ClojureScript and get it working. We'll take the web application we started in the *Serving data with Ring and Compojure* and *Creating HTML with Hiccup* recipes and add an alert to the index page. This isn't anything more than a *hello world* application, but this will prove that ClojureScript is working in our application.

## Getting ready

To add ClojureScript to our project, we'll first add a dependency on ClojureScript. Now, this is how the `:dependencies` section of the `project.clj` file will look:

```
:dependencies [[org.clojure/clojure "1.6.0"]
               [ring/ring-core "1.3.1"]
               [ring/ring-jetty-adapter "1.3.1"]
               [compojure "1.2.0"]
               [hiccup "1.0.5"]
               [org.clojure/clojurescript "0.0-2371"]]
```

Next, we'll add the `lein-cljsbuild` plugin to our Leiningen `project.clj` file. Now, our `:plugins` directive should look similar to this:

```
:plugins [[lein-ring "0.88.3"]
          [lein-cljsbuild "11.0.3"]]
```

## How to do it...

To set up ClojureScript, most of what we need to do is configuration. We have to tell the ClojureScript compiler where to find the input and where to put the output. We'll go into details on this in a minute.

1. First, we'll just add this key-value pair to our `project.clj` configuration file:

```
:cljsbuild {:builds
            [{:source-paths ["src-cljs"],
              :compiler
              {:pretty-print true,
               :output-to "resources/js/script.js",
               :optimizations :whitespace}}]}
```

2. Now, let's go to the command prompt and create the directories we'll use:

```
$ mkdir -p src-cljs/webviz
$ mkdir -p resources/js
```

3. Create the `src-cljs/webviz/core.cljs` file. This will look a lot like a regular Clojure file:

```
(ns webviz.core)
(defn ^:export hello [world]
  (js/alert (str "Hello, " world)))
```

4. From the command line, enter this command. This will start the ClojureScript compiler that watches all the ClojureScript files and automatically compiles them whenever we save one:

```
$ lein cljsbuild auto
Compiling ClojureScript.
Compiling "resources/js/scripts.js" from "src-cljs"...
Successfully compiled "resources/js/script.js" in 4.707129
seconds.
```

5. Next, we'll add our compiled ClojureScript file to our Hiccup template. Let's open src/web_viz/web.clj again and change the index-page function to look as shown here:

```clojure
(defn index-page []
  (html5
    [:head
     [:title "Web Charts"]]
    [:body
     [:h1 {:id "web-charts"} "Web Charts"]
     [:ol
      [:li [:a {:href "/data/census-race.json"}
            "2010 Census Race Data"]]]
     (include-js "js/script.js")
     (javascript-tag
       "webviz.core.hello('from ClojureScript!');")]]))
```

Now when we start the Ring server and look at the main page, we should see the following screen:

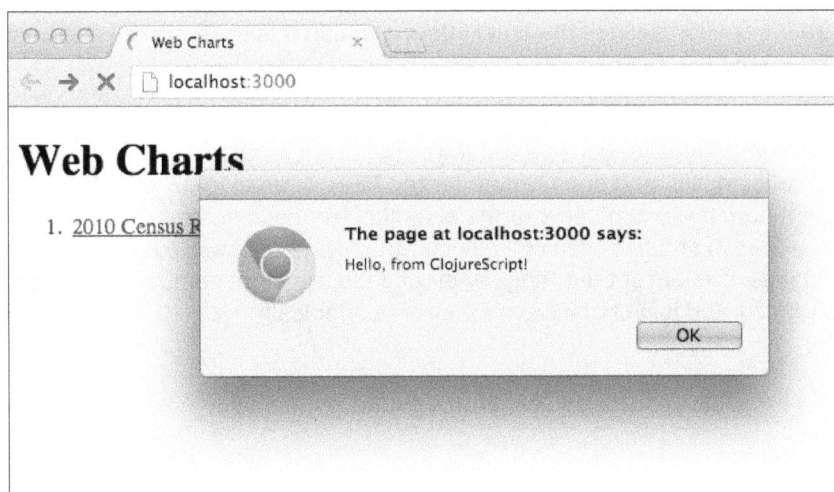

## How it works...

A lot took place in this recipe, and there's a lot that we need to talk about in a little more detail.

First, we need to talk about ClojureScript. If we open up the generated file, `resources/js/script.js`, we'll see a lot that's not in our code. Why is there so much more in there?

The explanation is pretty simple. ClojureScript doesn't just target JavaScript as a compilation platform. It targets the `Google-Closure-compiler-advanced-mode` JavaScript. Because of this, it includes most of the Google Closure libraries, so we have these immediately available, and we'll use them in the upcoming recipes. Also, we can run our output through the Closure compilers by changing the `:optimizations` parameter in the `:cljsbuild` options, and it will shake out the parts of the code that we don't use. This not only includes our code but also the parts of the Clojure libraries and the Google Closure libraries that we don't use. In the end, this is a huge win. Unfortunately, not all libraries can be used with the Closure compiler's advanced mode; D3, for example, requires a file that lists all the functions it exports. The *d3-externs* project (`https://github.com/shripadk/d3-externs`) is an attempt to provide this interface file for the Closure compiler.

Also, note that the `hello` function is annotated with the `^:export` metadata. This signals the ClojureScript compiler that it needs to make this function available to the outside world. This is a good, lightweight way of enforcing scoping according to JavaScript's best practices.

Also, inside the `hello` function, the `alert` function is called from the `js` namespace (`js/alert`). This namespace represents the global JavaScript context. Whenever we call a JavaScript object from the global context (when working in the `window` browser), we have to prefix it with the `js/` namespace in ClojureScript.

Next, we should take a look at the `:cljsbuild` configuration in the `project.clj` file. This configuration section defines the build information. In this case, we tell it to compile everything in `src-cljs/` to `js/script.js`.

Finally, I will also make a note here about the workflow. If you're keeping count, you probably have at least three terminal or console windows open. One for the Ring server, one for the ClojureScript compiler, and one or more for the REPL or shell to work in. That's what I have going right now. If you can use a terminal multiplexer such as tmux (`http://tmux.sourceforge.net/`) or Screen (`http://www.gnu.org/software/screen/`), this can simplify things. You can set the Ring server and ClojureScript compiler running in a background window and just check them for errors periodically.

## There's more...

▶ ClojureScript ships with the Google Closure library. It's a fully-featured library, and it's there, so you might as well use it. You can learn more about it at `https://developers.google.com/closure/`.

▶ For more information about the configuration options available, see `https://github.com/emezeske/lein-cljsbuild/blob/master/sample.project.clj`.

▶ The home page for Screen is (`http://www.gnu.org/software/screen/`). The best tutorial I've found for this is at `http://www.kuro5hin.org/story/2004/3/9/16838/14935`.

▶ If you're interested in using tmux, the best tutorial I've found is `http://blog.hawkhost.com/2010/06/28/tmux-the-terminal-multiplexer/`. Another good tutorial is available at `http://lukaszwrobel.pl/blog/tmux-tutorial-split-terminal-windows-easily`.

# Creating scatter plots with NVD3

If you've been following along from the previous recipes in this chapter, you'll now have a complete web application stack ready, and you can use it to create charts and graphs for the Web.

For this recipe, we'll create a scatter plot of the US census racial data that we saw in *Chapter 6*, *Workin with Incanter DataSets*, in the *Grouping data with $group-by* recipe. In fact, this will be the same recipe as we saw in *Chapter 10*, *Working with Unstructured and Textual Data*, only this time we'll create a web page.

To do this, we'll use the D3 JavaScript library (`http://d3js.org/`). **D3** stands for **Data-Driven Documents**, and this library makes it easy to load data and create HTML and SVG structures from data. You can use it to transform data into tables or charts. It is pretty low-level though. With D3, we will create many of the actual elements. We'll do this in a later recipe, but for now, we'll use the NVD3 library (`http://nvd3.org/`), which is a collection of prebuilt charts. We can set a few parameters, pass them our data, and immediately get a great looking chart back out.

## Getting ready

We'll again build on the previous recipes in this chapter, so make sure you have the environment and web application described in the *Setting up to use ClojureScript* recipe running.

We can use the same namespace declaration that we did in the *Creating HTML with Hiccup* recipe.

I've transformed the CSV data into JSON, so we can serve it statically. You can download this from `http://www.ericrochester.com/clj-data-analysis/data/census-race.json` and put it into the `resources/data/` directory in your project.

## How to do it...

There are a number of steps that need to be performed to add a resource to a web application, as shown here:

1. Before we get started, we need to download the NVD3 style sheet from `https://raw.github.com/novus/nvd3/master/src/nv.d3.css` and save it into `resources/css`.

2. We'll also need the NVD3 JavaScript library itself from `https://raw.github.com/novus/nvd3/master/nv.d3.min.js`. Save it to `resources/js`.

3. Now, let's add a Hiccup template function to the `src/web_viz/web.clj` file. We can pass it a title and some content, and it will fill in the rest of the page:

```clojure
(defn d3-page
  [title js body & {:keys [extra-js] :or {extra-js []}}]
  (html5
    [:head
     [:title title]
     (include-css "/css/nv.d3.css"))
     (include-css "/css/style.css")]
    [:body
     (concat
       [body]
       [(include-js "http://d3js.org/d3.v3.min.js")
        (include-js "/js/nv.d3.min.js")]
       (map include-js extra-js)
       [(include-js "/js/script.js")
        (javascript-tag js)])])))
```

4. Let's also add some ClojureScript infrastructure. This function will abstract out the boilerplate to create NVD3 and D3 charts. We'll put this and the next few definitions into `src-cljs/webviz/core.cljs`, as shown here:

```clojure
;;; A group of values. Each group has a key/label and
;;; a JS array of point values.
(deftype Group [key values])
;;; A point. Each point has a location (x, y) and a
;;; size.
(deftype Point [x y size])
```

5. We'll also define some functions to help build the chart:

```
(defn add-label [chart axis label]
  "This sets an axis' label if not nil."
  (when-not (nil? label)
    (.axisLabel (aget chart axis) label)))
(defn add-axes-labels [chart x-label y-label]
  "Add axes' labels to the chart."
  (doto chart
    (add-label "xAxis" x-label)
    (add-label "yAxis" y-label)))
(defn populate-node [selector chart groups transition
                     continuation]
  "This builds the chart from the selector."
  (-> (.select js/d3 selector)
    (.datum groups)
    (.transition)
    (.duration (if transition 500 0))
    (.call chart)
    (.call continuation)))
```

6. We'll also create some data structures to represent points and groups of points. This is how NVD3 wants the input data represented:

```
(defn create-chart
  [data-url selector make-chart json->groups &
   {:keys [transition continuation x-label y-label]
    :or {transition false, continuation (fn [_])
         x-label nil, y-label nil}}]
  "Create a chart with the data's URL, a selector, and
functions to create the chart and transform the data."
  (.json
    js/d3 data-url
    (fn [error data]
      (when data
        (.addGraph
          js/nv
          (fn []
            (let [chart (make-chart)]
              (add-axes-labels chart x-label y-label)
              (populate-node selector chart
                             (json->groups data)
                             transition continuation)
              (.windowResize js/nv.utils
                             #(.update chart)))))))))
```

With these bits of infrastructure, we can create the plot, as follows:

1. We'll define a handler for the page itself, in the `src/web_viz/web.clj` file, using the `d3-page` function. This will embed the JavaScript to create the chart and create an SVG element to contain it:

```
(defn scatter-charts []
  (d3-page "Scatter Chart"
          "webviz.scatter.scatter_plot();"
          [:div#scatter.chart [:svg]]))
```

2. Next, we'll define the routes for it. You can add the highlighted routes to the current set, as follows:

```
(defroutes
  site-routes
  (GET "/scatter" [] (scatter-charts))
  (GET "/scatter/data.json" []
    (redirect "/data/census-race.json"))
  (route/resources "/")
  (route/not-found "Page not found"))
```

3. Let's add a little style to the chart. Create `resources/css/style.css` and add this:

```
div.chart {
    height: 450px;
    width: 650px;
}
body {
    font-family: Helvetica, Arial, sans-serif;
    font-size: smaller;
}
```

4. Now, let's create a new file named `src-cljs/webviz/scatter.cljs`. The namespace declaration for this is given as follows:

```
(ns webviz.scatter
  (:require [webviz.core :as webviz]))
```

5. We'll need to summarize the data in order to get the totals for the white and African-American populations by state. The following functions will take care of this:

```
(defn sum-by [key-fn coll]
  "This maps the values in a collection and sums the
  results."
  (reduce + 0 (map key-fn coll)))
(defn sum-values [key-fn coll]
```

```
    "This takes a function and a map associating a label
    with a sequence of values. It replaces those values
    with their sums after passing them through the function."
    (reduce
      (fn [m [k vs]] (assoc m k (sum-by key-fn vs)))
      {}
      coll))
(defn sum-data-fields [json]
  "This generates by-state sums for different groups."
  (let [by-state (group-by #(.-state_name %) json)
        white-by-state (sum-values #(.-white %) by-state)
        afam-by-state (sum-values #(.-black %) by-state)
        total-by-state (sum-values #(.-total %) by-state)]
    (map #(hash-map :state %
                    :white (white-by-state %)
                    :black (afam-by-state %)
                    :total (total-by-state %))
        (keys by-state))))
```

6. NVD3 expects the data to be in points and groups. We'll use the types we defined in `webviz.core`. These functions will convert the summarized data into the objects that NVD3 expects, as shown here:

```
(defn ->nv [item]
  (let [{:keys [white black]} item]
    (webviz/Point. (/ white 1000) (/ black 1000) 1)))
(defn ->nv-data [key-name data]
  (->> data
    sum-data-fields
    (map ->nv)
    (apply array)
    (webviz/Group. key-name)
    (array)))
```

7. This function will actually create the chart and set the options and formatting for it:

```
(defn make-chart []
  (let [c (-> (.scatterChart js/nv.models)
              (.showDistX true)
              (.showDistY true)
              (.useVoronoi false)
              (.color (.. js/d3 -scale category10 range)))]
    (.tickFormat (.-xAxis c) (.format js/d3 "d"))
    (.tickFormat (.-yAxis c) (.format js/d3 "d"))
    c))
```

8. Actually, pulling all of this together is pretty simple:

```
(defn ^:export scatter-plot []
  (webviz/create-chart
    "/scatter/data.json"
    "#scatter svg"
    make-chart
    (partial ->nv-data "Racial Data")
    :x-label "Population, whites, by thousands"
    :y-label (str "Population, African-Americans, "
                  "by thousands")
    :transition true))
```

Now when we visit `http://localhost:3000/scatter`, we will get a good-looking chart, as shown in the following screenshot:

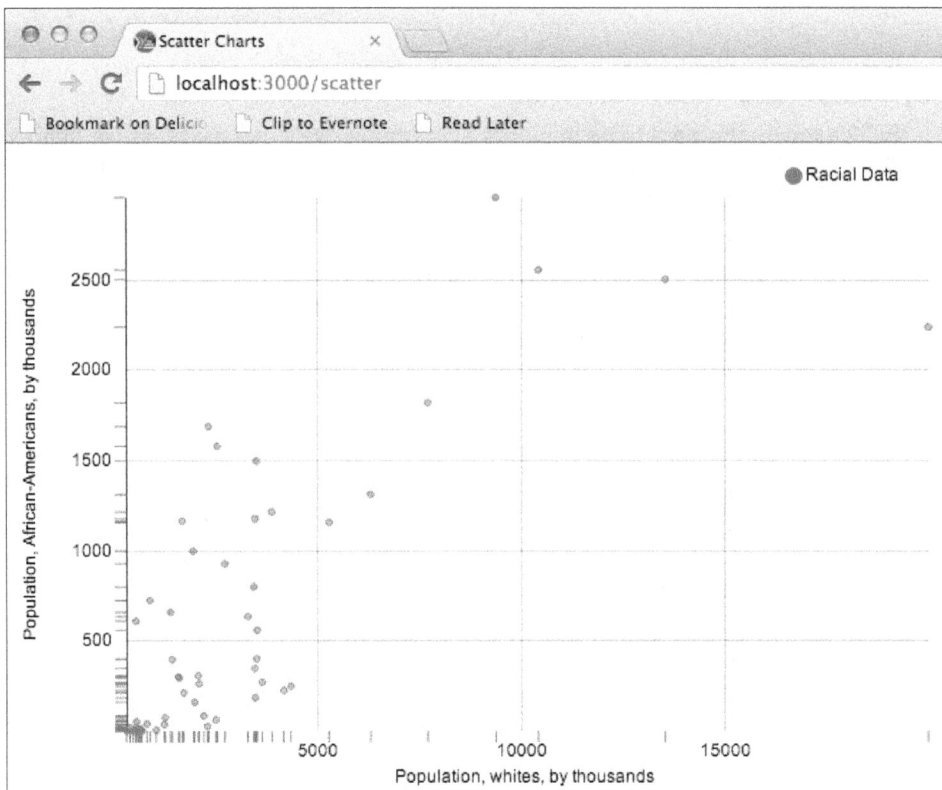

## How it works...

NVD3 expects the data to be in a specific format. We create an adapter function for the data and a function to create and configure the specific plot we want. With these functions, we call `webviz/create-chart` to actually populate the HTML elements and display the chart.

The `create-chart` function takes a URL to load the data, the path to select the element to create the chart in, a function to create the chart, and a function to convert the data into points and groups. The `create-chart` function uses these parameters to request the data, create the chart, and associate the data with it. Those steps are common to any chart built with NVD3, so abstracting them out will save us in the long run.

## There's more...

▶ The page for D3 is at `http://d3js.org/`. The gallery here is a good place to start looking, to take inspiration from, and to learn what the library is capable of.

▶ The page for NVD3 is `http://nvd3.org/`.

▶ An alternative to D3 and NVD3 is Kevin Lynagh's C2 (`http://keminglabs.com/c2/`). This allows a more declarative approach to creating HTML and SVG structures and to using Hiccup-style data structures in the browser.

# Creating bar charts with NVD3

Bar charts are good for comparing the sums or counts of categories of data in a dataset. For example, in this recipe, we'll create a chart that compares the weight of chicks being fed one of four diets.

Like most of the recipes in this chapter, this one builds on the previous ones. It will take the foundation from the *Setting up to use ClojureScript* recipe, along with the infrastructure added in the *Creating scatter plots with NVD3* recipe, and build the bar chart on it.

Let's get started.

## Getting ready

We'll use the same dependencies and plugins in our `project.clj` file as we did in the *Creating scatter plots with NVD3* recipe. We'll also use the `sum-by` function from that recipe.

We'll use the chicks' weight dataset that we've seen before. I've transformed it into JSON, and you can download it from `http://www.ericrochester.com/clj-data-analysis/data/chick-weight.json`. Save it into the `resources/data/` directory of your project.

## How to do it...

We'll follow the same workflow as we did in the last recipe: write a handler, add a route, and write the client-side ClojureScript. To do this, perform the following steps:

1. The handler will return a D3 page, complete with the code to create the DIV and SVG elements and to call the ClojureScript function that we'll define in a minute:

```
(defn bar-chart []
  (d3-page "Bar Chart"
           "webviz.barchart.bar_chart();"
           [:div#barchart.chart [:svg]]))
```

2. Next, we'll add the routes for this chart:

```
(defroutes
  site-routes
  (GET "/barchart" [] (bar-chart))
  (GET "/barchart/data.json" []
       (redirect "/data/chick-weight.json"))
  (route/resources "/")
  (route/not-found "Page not found"))
```

3. Now, we'll create the ClojureScript. Create a `src-cljs/webviz/barchart.cljs` file and add this namespace declaration:

```
(ns webviz.barchart
  (:require [webviz.core :as webviz]))
```

4. We'll convert the data into two categories of the `Group` and `Point` data structures that NVD3 expects. For the first category, `get-diet-counts` expects a hash table that associates a diet code with the items from the dataset that have this diet code. The *y* value for the point is the count of those items:

```
(defn count-point [pair]
  (let [[diet items] pair]
    (webviz/Point. diet (count items) 1)))
(defn get-diet-counts [diet-groups]
  (apply array (map count-point diet-groups)))
```

5. We'll add a pair of functions for the other category. The *y* value for these points will be the sum of the weights, as shown here:

```
(defn sum-by [key-fn coll]
  (reduce + 0 (map key-fn coll)))
(defn weight-point [pair]
  (let [[diet items] pair
```

```
          weight-total (sum-by #(.-weight %) items)]
      (webviz/Point. diet weight-total 1)))
  (defn get-diet-weights [diet-groups]
    (apply array (map weight-point diet-groups)))
```

6. Here's the function that will transform the JSON input into JavaScript objects for NVD3:

```
(defn json->nv-groups [json]
  (let [diet-groups (group-by #(.-diet %) json)]
    (array (webviz/Group.
             "Chick Counts"
             (get-diet-counts diet-groups))
           (webviz/Group.
             "Chick Weights"
             (get-diet-weights diet-groups)))))
```

7. Finally, here's the function that ties it all together and creates the chart (with the help of `create-chart`):

```
(defn ^:export bar-chart []
  (webviz/create-chart "/barchart/data.json"
                       "#barchart svg"
                       #(.multiBarChart js/nv.models)
                       json->nv-groups))
```

When we visit `http://localhost:3000/barchart`, here's what we will get:

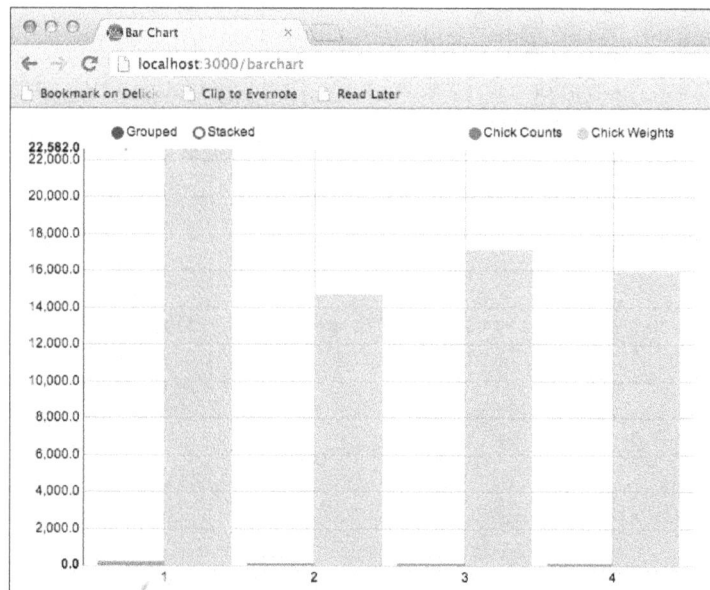

## How it works...

At this point, we can see some payoff for all of the work and code we put into the *Creating scatter plot with NVD3* recipe. As we could leverage the `create-chart` function, we avoided a lot of the boilerplate involved in creating graphs.

However, setting up a web resource in this manner still involves a number of standard steps, as follows:

1. Define the resource on the server (`bar-chart`).
2. Define the routes to access this resource.
3. Create the ClojureScript file.
4. In ClojureScript, write functions to transform the data.
5. In ClojureScript, create the chart.

# Creating histograms with NVD3

To show the distribution of our data, we generally use a histogram. In this recipe, we'll use a histogram to display the distribution of lengths in the abalone dataset.

## Getting ready

We'll use the same dependencies and plugins in our `project.clj` file as we did in the *Creating scatter plots with NVD3* recipe. Also, we'll use the framework we've created in the recipes in this chapter upto the *Creating scatter plots with NVD3* recipe.

For the data, we'll use the abalone dataset from the *Creating histograms with Incanter* recipe. I've transformed the data to JSON, and you can download it from `http://www.ericrochester.com/clj-data-analysis/data/abalone.json`. Save it to the `resources/data/` directory in your web application.

## How to do it...

We'll create the handler and the routes and then we'll spend most of this recipe in adding the ClojureScript to create the graph. To do this, perform the following steps:

1. For the handler, we'll pass the options for this chart to the `d3-page` function, as shown here:

```
(defn hist-plot []
  (d3-page "Histogram"
           "webviz.histogram.histogram();"
           [:div#histogram.chart [:svg]]))
```

2.  We'll add that and the data URL to the routes:

```
(defroutes
  site-routes
  (GET "/histogram" [] (hist-plot))
  (GET "/histogram/data.json" []
       (redirect "/data/abalone.json"))
  (route/resources "/")
  (route/not-found "Page not found"))
```

3.  Now, for the ClojureScript file, we'll open `src-cljs/webviz/histogram.cljs` and add the following namespace declaration:

```
(ns webviz.histogram
  (:require [webviz.core :as webviz]))
```

4.  We'll need a function to group the data into buckets:

```
(defn get-bucket-number [mn size x]
  (Math/round (/ (- x mn) size)))
(defn inc-bucket [mn size buckets x]
  (let [b (get-bucket-number mn size x)]
    (assoc buckets b (inc (buckets b)))))
(defn get-buckets [coll n]
  (let [mn (reduce min coll)
        mx (reduce max coll)
        bucket-size (/ (- mx mn) n)
        first-center (+ mn (/ bucket-size 2.0))
        centers (map #(* (inc %) first-center)
                     (range n))
        initial (reduce #(assoc %1 %2 0) {}
                        (range n))]
    (->> coll
      (reduce (partial inc-bucket mn bucket-size)
              initial)
      seq
      (sort-by first)
      (map second)
      (map vector centers))))
```

5.  Here are two functions to take the JSON, put it into buckets, and convert it to points and groups:

```
(defn ->point [pair]
  (let [[bucket count] pair]
    (webviz/Point. (inc bucket) count 1)))
(defn data->nv-groups [data]
```

```
(let [lengths (map #(.-length %) data)
      buckets (apply array
                     (map ->point
                          (get-buckets
                           lengths 10)))]
  (array (webviz/Group. "Abalone Lengths" buckets))))
```

6. It is simple to initialize the chart. We just want a standard multibar chart, as shown here:

```
(defn make-chart [] (.multiBarChart (.-models js/nv)))
```

7. Creating the chart just involves tying these together with `create-chart`:

```
(defn ^:export histogram []
  (webviz/create-chart
    "/histogram/data.json"
    "#histogram svg"
    make-chart
    data->nv-groups
    :transition true))
```

Now, when we visit `http://localhost:3000/histogram`, we can see the following histogram:

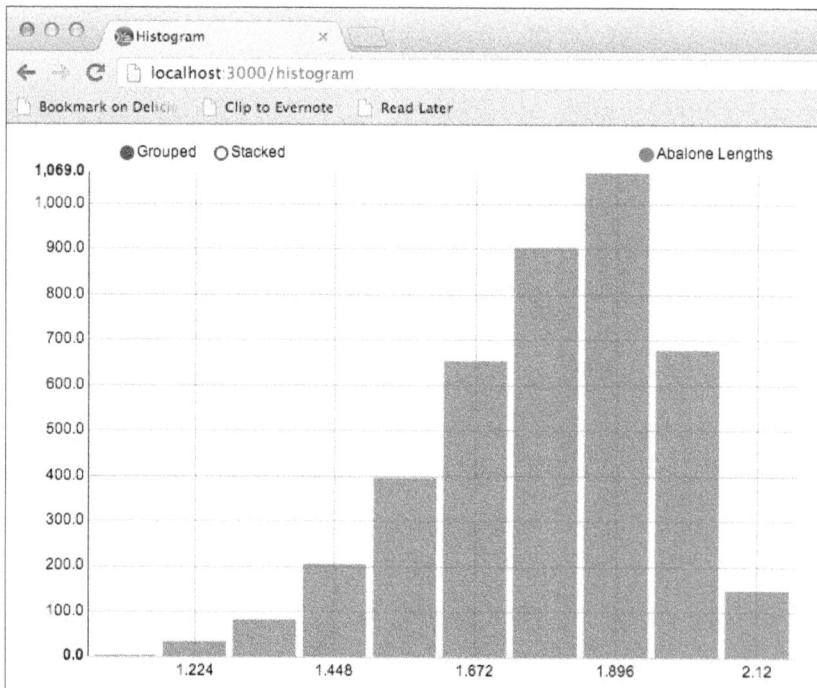

## How it works...

For the most part, this recipe's very similar to the preceding ones. The interesting difference here is that we partition the data into buckets.

To do this, we get the minimum and maximum values in the data and divide the difference between them by the number of buckets. This gives us the width of each bucket in the data.

We use this to determine which bucket each data point goes into, and we count the number of data points in each bucket.

We also get the center value for each bucket, and we use this to label the columns in the graph.

# Creating time series charts with D3

So far in this chapter, all the charts that we've created have used a utility library, NVD3, to do a lot of heavy lifting for us. However, we can also create a lot of these charts directly with D3. We'll see how to do this to use graphs with time series data.

## Getting ready

We'll use the same dependencies and plugins in our `project.clj` file as we did in the *Creating scatter plots with NVD3* recipe. Also, we'll use the framework we created in the recipes in this chapter upto the *Creating scatter plots with NVD3* recipe.

For data, we'll use IBM's stock prices from the end of November 2001 to November 2012. You can download this dataset from `http://www.ericrochester.com/clj-data-analysis/data/ibm.csv`. Save the file into `resources/data/ibm.csv`.

## How to do it...

Our procedure will largely follow the pattern that we've established in the previous recipes. However, we'll also redefine some functions to make sure that we don't load NVD3. To do this, perform the following steps:

1.  First, we'll define a function that uses `d3-page` to create the page containing the stock price graph:

    ```
    (defn time-series []
      (d3-page
        "IBM Stock Data"
        "webviz.time.ibm_stock();"
        [:div#time.chart [:svg]]))
    ```

2. Now, we'll add the URLs for this page and its data to the routes we've been working with:

```
(defroutes site-routes
  (GET "/ibm-stock" [] (time-series))
  (GET "/ibm-stock/data.csv" [] (redirect "/data/ibm.csv"))

  (GET "/" [] (index-page))
  (route/resources "/")
  (route/not-found "Page not found"))
```

3. We'll also want to add some style-related information to make the chart look good. We can do this by adding the following lines to `resources/css/style.css`:

```
#time .axis path {
    fill: none;
    stroke: #000;
    shape-rendering: crispedges;
}

#time .axis line {
    fill: none;
    stroke: #000;
    shape-rendering: crispedges;
}

#time .x.axis path {
    displays: none;
}

#time .line {
    fill: none;
    stroke: steelblue;
    stroke-width: 1.5px;
}
```

4. For the graph, the rest of this will take place in a new file. We'll open `src-cljs/webviz/time.cljs`. This will contain the following namespace declaration:

```
(ns webviz.time)
```

5. Now, let's start creating parts of the graph. First, we'll have one that takes the margins and returns the dimensions of the graph:

```
(defn get-dimensions [margin]
  [(- 960 (:left margin) (:right margin))
   (- 500 (:top margin) (:bottom margin))])
```

6. We'll use D3's facilities to scale the values onto the graph. These objects will be created by `get-scales`:

```
(defn get-scales [width height]
  [(.. js/d3 -time scale (range #js [0 width]))
   (.. js/d3 -scale linear (range #js [height 0]))])
```

7. D3 also provides helpers to calculate and draw the axes:

```
(defn get-axes [x y]
  [(.. js/d3 -svg axis (scale x) (orient "bottom"))
   (.. js/d3 -svg axis (scale y) (orient "left"))])
```

8. The graph's line itself will be created by getting the date and the closing price and scaling these by the appropriate scales ($x$ or $y$), as follows:

```
(defn get-line [x y]
  (.. js/d3 -svg line
      (x #(x (.-date %)))
      (y #(y (.-close %)))))
```

9. The main SVG element will be populated using the `get-svg` function:

```
(defn get-svg [margin width height]
  (.. js/d3 (select "svg")
      (attr "width" (+ width (:left margin)
                          (:right margin)))
      (attr "height" (+ height (:top margin)
                           (:bottom margin)))
      (append "g")
      (attr "transform" (str "translate(" (:left margin)
                                \, (:top margin) \)))))
```

10. The next several functions will apply the data to the graph in order to populate the axes and the line. However, the first two functions that directly deal with the data will simply make sure that the data values are of the right type and calculate the domains:

```
(defn coerce-datum [parse-date d]
  (aset d "date" (parse-date (.-date d)))
  (aset d "close" (js/parseFloat (.-close d))))
(defn set-domains [x y data]
  (.domain x (.extent js/d3 data #(.-date %)))
  (.domain y (.extent js/d3 data #(.-close %))))
```

11. The next two functions will use the data to draw the $x$ and $y$ axes:

```
(defn build-x-axis [height svg x-axis]
  (.. svg (append "g")
      (attr "class" "x axis")
```

```
        (attr "transform" (str "translate(0," height \)))
        (call x-axis)))
(defn build-y-axis [svg y-axis]
  (.. svg (append "g")
      (attr "class" "y axis")
      (call y-axis)
      (append "text")
      (attr "transform" "rotate(-90)")
      (attr "y" 6)
      (attr "dy" ".71em")
      (style "text-anchor" "end")
      (text "Price ($)")))
```

12. The last part of the graph that we'll deal with here is the line that traces out the data's values:

```
(defn add-line [svg line data]
  (.. svg (append "path")
      (datum data)
      (attr "class" "line")
      (attr "d" line)))
```

13. Now, we'll assemble all of these together to create the graph, as shown here:

```
(defn ^:export ibm-stock []
  (let [margin {:top 20, :right 20, :bottom 30, :left 50}
        [width height] (get-dimensions margin)
        parse-date (.. js/d3 -time (format "%d-%b-%y") -parse)
        [x y] (get-scales width height)
        [x-axis y-axis] (get-axes x y)
        line (get-line x y)
        svg (get-svg margin width height)]

    (.csv js/d3
      "/ibm-stock/data.csv"
      (fn [error data]
        (.forEach data
          #(coerce-datum parse-date %))

        (set-domains x y data)

        (build-x-axis height svg x-axis)
        (build-y-axis svg y-axis)
        (add-line svg line data)))))
```

With these in place, we can now visit the page with our browser and view the graph, as shown in the following screenshot:

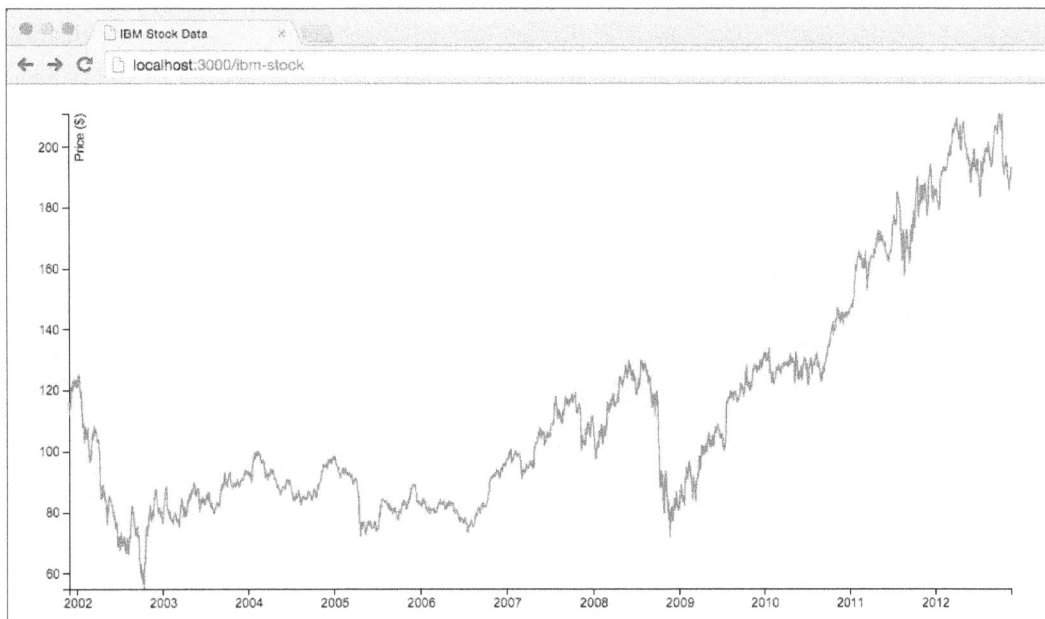

## How it works...

This recipe makes it clear that working with D3 directly is often much lower-level than using NVD3. In this recipe, we're using D3 to create the actual SVG elements, with the appropriate attributes and content, to display the graph. We can see this clearly in `add-line`, for instance.

Let's take a look at that function line-by-line (almost):

```
(defn add-line [svg line data]
  (.. svg (append "path")
      (datum data)
```

In this snippet, D3 will add an SVG `path` element for each datum. This just creates an empty element and associates it with a datum:

```
      (attr "class" "line")
```

This line adds the `class` attribute with the value *line*. We used this in the CSS style sheet to set the line's color:

```
(attr "d" line)))
```

This sets the d attribute to be the value of the `line` function called on this element's datum. The `line` function is created by `get-line`, and it knows how to get its coordinates from the data's `date` and `close` properties.

## There's more...

The Mozilla Developer Network has a good reference to SVG at `https://developer.mozilla.org/en-US/docs/Web/SVG`.

# Visualizing graphs with force-directed layouts

One popular way to visualize graphs of data is to use a force-directed layout. This employs a physical simulation of charged particles and springs to create an aesthetically pleasing visualization. It minimizes crossed lines while keeping all the edges more or less of the same length. This makes the relationships in the graph immediately clear, at the expense of expressing the distances between nodes. For example, consider the following diagram. On the left, we have a graph that is randomly laid out. On the right, it's laid out using a force-directed layout. Each of the edges is approximately as long as the others, and each node is as far away from its neighbors as it can get:

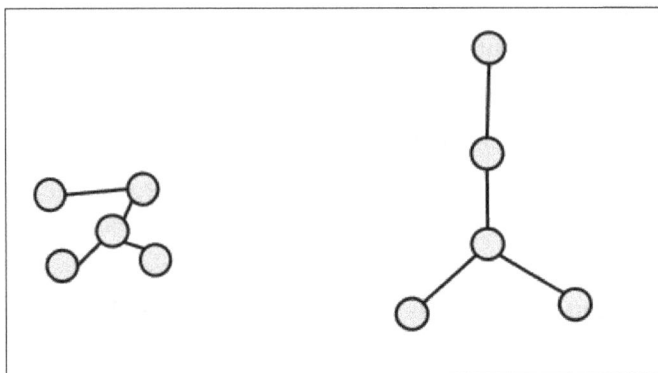

In this recipe, we'll create a force-directed graph visualization for a K-Means cluster of the US census race data aggregated by state.

## Getting ready

We'll use the same dependencies and plugins in our `project.clj` file as we did in the *Creating scatter plots with NVD3* recipe.

As I just mentioned, we'll use a graph of clusters of US census race data by state. I've already compiled this, and you can download it from `http://www.ericrochester.com/clj-data-analysis/data/clusters.json`. Place it in the `resources/data/` directory of your project and you should be ready.

## How to do it...

This recipe will follow the same pattern that we've seen in the last few recipes. We'll define a handler, routes, and then the ClojureScript. To do this, perform the following steps:

1. The handler is similar to what we've seen so far, and it uses the `d3-page` function too:

```
(defn force-layout-plot []
  (d3-page "Force-Directed Layout"
           "webviz.force.force_layout();"
           [:div#force.chart [:svg]]))
```

2. The routes are also as we'd expect them to be:

```
(defroutes
  site-routes
  (GET "/force" [] (force-layout-plot))
  (GET "/force/data.json" []
       (redirect "/data/clusters.json"))
  (route/resources "/")
  (route/not-found "Page not found"))
```

3. We'll also need some style. Open `resources/css/style.css` and add these lines:

```
#force { width: 650px; height: 500px; }
#force .node { stroke: #fff; stroke-width: 1.5px; }
#force .link { stroke: #999; stroke-opacity: 1; }
```

4. Now, let's create the ClojureScript file. Open `src-cljs/webviz/force.cljs` and add this for the namespace declaration:

```
(ns webviz.force)
```

5. First, we'll create the force diagram, as shown here:

```
(defn create-force [width height]
  (-> js/d3 .-layout
    (.force)
    (.charge -120)
    (.linkDistance 30)
    (.size (array width height))))
```

6. Now, we'll create the SVG element to contain it:

```
(defn create-svg [width height]
  (-> js/d3
    (.select "#force svg")
    (.attr "width" width)
    (.attr "height" height)))
```

7. With the force diagram, we need to set the nodes and edges and start the animation:

```
(defn start-force [force graph]
  (-> force
    (.nodes (aget graph "nodes"))
    (.links (aget graph "links"))
    .start))
```

8. We also need to create the lines for the edges and the circles for the nodes:

```
(defn create-links [svg graph]
  (-> svg
    (.selectAll "line.link")
    (.data (aget graph "links"))
    (.enter)
    (.append "line")
    (.attr "class" "link")
    (.style "stroke-width"
            #(.sqrt js/Math (inc (aget % "value"))))))
(defn create-nodes [svg force color graph]
  (-> svg
    (.selectAll "circle.node")
    (.data (aget graph "nodes"))
    (.enter)
    (.append "circle")
    (.attr "class" "node")
    (.attr "r" 5)
    (.attr "data-n" #(aget % "n"))
    (.style "fill" #(color (aget % "group")))
    (.call (aget force "drag"))))
```

9. The `tick` handler transfers the animation from the force chart's objects to the SVG elements, displaying them:

```
(defn on-tick-handler [link node]
  (fn []
    (-> link
      (.attr "x1" #(-> % .-source .-x))
      (.attr "y1" #(-> % .-source .-y))
      (.attr "x2" #(-> % .-target .-x))
      (.attr "y2" #(-> % .-target .-y)))
    (-> node
      (.attr "cx" #(aget % "x"))
      (.attr "cy" #(aget % "y")))))
```

10. We'll add a `title` element to the nodes for a tooltip:

```
(defn set-title [node]
  (-> node
    (.append "title")
    (.text #(aget % "name"))))
```

11. Now, we use all of these to render the graph. We'll also save the input graph that we are visualizing. We'll query this to make the visualization interactive in the next recipe, *Creating interactive visualizations with D3*. If you don't care about that, you can remove the call to `swap!`:

```
(def census-graph (atom nil))
(defn render-graph [color force svg graph]
  (swap! census-graph (fn [] graph))
  (start-force force graph)
  (let [link (create-links svg graph)
        node (create-nodes svg force color graph)]
    (set-title node)
    (.on force "tick" (on-tick-handler link node))))
```

12. Here's the function that we'll export. It makes the AJAX call to download the JSON, creates the base objects, and calls `render-graph`:

```
(defn ^:export force-layout []
  (let [width 650, height 500]
    (.json js/d3 "force/data.json"
           (partial
             render-graph
             (.category20c (aget js/d3 "scale"))
             (create-force width height)
             (create-svg width height)))))
```

When we visit `http://localhost:3000/force`, we will get the following visualization:

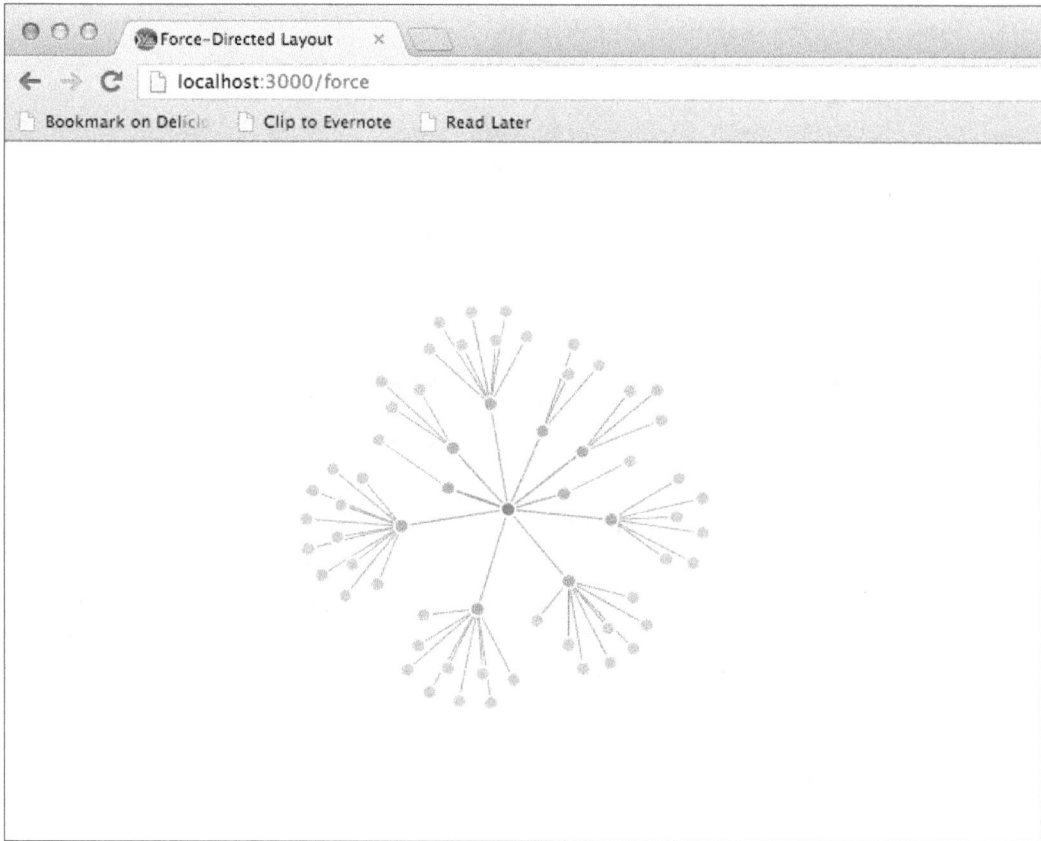

## How it works...

This is a good example of a pure D3 visualization, without NVD3. We've broken the task up into functions to make them easier to understand, but let's take a look at the typical D3 visualization process that we outlined at the end of the *Creating time series charts with D3* recipe and see how the functions in this recipe fit into it, as follows:

1. **Create the chart**: `create-force` takes care of creating the controller for the chart.

2. **Call select on the container**: `create-svg` selects the SVG elements to render the graph.

3. **Call selectAll on the element we want created to contain each data point**: Two functions, `create-links` and `create-nodes`, start by calling `selectAll` on line nodes and circle nodes.

4. **Associate the data with the chart**: This happens in three places. The `create-links` and `create-nodes` functions associate the edges and nodes with their elements, and `start-force` passes a copy of both to the `force` object.

5. **Enter each data point and create the HTML using append and attr**: Again, the `create-links` and `create-nodes` functions do this for their respective data types.

All of these work together to create the graph. Additionally, since the force-directed layout is animated, we also create a `tick` handler to update the browser with the latest positions of the objects.

## There's more...

For more about D3, see its website at `http://d3js.org/`.

# Creating interactive visualizations with D3

One of the great things about working on the Web is how easy it is to make things interactive. Also, since D3 exposes the underlying HTML elements— in fact, it often forces you to work in them—making a D3 graph interactive is pretty straightforward; we just use standard HTML events.

For this recipe, we'll take the force-directed layout visualization of the US census data that we did in the last recipe, *Visualizing graphs with force-directed layout*, and make it interactive. We'll add a data panel to the right-hand side of the graph, and whenever the user hovers over a node, the page will display the census data from that node in the data panel.

## Getting ready

We'll start with the visualization from the last recipe, *Visualizing graphs with force-directed layout*, and add to it.

## How to do it...

Even though we're adding to an existing graph, we'll do it on a new URL, so we'll also need to add a handler, route, and ClojureScript for it. To do this, perform the following steps:

1. Here's the handler, which also includes the HTML for the data panel:

```
(defn interactive-force-plot []
  (d3-page "Interactive Force-Directive Layout"
           (str "webviz"
                ".int_force"
```

```
              ".interactive_force_layout();")
        [:div
         [:div#force.chart [:svg]]
         [:div#datapane]]]))
```

2. We'll use the following route:

```
(defroutes
  site-routes
  (GET "/int-force" [] (interactive-force-plot))
  (GET "/int-force/data.json" []
       (redirect "/data/clusters.json"))
  (route/resources "/")
  (route/not-found "Page not found"))
```

3. We'll need extra styles for the data panel. Open up `resources/css/style.css` and add these lines:

```
#datapane { float: right; width: 250px; }
#datapane dt { font-weight: bold; }
```

4. Now, for this graph, let's open `src-cljs/webviz/int_force.cljs` and add this namespace declaration:

```
(ns webviz.int-force
  (:require [clojure.browser.dom :as dom]
            [webviz.force :as force]
            [goog.events :as gevents]))
```

5. In the data panel, for each census item, we'll add a DT/DD element combination. We'll encapsulate this into a function since we'll define a number of these:

```
(defn dl-item [title data key]
  (let [val2000 (aget data (str key "-2000"))]
    (str "<dt>" title "</dt>"
         "<dd>" (.round js/Math (aget data key))
         " <em>(2000: "
         (.round js/Math val2000)
         ")</em>"
         "</dd>")))
```

6. The most complicated function builds the HTML to populate the data panel, as shown here:

```
(defn update-data [node]
  (let [data (aget node "data")
        content
```

```
              (str "<h2>" (aget node "name") "</h2>"
                   "<dl>"
                   (dl-item "Total" data "race-total")
                   (dl-item "White" data "race-white")
                   (dl-item "African-American" data
                            "race-black")
                   (dl-item "Native American" data
                            "race-indian")
                   (dl-item "Asian" data "race-asian")
                   (dl-item "Hawaiian" data "race-hawaiian")
                   (dl-item "Other" data "race-other")
                   (dl-item "Multi-racial" data
                            "race-two-more")
                   "</dl>")]
      (dom/remove-children :datapane)
      (dom/append
        (dom/get-element :datapane)
        (dom/html->dom content)))))
```

7. Our `mouseover` event, which will get called whenever the user hovers over a node, pulls the `CIRCLE` element out of the event, gets the index of the node from the element, and pulls the data item out of the graph:

```
(defn on-mouseover [ev]
  (let [target (.-target ev)]
    (if (= (.-nodeName target) "circle")
      (let [n (+ (.getAttribute target "data-n"))]
        (update-data
          (aget (.-nodes @force/census-graph) n))))))
```

8. Now, we create the chart using the `force-layout` function from the last recipe and then we add an event handler to the chart's parent:

```
(defn ^:export interactive-force-layout []
  (force/force-layout)
  (gevents/listen (dom/get-element "force")
                  (.-MOUSEOVER gevents/EventType)
                  on-mouseover))
```

When we visit `http://localhost:3000/int-force` and hover over one of the circles, we will get the following screenshot:

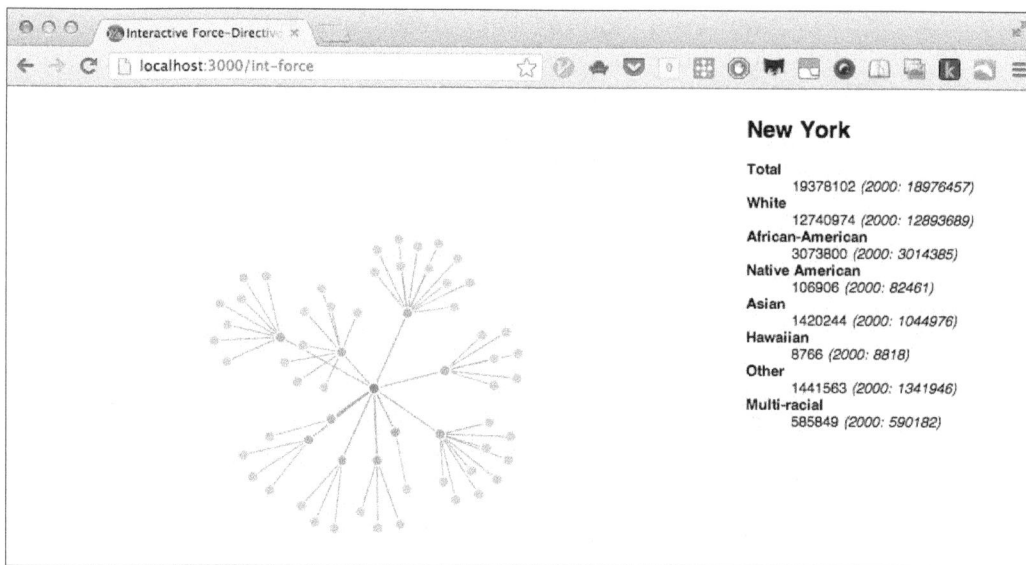

## How it works...

This recipe works in the same way as an interaction works on any web page. We listen to events that the user generates on certain HTML tags. In this case, we pay attention to whenever the mouse moves over a node on the graph. We bind our event handler to this event in step 7.

When the event is triggered, the event handler is called. In our example, the event handler function, `on-mouseover`, is defined in step 6.

The event handler retrieves the data for the node that the user moved their mouse cursor over, and it calls `update-data` and `dl-item` to build the HTML structure in order to display data about this node.

We've mentioned before that the Google Closure library comes with ClojureScript. In this recipe, we use its events module (`http://docs.closure-library.googlecode.com/git/namespace_goog_events.html`) to bind `on-mouseover` to the appropriate event.

We also use the ClojureScript `clojure.browser.dom` namespace to delete and create HTML elements on the fly. This namespace is a thin, Clojure-friendly wrapper around the Closure library for manipulating the DOM, goog.dom (`http://docs.closure-library.googlecode.com/git/namespace_goog_dom.html`).

Finally, we also interface a few times with JavaScript itself. We do this by prefixing the name of the JavaScript object or module with js, `js/Math`, for example.

## There's more...

▶ Google's Closure library is bundled with ClojureScript and provides a lot of functionality to manipulate the DOM and other common tasks for writing in-browser web apps. You can learn more about this library at `https://developers.google.com/closure/library/`.

▶ The standard ClojureScript namespace, `clojure.browser.dom`, provides a Clojure-like wrapper over some of the Closure library's DOM manipulation functionality. You can see what's in this library by browsing it at `https://github.com/clojure/clojurescript/blob/master/src/cljs/clojure/browser/dom.cljs`.

▶ A good resource to work with HTML, CSS, and JavaScript is the Mozilla Developer Network. You can find it at `https://developer.mozilla.org/`.

# Index

# C

## E

edit-distance parameter  52
embedded domain-specific
        language (EDSL)  33
Enlive
    URL  21
ensure function
    about  85
    consistency, maintaining with  85-88
equations
    adding, to Incanter charts  290, 291
error handler  98
error mode  98
errors
    continuing on  99
    custom error handler, using  99
    failing on  98
    recovering, in agents  98
EuroClojure 2012
    URL  118
Excel, with Incanter
    data, reading from  14, 15
exchange rates
    scraping  39-41

## F

FASTA data
    URL  68
FASTA format
    URL  68
filter operators
    creating  149
force-directed layouts
    graphs, visualizing with  334-339
function calls
    combining, with reducers  116-118
function plots
    creating, with Incanter  288-290
functions
    creating, from Mathematica  218
function words  260
fuzzy-dist  52

## G

get-corpus-terms function  268
get-dataset function
    about  157
    URL  157
get-idf-cache function  268
Google Closure library
    URL  317
Google Finance
    URL  184
graphs
    visualizing, with force-directed
        layouts  334-339
Graphviz
    URL  247
groups of data
    discovering, K-Means clustering
        used  235-238

## H

Hadoop
    initializing, for distributed
        processing  133-136
    URL  132
hadoop command  141
Hadoop Distributed File System (HDFS)  133
handlers
    about  310
    defining  308
Harvard
    URL  177
Heroku
    URL  306
Hiccup
    HTML, creating with  311-313
    URL  306, 313
hierarchical clustering
    URL  243
hierarchical clusters
    finding, in Weka  241-243
histograms
    creating, with Incanter  287, 288
    creating, with NVD3  326-329
HTML
    creating, with Hiccup  311-313

## I

**ID3 algorithm**
URL 248
**Incanter**
dynamic charts, creating with 304
function plots, creating with 288-290
histograms, creating with 287, 288
infix formulas, using 163, 164
processing, parallelizing with 106
scatter plots, creating with 282-284
SOMs, clustering with 244, 245
URL 8, 156, 202
**Incanter charts**
equations, adding to 290
**Incanter datasets**
CSV data, reading into 9-11
JSON data, reading into 12, 13
XML data, reading into 18-20
**Incanter Zoo**
time series data, working with 184-186
**infix formulas**
used, in Incanter 163, 164
**Infochimps**
URL 13, 139
**insert-split function 67**
**interactive visualizations**
creating, with D3 339-343
**ionosphere dataset**
URL 254

## J

**Java data types, R**
URL 225
**Java Development Kit**
URL 212
**JavaDocs**
URL 143
**JavaDocs, for Pattern class**
URL 48
**JavaScript Object Notation (JSON)**
URL 12
**Java tutorial, on regular expressions**
URL 48

**JDBC databases**
data, reading from 15-17
**Jetty**
URL 306
**JFreeChart**
charts, customizing with 293-296
**Joda Java library**
URL 57
**JSON**
and XML, comparing 21
data, saving 173
reading, into Incanter datasets 12, 13

## K

**K-Means clustering**
about 235
macros, building 240
results, analyzing 239, 240
used, for discovering groups of data 235-238
**kr Clojure library**
URL 29

## L

**large data sets**
processing 59-61
sampling 61
sampling, by percentage 62
sampling, for exact count 62, 63
**large inputs**
managing, with sized queues 100
**least squares linear regression 194**
**Leiningen**
URL 8, 9
**lein new command 8**
**linear regression 192**
**linear relationships**
modeling 192-194
**lines**
adding, to scatter charts 292, 293
**Linux**
Mathematica, setting up for 208-212

# O

**online summary statistics**
generating, for data streams with
    reducers 121-123
**online tester, RegexPlant**
URL 48
**OpenNLP**
URL 258
**Open Secrets**
URL 80
**optimal partition size**
finding, with simulated annealing 112-115
**output-points function 103**

# P

**parallel aggregate operators**
composing 151-153
creating 150
**Parallel Colt Java library**
URL 106
**parallelism 74**
**parallelization 102**
**people**
finding, with NER 270-272
**Pig 133**
**pipeline processing 20, 21**
**places**
finding, with NER 270-272
**pmap**
processing, parallelizing with 102-105
**POI Factory**
URL 10
**Political Action Committee (PAC) 80**
**processing**
monitoring, with watchers 94-96
parallelizing, with Incanter 106, 107
parallelizing, with pmap 102-105
**program complexity**
managing, with agents 79-82
managing, with STM 75-79
**project**
creating 8, 9
**Project Gutenberg**
URL 187

# Q

**qr**
URL 222

# R

**R**
plotting, from Clojure 226, 227
setting up 219
URL 156, 208, 219
vectors, passing into 222, 223
**RDF data**
querying, with SPARQL 33-37
reading 29-32
**Reduce operation 132**
**reducers**
function calls, combining with 116-118
online summary statistics, generating for
    data streams with 121-123
parallelizing with 118-121
**regular expressions**
about 47, 48
data, cleaning with 46-48
**relative values**
calculating 55, 56
**REPL 8**
**replace-split function 67**
**Resource Description Format (RDF) 32**
**results**
analyzing 239, 240
**R files**
evaluating, from Clojure 224, 225
**R functions**
calling, from Clojure 221
**R gallery**
URL 227
**Ring**
about 306
adapters 310
data, serving with 306, 307
handlers 310
middleware 310
URL 306, 309

**TF-IDF**
document frequencies, scaling with  266-270
**tf-idf-freqs function  268**
**things**
finding, with NER  270-272
**thread starvation  89**
**thunk  77**
**times**
parsing  57-59
**time series charts**
creating, with D3  329-334
**time series data**
working, with Incanter Zoo  184-186
**tmux**
URL  316, 317
**to-dataset function  159**
**tokenization  258**
**to-matrix function  162**
**topic modeling**
about  274
performing, with MALLET  274-277
**transpose-char function  67**
**triple store**
creating  39
**type hints**
using  124-127

# U

**UCI datasets**
URL  246
**update-totals function  76**

# V

**validators**
data consistency, maintaining with  91-93
**Valip**
data, validating with  70-72
URL  71
**values, change**
working with  180-182
**variable binding**
URL  138

**variable relationships**
simplifying, for scaling variables  182, 183
**variables**
scaling, to simplify variable
relationships  182, 183
smoothing, to decrease variation  186-189
**variation**
decreasing, for smoothing
variables  186-189
**vectors**
passing, into R  222, 223
**vector space representation**
documents, mapping to  272, 273
**view**
datasets, viewing with  159, 160

# W

**watchers**
about  94
concurrent programs, debugging with  96, 97
processing, maintaining with  94-96
**web application**
configuring  307, 308
setting up  307, 308
**web pages**
data, scraping from tables  21-25
textual data, scraping from  25-28
**Weka**
ARFF file, loading into  230-232
columns, deleting  232, 233
columns, filtering  232, 233
columns, renaming  232, 233
CSV file, loading into  230-232
hierarchical clusters, finding  241-243
URL  230, 232
**Weka datasets**
URL  252
**Weka documentation**
URL  256
**Weka library  8**
**Windows**
Mathematica, setting up for  212-214

# [PACKT] PUBLISHING   open source*
community experience distilled

## Thank you for buying
## Clojure Data Analysis Cookbook
### Second Edition

## About Packt Publishing

Packt, pronounced 'packed', published its first book, *Mastering phpMyAdmin for Effective MySQL Management*, in April 2004, and subsequently continued to specialize in publishing highly focused books on specific technologies and solutions.

Our books and publications share the experiences of your fellow IT professionals in adapting and customizing today's systems, applications, and frameworks. Our solution-based books give you the knowledge and power to customize the software and technologies you're using to get the job done. Packt books are more specific and less general than the IT books you have seen in the past. Our unique business model allows us to bring you more focused information, giving you more of what you need to know, and less of what you don't.

Packt is a modern yet unique publishing company that focuses on producing quality, cutting-edge books for communities of developers, administrators, and newbies alike. For more information, please visit our website at www.packtpub.com.

## About Packt Open Source

In 2010, Packt launched two new brands, Packt Open Source and Packt Enterprise, in order to continue its focus on specialization. This book is part of the Packt open source brand, home to books published on software built around open source licenses, and offering information to anybody from advanced developers to budding web designers. The Open Source brand also runs Packt's open source Royalty Scheme, by which Packt gives a royalty to each open source project about whose software a book is sold.

## Writing for Packt

We welcome all inquiries from people who are interested in authoring. Book proposals should be sent to author@packtpub.com. If your book idea is still at an early stage and you would like to discuss it first before writing a formal book proposal, then please contact us; one of our commissioning editors will get in touch with you.

We're not just looking for published authors; if you have strong technical skills but no writing experience, our experienced editors can help you develop a writing career, or simply get some additional reward for your expertise.

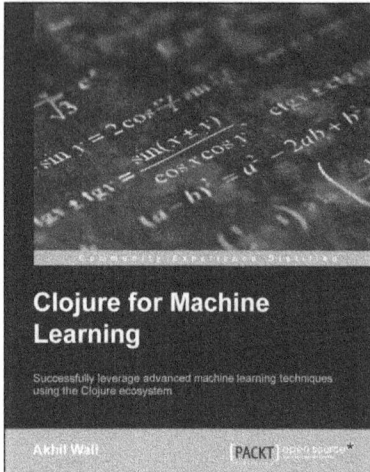

# Clojure for Machine Learning

ISBN: 978-1-78328-435-1          Paperback: 292 pages

Successfully leverage advanced machine learning techniques using the Clojure ecosystem

1.  Covers a lot of machine learning techniques with Clojure programming.

2.  Encompasses precise patterns in data to predict future outcomes using various machine learning techniques.

3.  Packed with several machine learning libraries available in the Clojure ecosystem.

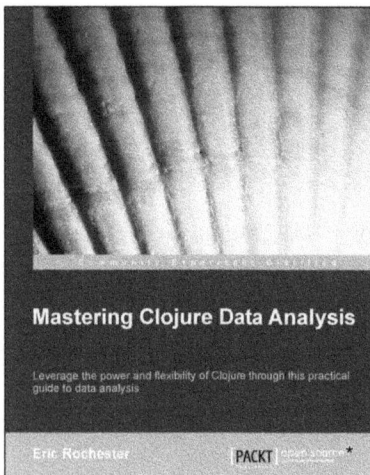

# Mastering Clojure Data Analysis

ISBN: 978-1-78328-413-9          Paperback: 340 pages

Leverage the power and flexibility of Clojure through this practical guide to data analysis

1.  Explore the concept of data analysis using established scientific methods combined with the powerful Clojure language.

2.  Master Naïve Bayesian Classification, Benford's Law, and much more in Clojure.

3.  Learn with the help of examples drawn from exciting, real-world data.

Please check **www.PacktPub.com** for information on our titles

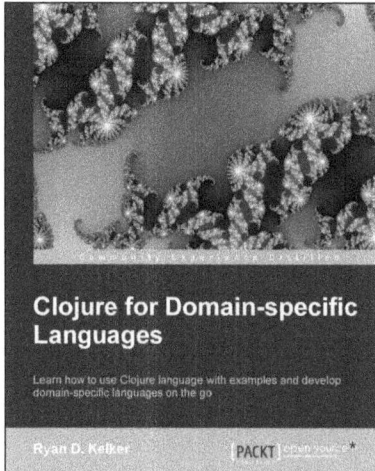

## Clojure for Domain-specific Languages

ISBN: 978-1-78216-650-4          Paperback: 268 pages

Learn how to use Clojure language with examples and develop domain-specific languages on the go

1. Explore DSL concepts from existing Clojure DSLs and libraries.

2. Bring Clojure into your Java applications as Clojure can be hosted on a Java platform.

3. A tutorial-based guide to develop custom domain-specific languages.

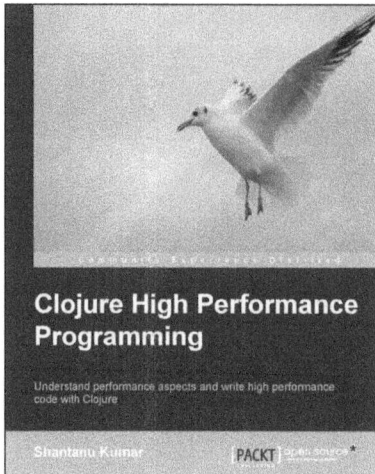

## Clojure High Performance Programming

ISBN: 978-1-78216-560-6          Paperback: 152 pages

Understand performance aspects and write high performance code with Clojure

1. See how the hardware and the JVM impact performance.

2. Learn which Java features to use with Clojure, and how.

3. Deep dive into Clojure's concurrency and state primitives.

Please check **www.PacktPub.com** for information on our titles

www.ingramcontent.com/pod-product-compliance
Lightning Source LLC
Chambersburg PA
CBHW080714220326
41598CB00033B/5419